Allon & Jean Oswo
and Family

EXPLORING BRITAIN

SCENIC WONDERS

SCENIC WONDERS
WAS EDITED AND DESIGNED BY
THE READER'S DIGEST ASSOCIATION LIMITED, LONDON

FIRST EDITION COPYRIGHT © 1984
THE READER'S DIGEST ASSOCIATION LIMITED, 25 BERKELEY SQUARE,
LONDON W1X 6AB

REPRINTED 1986

COPYRIGHT © 1984
READER'S DIGEST ASSOCIATION FAR EAST LIMITED
PHILIPPINES COPYRIGHT 1984
READER'S DIGEST ASSOCIATION FAR EAST LTD

PRINTED IN HONG KONG

CONTRIBUTORS

MAIN TEXT BY EDWARD GREY
GAZETTEER BY RON FREETHY

EXPLORING BRITAIN
SCENIC WONDERS

PUBLISHED BY THE READER'S DIGEST ASSOCIATION LIMITED
LONDON NEW YORK MONTREAL SYDNEY CAPE TOWN

—CONTENTS—

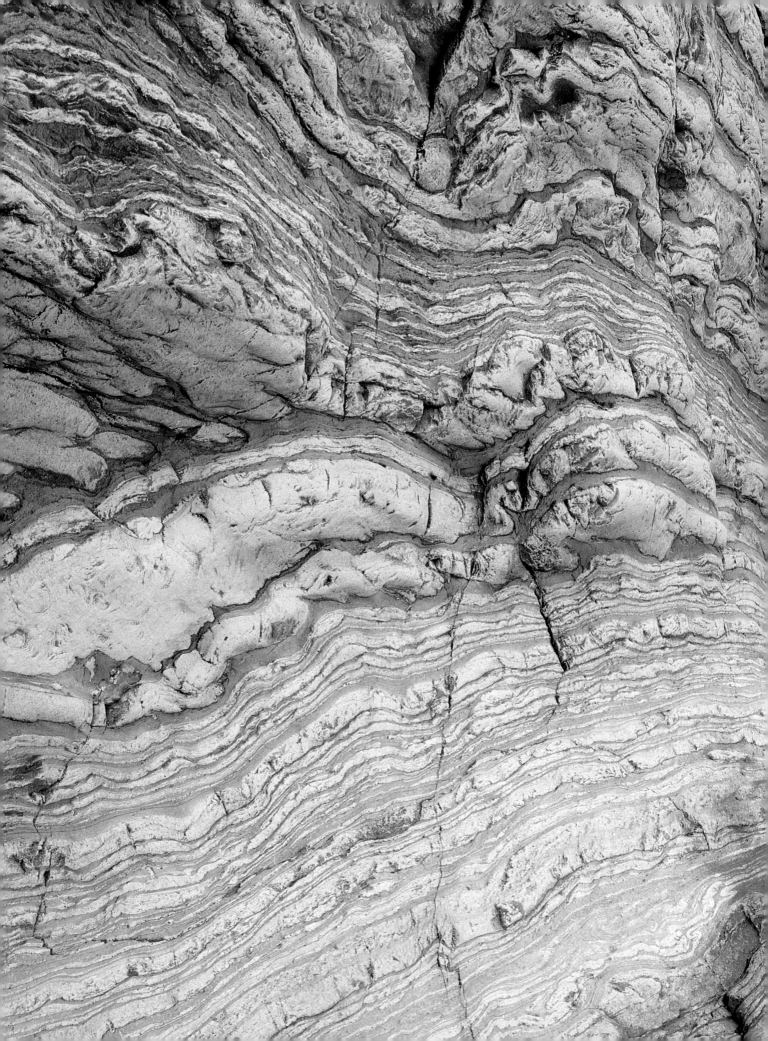

A MASTERPIECE OF NATURE

Britain is a notoriously crowded island. Yet few countries have such a concentrated diversity of scenery. There are still wild acres of bleak, unpeopled moorland; tranquil sheep-nibbled dales; craggy mountains whose teeth rake the sky; and flat, deserted marshlands fringed by waving reedbeds. Writing some 400 years ago, the antiquary William Camden described Britain as a masterpiece of Nature, 'a little world by itself'.

This book explores the beauty of our land through its 6,000 miles of matchless coastline, its mountain peaks and passes, its heather-carpeted moorlands, its rolling downs and wooded hills, its sparkling rivers and romantic lakes. Each of these five types of landscape is the subject of a separate chapter in which seven natural wonders are described in detail. To do justice to the amazingly varied interest of the British landscape, a further 180 locations are briefly described in a separate gazetteer at the end of the book. Many are marvels shaped entirely by Nature. At Fingal's Cave, for example, is a fantastic basalt wonderland created by floods of lava. At Cheddar Gorge, gaunt limestone cliffs soar 450 ft above an abyss contoured by a long-vanished river. At Brimham Rocks, a gritstone plateau is peopled with monstrous rock statues shaped by searing sandstorms.

Yet the British rural scene is deeply ingrained with evidence of human presence. Where the finest relics of man have survived in unspoiled surroundings they have acquired a timeless quality. The ribbed immensity of Maiden Castle and the sinuous line of Hadrian's Wall have become landscape wonders in their own right. So, too, have the breathtakingly beautiful ruins of Rievaulx Abbey, nestling in the wooded valley of the Rye, and Thomas Telford's airy cast-iron aqueduct at Pont Cysyllte.

The landscape is enriched too with invisible assets through association with the writers who have loved it. It enhances the dark magic of Rannoch Moor, for example, to know that Robert Louis Stevenson imagined the hero of his *Kidnapped* fleeing across the peaty wilderness pursued by a company of troopers. Ullswater's flowered banks gain an extra dimension of enchantment through the knowledge that Wordsworth was inspired by them to compose the poem now known as *Daffodils*.

For in reality, wonder is a human quality – a response to the exceptional, whether grand, or beautiful or even terrifying. And the scenic wonders of Britain are sites of exceptional interest in a land that is changed since Camden's day – but still remains a masterpiece of Nature.

FLIMSTON BAY, DYFED

WHERE
WAVES BREAK

If one image embodies all the restless energy of nature it is surely that of the sea, incessantly heaving, rolling and breaking at the margins of the land. Sometimes that energy finds release in fearsome assault, when surf-laden rollers rush full tilt at the coastline to burst in thunder against cliff or headland. Sometimes it is expressed in the tranquil rhythms of waves uncurling on a sandy beach. And always as it moves, with patience or ferocity, it is modifying the edges of Britain. The British have long been famed as a nation of seafarers. But to experience the full glory of the sea, in savage grandeur or limpid calm, you need travel no further than the land's edge.

FINGAL'S CAVE

Strathclyde

The whole fantastic cavern belongs to the architecture of dreams. An elegant forest of slender basalt columns rises to heights of 60 ft, supporting a monstrous arched roof of rock. Sweeping into the cave's yawning mouth is a natural causeway of massive stepping-stones, each shaped with an immaculate geometry of planes and angles. The tapering grotto reaches 227 ft into the bowels of its island, yet the dark, fluted walls are curiously luminous, glistening with yellow stalactites. The cave is 42 ft wide at its mouth and the air is fresh, scourged by the flux of tides which surge into its deepest recess.

Fingal's Cave is named after Fion-na-Gael, a giant hero of Celtic folklore who is said to have formed the cavern. Certainly, it looks like the work of giants; the poet John Keats imagined them bundling up the pillars like matchsticks and hacking out the grotto with immense axes. Yet the cavern was shaped entirely by nature. Ancient volcanoes, spewing floods of molten lava, fashioned the colonnades and paving stones. The sea gouged out the chamber, shattering columns to leave only stumps and imprints in the roof. But the waves allowed a perilous section of the Causeway to survive on the eastern side, as if inviting only the bravest to examine their handiwork. In all, the effects are unearthly.

The cave is situated at the southern end of Staffa, an island off the west coast of Scotland. The island is less than a mile long by a quarter of a mile wide, and is uninhabited today except by gulls, seals, and the sheep which are brought to pasture on its green tableland. However, Staffa has not always been so deserted, for in the south-west are the ruins of what seems to have been a 13th-century chapel. The sacred isle of Iona is only 6 miles to the south, and Mull is about the same distance to the east. Though isolated, Staffa is not entirely remote from ancient centres of habitation.

THE SHRINE OF ROMANCE

Staffa derives its name from a Norse term meaning 'Isle of Staves or Columns'. The title well suits its pillared southern face, which looks from the sea like a giant bundle of rods supporting a taut canopy of slag above. The island is wholly basaltic, formed by lava eruptions which burst from the earth millions of years ago. As the molten rock cooled, it contracted and solidified at different rates.

At Fingal's Cave three lava zones are clearly visible. The roof is the upper level, an amorphous crust of slag which cooled very quickly in contact with the air at the top. The pillared walls are the middle level,

GIANT'S CREATION *The serried columns that frame the entrance, and the symmetrical flags that lead inside, convinced early travellers that the great sea cave on Staffa had been fashioned by Fion-na-Gael, mightiest of the Celtic giants and wonder-workers.*

where the lava cooled more slowly. The Causeway is the lowest zone, which was formed only when the searing heat from below began to diminish.

Basalt is a dark, fine-grained volcanic rock whose colour was well described by Keats after his visit to Fingal's Cave; he spoke of the columns being 'a sort of black with a lurking gloom of purple therein'. It is not uncommon for the rock to form hexagonal or six-sided columns in cooling. Basalt cliffs can be seen

elsewhere, and a natural pavement of hexagonal slabs exists at the Giant's Causeway in Ireland.

But at Fingal's Cave the lava zones have combined to create something quite unique. Although the grotto has been known locally from ancient times, it was only in 1772, when Sir Joseph Banks visited the site, that it aroused widespread interest. Banks was the president of the Royal Society, an eminent botanist and geologist who had accompanied Captain Cook on his first

THE MELODIOUS CAVE

As the waves rush through the vaulted grotto, an eerie and resonant sound emanates from below. The earliest visitors must have noticed it, for a Gaelic name of Fingal's Cave – *Uamh Binn* – means 'Melodious Cave'.

One figure with whom the site is especially associated is Felix Mendelssohn, the German composer, who visited Staffa in August 1829.

After a nightmarish voyage, he approached the island by rowing boat. Walking up to the cave as the waves crashed on the rocky shore, Mendelssohn was inspired. Immediately, he scrawled down a melody which captured the descending roar of the tide.

The tune, no more than two bars long, was to provide the recurrent motif of his famous overture *The Hebrides*, otherwise known as *Fingal's Cave*. A critic wrote that it 'brought the perils of nature straight into the concert hall'

ECHOING SHADES *The eerie symmetry of the rocks outside is repeated within the cave where it is enhanced by the shadows and the echoing melody from the sea.*

round-the-world voyage. He learned of the wonders of Staffa quite by chance while sheltering in the Sound of Mull on his way to Iceland. Deciding to make an excursion, he was staggered by the cave which he thought finer than any ever previously described. 'Compared to this what are the cathedrals and the palaces built by men!' he wrote.

In the decades which followed, hundreds made a pilgrimage to Fingal's Cave. Dr Johnson, on his famous tour of the Hebrides, visited the site but was prevented from landing by rough seas. Keats went, and so did Scott and Wordsworth. Turner painted the island from the sea, and also ventured into the cave to sketch the interior. For the Romantics, the place became a kind of cult shrine, where the Gothic forces of nature could be seen at their most fantastic.

And the cave did not only appeal to artistic temperaments. In 1847, Queen Victoria and Prince Albert landed on the island, the queen recording her impressions in her diary. At least one prime minister has waxed lyrical at the site. Sir Robert Peel was moved to write that he 'had seen the temple not made with hands, had felt the majestic swell of the ocean – the pulsation of the great Atlantic – beating in its inmost sanctuary'.

The whole southern face of Staffa is a petrified tribute to the perils of nature, and the hardened lava flows have produced a variety of effects. If you stand on the Causeway outside the cave you can see the Bending Columns, which seem to have buckled under the weight of the slag. Along the stepped path of

hexagonal columns is a throne of rock known as Fingal's Chair, credited with granting the wishes of those who sit in it. Jutting from the sea just offshore is a pyramid of pillared rock which rises to 30 ft; it is known as *Am Buachaille* – 'the Herdsman' – because it is said to resemble a shepherd's conical hat.

Fingal's Cave is not the only grotto on the island. Climb from the Causeway to the top of the cliffs and the inaccessible Clamshell comes into view, a cave 130 ft deep, whose basalt columns are weirdly splayed like the ribs of a giant scallop. To the west of Fingal's Cave is the Boat Cave, so named because it can be entered only by sea. Further west still is Mackinnon's Cave, reaching 224 ft into the island, slightly shorter than Fingal's but broader at the mouth. It is named after John Mackinnon, a 15th-century Abbot of Iona, who is buried in the sacred isle's cathedral. Legend tells how the abbot fell in love with a mermaid and was banished to the cave on Staffa; but the roar of the waves so disquieted him that he moved to more spacious premises – a larger cave on Mull which also bears his name.

For early visitors, a voyage to Staffa was fraught with danger. But today a passenger-boat service runs from Mull, and the island is much visited in summer. The sea trip is short, taking only 45 minutes, and is in itself a glorious experience which encompasses the majestic coastline of Mull where the mountains slope down to the sea. But it is Fingal's Cave which draws like a magnet, a fluted, fantastic cavern which rings to the music of the tide.

THE HERDSMAN *Rising from the sea close to the entrance of the cave is a small mound of basalt columns, some upright, reaching down into the sea, others just lying there. They look for all the world like a pile of left-over materials on a building site – something the giant Fion-na-Gael had no further use for when he had finished building his cave. The mound's Gaelic name,* Am Buachaille, *has a romantic ring to it, but translates, prosaically, into 'the Herdsman'.*

KYNANCE COVE

Cornwall

White sand and turquoise sea, green turf and dark, glittering rock – the colours are Kynance's glory. At sunrise and sunset the views from above are unearthly – the very rock seems lit with strange fires. Climb down from the cliffs to explore the cove and the wonder only increases. There are jagged stacks, islands and bay-windowed caves, all shimmering with the same iridescence. And the streaking hues are no trick of the atmosphere, for in Kynance's rock there are rainbows.

The cove lies close to Lizard Point, the southernmost tip of mainland Britain. Among seamen, the Cornish headland is notorious for its murderous reefs, knives which have ripped open the flanks of countless ships and sent many a sailor to his doom. At Kynance itself, the Atlantic can break with awesome fury over a broken rampart of offshore stacks and islands. The cliffs weather slowly, but with patient ferocity the waves have mauled and contorted them to expose a radiant core.

THE SERPENTINE COAST

Kynance Cove is one riven mass of serpentine, an igneous rock rare in Britain and distinguished by its multicoloured hues. The dominant tone is a deep olive-green, but it is veined and mottled with dark red, yellow and purple, sometimes spangled with bronze crystals. When polished, the surface shimmers like the scaly skin of a snake – hence the reptilian name.

The heart of the Lizard peninsula is a swathe of serpentine, and making ornaments from the rock has long been an important local industry. One wedge of the mass reaches the coast around Kynance Cove, and its variegated hues are found here in exceptionally rich concentrations.

The rock is all about. On the path which winds steeply down from the cliffs there are jagged outcrops piercing the heather. On the surf-lapped whitesand beach you can find exquisite pebbles polished smooth by the waves. And grouped all around are extraordinary rock formations, eroded by the wrathful sea along natural lines of weakness. The Cornish coastline is famed for its caves, stacks and blowholes, and Kynance has wonderful examples. What gives the setting a special magic is that radiant lustre of snakeskin.

At Kynance, the views and formations are so varied that it takes you a while to get your bearings. Lord Leighton, a Victorian artist with a special eye for sculptural effects, called the setting 'perfectly unique;

AWESOME BEAUTY *In still weather and sunshine Kynance Cove is a place of tranquil beauty. But beside the sea, nothing is constant. The wind changes, the tide turns and a smooth blue mirror breaks into a seething turbulence of grey water and white spume scouring the sand and pounding the rock. But beauty remains, in a new, if awesome, guise.*

DREAM ISLAND *Rising from the waters of Mount's Bay, the conical castle-topped mass of St Michael's Mount shows the ideal island shape, beloved of artists. Even had it not existed, it would have often been painted just the same.*

RARE FLOWERS

In spring and summer the cliffs above Kynance Cove are bright with myriads of wild flowers, many of them rare in other parts of Britain. Among these are the squills. The sky-blue, star-shaped flowers of vernal squill appear from April to June. In August and September it is the turn of the autumnal squill, which has similar flowers, only purplish, borne on bare stems.

Vernal squill
Scilla verna

Autumnal squill
Scilla autumnalis

a lovely picture, the finest cove in the kingdom'.

Guarding the cave's mouth to the east is the Lion Rock, while to the west are two islands: Gull Rock, off shore, and Asparagus Island connected to the coast by a sandy causeway exposed at low tide. The island's name comes from the asparagus that once grew wild on its slopes, and in its hulking flanks nature has created an effect of pure caprice: the Devil's Letterbox and Bellows. The sea has undermined the island so that the incoming tide is sucked noisily in through a narrow hole, then spewed out in cascades of spray. (You can watch pieces of driftwood disappear like letters into the vent.)

Rising sheer from the beach are a number of stacks: the Sugarloaf, towering Steeple Rock, and the Bishop's Rock with its human profile and mitred head. Round every serpentine mass new angles open up, each with its own appeal. Kynance is a three-dimensional wonder, and no single picture can quite do it justice. Nevertheless, the views from inside the caves have a particular enchantment.

The caves have been given homely names: the Kitchen, the Parlour and the Drawing Room. The Parlour has a particularly shapely 'bay window' looking out on to the beach, while the Drawing Room, which also offers a splendid frame for the rocks, is exceptionally beautiful in its own right. Walled in green serpentine and floored with pale sand, it ranks among the finest sea caves in all Cornwall: only Merlin's Cave at Tintagel, and the Banqueting Hall at Porth quite compete for scenic grandeur.

Exploring the slippery rocks and caves can be dangerous, and visitors should take care not to be caught by the tide. The Ladies' Bathing Pool offers no hazards, however. A natural formation, it is quite safe to bathe in and its sheltered waters are always deliciously warmer than the wind-driven ocean. In contrast, there is nothing inviting about the Devil's Mouth, a dark cavity situated high above Bishop's Rock. The black mouth whispers menace from the heights, a reminder that for all its delights, Kynance Cove lies on a savage coast.

TO RAINBOW'S END

Seen from the cliffs, the sea at Kynance shelves from deep blue to turquoise, but beneath the surface there are razor-edged ridges. No harbour-works line the shore. And yet there is evidence of ancient settlement here, on a stream which runs down to the cleft bay. Only 600 yds inland, an important prehistoric site was excavated in 1953. It seems to have been first occupied in about 1300 BC by Bronze Age immigrants from Brittany, who made coarse, decorated pottery from the local clay. They were succeeded by Iron Age colonists from the same region. But the soil here is poor, and the stone huts were abandoned in about AD 100.

Today, only a tiny cluster of buildings rises from the heights. To the west is a jagged wall of cliffs, along the tops of which stretch some 4 miles of glorious walking. Treading this path, you are at the heel of the great Cornish 'boot' which reaches its toe at Land's End, and it faces the full wrath of the Atlantic. The sea has ripped the rock curtain to shreds: the whole coast is fretted with stacks, chasms, reefs and islets, hollowed rock arches and caves.

At Kynance Cliff is a wild headland known as The Rill from which, it is said, the Armada was first sighted. A little beyond is the dizzying crest of a fanged peninsula called the Horse. Further west still is the horrific sea chasm of Pigeon Ogo, where the ground plunges sheer away to a groaning cauldron of surf. Sea-birds haunt the narrow ledges and fissures, and you can watch them nesting from close to – if you have a head for heights.

At Predannack Head the cliffs rise vertically 200 ft from the sea, offering superb panoramas of Mount's Bay, with the hallowed vision of St Michael's Mount clearly in view. Inland, is a rugged and lonely heath, an area now preserved as a nature reserve. All of these cliffs are rich in wild flowers, which are part of their unique attraction.

SHELTERED HARBOUR

Beyond Predannack Head the coast path descends to Mullion Cove, with its distinctive sea stack and island offshore. Unlike Kynance, Mullion has a harbour – a tiny picture-postcard affair sheltered by a stone-jettied arm. This is a haven steeped in smugglers' lore, and it witnessed the last recorded fight between Moonlighters and Excise men.

The path from Kynance to Mullion is one of the grand set-pieces of the Cornish coastline, with a splendid cove at each extremity. And although there are fine walks on to Gunwalloe, this is the rainbow's end; for at Mullion, the serpentine rock peters out.

Kynance Cove is no undiscovered wonder; it has been something of a place of pilgrimage since the 18th century. The cove can be reached by a toll road from the Helston-Lizard road, and in summer it receives flocks of visitors. The beach offers fine bathing, though the white sands are only uncovered for limited periods (roughly 5 hours, twice a day, 2½ hours before and after low tide). But though the swimmers come with their rolled towels in August, the cove is quite unspoiled. It is protected, like much of the cliffs, by the National Trust, and that glittering rock is resilient; it has repulsed the elements for thousands of years and meets human invasion with equal defiance.

In autumn, the bathers are few and the sunsets are quite breathtaking. By winter, of course, the beach is deserted – and dangerous. The whole headland becomes a theatre of war where thundering rollers hurl bombs of salt spray against the cliffs and stacks. The tides are so violent that they can even strip the white sand from the cove, baring beds of raw rock to the sky.

In spring, the sands are restored, and this is perhaps the best time to experience Kynance's splendour. In April and May the heights come alive with wild flowers: blue squill and buttercups, the blossom of blackthorn and foxglove bells – breeze-blown garlands which match the rainbow rocks to produce scenic feasts of radiance.

SMUGGLERS' COVE *Until the middle of the 19th century the main attraction of Mullion Cove was not the beauty of its rocky cliffs and sunlit waters, but the fact that it provided a safe haven for generations of Cornish smugglers who ran contraband into its tiny harbour.*

LINDISFARNE

Northumberland

There is a mood of haunting solitude about the wilder reaches of Britain's North Sea coastline, and Lindisfarne shares that aura. A bare green spit off the Northumberland shore, the island is approached by a mile-long causeway uncovered only at low tide. The permanent inhabitants are few, and they are massively outnumbered by the flocks of sea-birds and waders that winter on its estuarial flats. Lindisfarne is a Shangri-la for birdwatchers, but it is as a place of true pilgrimage that the island is chiefly known. For Lindisfarne is the holiest site in England, the very cradle of a nation's Christian faith.

It was here that St Aidan founded the first enduring English Church; here, too, that St Cuthbert worked and prayed. Lindisfarne Priory, sheltered by a hollow in the dunes, is among the most moving monastic ruins in the country. And as if the sacred associations were not enough, the island's one dramatic upsurge of rock is crowned by a picture-book castle. On Lindisfarne, history, faith and the landscape have conspired to create a setting of enchantment.

THE LIGHT THAT DID NOT FAIL

The island is shaped like a long trawler net cast from the mainland. Tapering from a narrow neck in the west, it expands to reach its broadest bulk on the seaward side. The total land area is some 2 sq. miles, but the northern part known as the Snook is a wilderness of dunes and marram grass. The sites of historic interest are concentrated on the south-eastern shoreline where the priory, village, harbour and castle are all situated.

The 16th-century castle – so dominant and romantic a feature of the skyline today – was not built until 900 years after the island's first monastery was founded. Lindisfarne's fame dates back to the Dark Ages, when warrior kingdoms of Celt and Saxon were battling for supremacy across the face of England.

Christianity at that time was a frail light. Brought to Britain under the Roman occupation of the 2nd century, the faith was seriously threatened by Anglo-Saxon invasion. Reclusive bands of Celtic monks carried the torch during the years of heathen conquest. The southern English were partially converted by Pope Gregory's famous missions, and the Northumbrians by King Edwin in 625. But in a decade of bloodshed which followed, most of the country lapsed back into paganism.

It was in 635 that Northumbria's King Oswald determined to restore the faith. Having contacted Celtic missionaries from Iona, the holy island off

ENCHANTED CASTLE *Looming out of a haze-covered sea the romantic outline of Lindisfarne could serve as a model for King Arthur's many-towered Camelot. In fact, the castle which lends enchantment to the view is a newcomer to the island skyline. It dates only from 1548 – 900 years later than the first monastery.*

During the so-called Dark Ages, after the fall of Rome, Christian learning and artistry found supreme expression in the production of illuminated manuscripts. Only a few manuscripts have survived from the Holy Island, but among them is the finest example of early Anglo-Saxon work. It is known as the Lindisfarne Gospels.

On 258 pages of vellum, St Jerome's version of the four gospels is laid out with the Eusebian Canons and two epistles. The illustrations are sumptuous, and with 22,800 lines of exquisite script it is one of the most beautiful handwritten books in the world. It is thought that the whole magnificent creation was the work of one man – a monk named Eadfrith who became Bishop of Lindisfarne in 698.

Today the originals are in the British Museum, but a fine facsimile is on display at the parish church of Lindisfarne.

ST MATTHEW *The Apostle is shown writing the Gospel which bears his name.*

FINE START *An elaborate initial letter opens St Matthew's Gospel.*

Scotland's west coast, he was sent a pious monk named Aidan. Saint Aidan, as he was to become, arrived at the royal castle of Bamburgh and was offered any place in the kingdom to set up a monastery. He chose the island of Lindisfarne, not far from the castle, because it reminded him of Iona.

The Church in England owes its origins to Aidan's mission centre. For well over 200 years, Lindisfarne was to be a beacon of Christian piety and learning which lit the whole country. From it, one by one, the other English kingdoms were converted, beginning with Mercia and Essex. And this time the light did not fail, Christianity took root and flourished.

THE HERMIT

Among Aidan's successors as Bishop of Lindisfarne, one became especially revered. His name was Cuthbert, born of humble Scottish parents, and in his early years a shepherd boy, he was known for his extreme simplicity of life. Appointed Prior in 664, he spent some years in pastoral work but gradually withdrew more and more from human society.

He first took to a cell on Hobthrush Island, just off Lindisfarne's southern coast; later he moved to the more remote island of Inner Farne, 7 miles away. There he lived some ten years as a hermit, and the fame of the holy man spread throughout England.

Cuthbert was appointed Bishop of Lindisfarne towards the end of his life. Abandoning his lonely meditations, he carried out his duties for two years before, broken in health, he returned to his cell on Farne. He died there on March 20, 687, and his body was carried back to Lindisfarne for burial.

THE RUINED PRIORY

Hobthrush Island, also known as St Cuthbert's Isle, is separated from Lindisfarne at high tide but may still be visited. A stone cross marks the site of the saint's retreat, and the foundations of his chapel and cell have been uncovered. It is a bleak spot, and for most modern visitors the more imposing ruins are what is left of Lindisfarne Priory, situated in Holy Island village.

It is not the original monastery – that was sacked by the Vikings in a series of raids beginning in 793. The grim cycle of slaughter and flight continued until 875, when faced with yet another onslaught the monks abandoned Lindisfarne, taking with them most of their sacred treasures including the body of St Cuthbert. They carried the saint's corpse around the country for seven long years – and innumerable legends have grown up around the stations of their route.

Lindisfarne was derelict for some 200 years. But after the Norman Conquest a Benedictine priory was established where the old building had stood, and its ruins today are a noble sight. Much of the church survives, built of dark red sandstone, with the roofless shell of the west end rising impressively and one delicate arch of vaulting providing a beautiful frame for the sea and sky.

The new monastery flourished in peace until 1537 when, like others throughout England, it was dis-

solved by Henry VIII. And although the building crumbled, some of its stonework was re-used to construct Lindisfarne Castle, the exquisitely picturesque fort which can be seen from the ruins, rising across the harbour on the wonderful rock pinnacle of Beblowe Crag.

ON BEBLOWE CRAG

Beblowe means 'Bible Law', and it is easy to imagine that the startling hummock was heaped up by pious hands as a vantage point in an otherwise featureless landscape. In fact the crag is a natural phenomenon, formed thousands of years before St Aidan by a volcanic upsurge of molten dolerite. Seething in jets from the earth, the rock cooled to create striking outcrops across the whole breadth of Northumbria. Beblowe Crag is an extremity of the Great Whin Sill, the same dolerite ridge which confers its magic on the most dramatic sections of Hadrian's Wall.

Lindisfarne Castle was built on the crag in 1548, as a garrison fort for the Tudor fleet making expeditions against the Scots. It remained occupied during the 17th century, when a visitor described it as a 'dainty little fort' with 'neat, warm and convenient rooms'. The same visitor sketched a portrait of its governor, a certain Robert Rugg, famed as much for his generous hospitality as for his 'great bottle nose, which is the largest I have seen'.

Rugg was a royalist during the Civil War, who waggishly described himself in verse to King Charles as:

The great commander of the cormorants,
The geese and ganders of these hallowed lands.

He surrendered the fort to Parliament when, for all his wit and loyalty, he received no payment for serving his sovereign.

In 1819, the garrison was withdrawn and the fort became a coastguard station. By the end of the Victorian era it had fallen into ruin, and was bought in 1903 by Edward Hudson, the founder of the magazine *Country Life*. He brought the architect Edwin Lutyens in to restore it as a private house, and the building was more than just reassembled. With much vision, Lutyens partially transformed what must have looked something like a blockhouse into the romantic creation seen today.

Perched on its isolated knoll, the building commands wonderful panoramas in every direction: of the farmlands, village and priory on the island, the bay and harbour below, and, in the distance, the magnificent profile of Bamburgh jutting proud from the Northumbrian coast. The view connects two of the finest castles in Britain – the fantasy on Beblowe Crag with the hulking giant of the mainland.

THE RACING TIDES

Lindisfarne has retained its character despite the seasonal invasions of pilgrims and tourists who come to marvel at its sights. There are about 200 permanent inhabitants, many of them farmers and fishermen.

The island's tranquillity is due in part to its racing,

deceptive tides. The metalled causeway from Beal on the mainland is completely submerged twice a day, and visitors have to check timetables in advance with great care. Vehicles still get stranded on the road, and there is a refuge box for emergencies. Before the causeway was built, there were other approaches across the sands. One, known as the Pilgrims' Way, is marked today by wooden posts. Special care should be taken by hikers attempting this approach.

The tidal races have caused many a ship to founder on the rocks and sands to the east. But if the shores have proved hazardous for shipping, they have made the island a haven for birds. The variety is quite astonishing – over 300 species have been recorded on or around Lindisfarne. Birds that breed there include eider ducks, fulmars, gannets, kittiwakes, guillemots, puffins, cormorants and shags. In addition, vast numbers of ducks, geese and waders congregate on the island in winter: wigeon, shovelers, teal, greylag and Brent geese, whooper and Bewick's swans. Among the waders, dunlins have been recorded in flocks numbering 20,000 with knots and bar-tailed godwits in scarcely smaller groups.

The east-coast path from the castle to Emmanuel Head offers staggering scenes in winter, and grey seals are commonly seen basking here. Part of the island is protected as a National Nature Reserve. Lindisfarne is a sanctuary as well as a sacred place, and the teeming birdlife provides a living scenic wonder to match its hallowed sites.

CRADLE OF FAITH
Lindisfarne Priory glows in the afternoon sun as it has done for more than 900 years. The present building, started in 1082, replaces the one founded by St Aidan, the Irish missionary who restored Christianity to Northumbria in 635.

LOCH HOURN

Highland

PAINTED LOCH *It is midsummer and Loch Hourn wears its welcoming face of blue waters and green hillsides bright with flowers. But even at midsummer this can change in an instant when the clouds close up to cover the sun. Then, the whole scene turns grey and Loch Hourn lives up to its name which means Lake of Hell.*

Its name means Lake of Hell. A twisted arrowhead of seawater piercing the West Highland seaboard, Loch Hourn is shadowed by awesome walls of rock rising straight from the water's edge to reach heights of over 3,000 ft at the mountain tops. Seen under the slaty cloud cover characteristic of the region, the waters reflect only grey from grey rock and sky. The grandeur is bare and forbidding, and the vast silences, broken only by the roaring of stags or the murmuring of wild geese's wings, can become faintly terrible.

And yet, the maverick West Highland skies transform the scene in seconds. Sunlight daubs the loch with all the colours of the hillsides: the copper of bracken, the purple of heather, the deep green of the pines. Dusk brings glowing pink and orange to the surface – the whole water becomes a mosaic of colour. The Lake of Hell has also been called the Painted Loch, and its clear waters can reflect the mountains so deeply that you cannot tell where the contours of hard rock end and the inverted mirror of reality begins.

WHERE MOUNTAINS MEET THE SEA

You only have to glance at a map to notice the West Highland seaboard's distinctive character. The whole north-western coast of Scotland is a huge saw-blade of land serrated by countless headlands and inlets. Skye and the Western Isles look like offshore debris splintered from the mass, while the mainland coast is so jagged that if you rowed its full length, keeping to the shore, you would cover some 2,000 miles.

Discounting the innumerable bays and small inlets, there are some 30 great sea lochs, the longest reaching 40 miles into the Highlands. Flanked by rugged mountains and lit by moving skies, each has its own special attraction: Nevis, Torridon, Duich, Morar – each of the sea throats is so crammed with splendour that to select one for special attention

ROUGH COUNTRY *The rugged peninsula of Knoydart separates Loch Hourn from its southern 'twin' Loch Nevis, seen here in the morning sun with Loch Morar gleaming among the mountains beyond.*

might seem diminishing to the others. No such effect is intended; but Loch Hourn, unquestionably, is unique.

The inlet shares the essential characteristics of all the western sea lochs. It was formed thousands of years ago when the sea flooded a mountain glen running west from the heart of the Highlands. It is typical, too, in that the broad outer loch is separated by narrows from a more slender inner one. But here the resemblance ends. For Hourn's inner loch winds among precipitous crags which have conferred an extraordinary dark grandeur on the setting. Alone among all of the Highland sea lochs, it has the appearance of a Norwegian fiord.

The mountains rise so steeply above the inner water that its north-facing shore receives no direct sunlight for five months of the year. Even Kinloch Hourn, the tiny hamlet at the head of the water, is masked from late October to February. And it is at this eastern end that the most spectacular impressions are to be gained. The hamlet is approached by a minor road which skirts Sgurr á Mhaoraich, rising to 3,365 ft behind; from the mountain's slopes there are astonishing views down into the grey-blue chasm.

The road stops abruptly at the little stone jetty of Kinloch Hourn, and it is not possible to go any further by car. An old crofters' track follows the south bank, while another follows the north at some distance from the shore. Loch Hourn is one of the most secluded and unspoiled waters in all of Scotland, and the best way to explore its inner mysteries is by boat.

The Vikings knew this fiord, and it is not hard to picture their longships moving among its shadows. A lonely little island called Eilean Mhogh-sgeir is set like a dark jewel between two promontories; there are waterfalls on the northern shore, and countless crystal burns streaming in from all sides. Waders pad the narrow marshes, and the freshwater birds live side by side with seafarers – in one moment you may see a heron, in the next a cormorant.

Beyond the swirling narrows you come to the Bay of Barrisdale – and quite suddenly the whole scene changes. The mountains above the outer loch are set somewhat back from the water's edge; the loch broadens, the sky expands, and you enter a different world.

THE ROAD TO CORRAN

Outer Loch Hourn offers some of the finest seascapes in all of Scotland. It is scarcely more frequented than the inner fiord, and there is no road link between the two waters. For motorists, the only approach to the seaward end is by a rough minor road which runs round the peninsula from Glenelg to enter the loch from the west.

Glenelg itself is a historic village which has the unique distinction among Highland settlements of having a name which reads the same backwards as forwards. It was visited by Dr Johnson on his famous *Journey to the Western Islands of Scotland*, in 1775, and is much tidier today than in the 18th century. The good doctor spent an execrable night at the local inn;

it was bare, damp and dirty with 'a variety of bad smells'. He and Boswell quarrelled violently, and they slept on hay with only their coats as blankets.

From Glenelg, the road travels south down the coast, providing magnificent views over the Sound of Sleat to Skye. This is remote and mountainous terrain, but not entirely strange to human settlement. The road crosses Gleann Beag where, not far inland, are two famous Pictish brochs, or fortified homesteads, built some 2,000 years ago and the best preserved on the mainland. The coastline begins to bend into the loch at Sandaig Bay, where Gavin Maxwell wrote *Ring of Bright Water*; his otters played on the beach below the road and the setting is evoked in the first chapter of the book:

'The landscape and seascape that lay spread below me was of such beauty that I had no room for it all at once; my eye flickered from the house to the islands, from the white sands to the flat green pasture round the croft, from the wheeling gulls to the pale satin sea and on to the snow-topped Cuillins of Skye in the distance.'

The views become more and more splendid as the road descends steeply down past the scree-littered slopes of 3,196 ft Beinn Sgritheall. There has been much Forestry Commission planting since the time when Maxwell wrote his book, but breaks in the conifers offer sudden frames for the splendours beyond. They are seen in a succession of breathtaking glimpses as the road approaches the loch-side village of Arnisdale.

CLUES TO THE VIKINGS

The Vikings must have been here. One of the ways in which their routes have been traced is the study of place-names, and the *dale* in Arnisdale is a clear pointer to their presence. Today, much of Arnisdale's small population is engaged in forestry work, but in the 18th century it supported a thriving community of fishermen who worked the loch for herring. The shoals dwindled in later years, and the population was badly hit by the potato blight of the mid-19th century. Little today suggests the 'busy haunt of men and ships' which one 18th-century visitor was startled to discover in this wild and romantic setting.

Beyond Arnisdale the road penetrates only a little further into the narrowing throat of the loch. It reaches its loveliest stretch as, lined with wild roses and irises, it reaches the tiny *clachan* or crofting hamlet of Corran. Here is a superb panorama of sea, loch and mountain. The misty pinnacles of Skye rise dream-like across the Sound of Sleat – there is no clearer view of the famous Black Cuillin to be had on the mainland. And the scenic feast can be enjoyed in the setting of one of Scotland's most beautiful clachans, nestling between the fresh waters of the little river Arnisdale and the blue enamelled sweep of the sea.

The road ends here, beside the neat cottage gardens. Beyond is only a short stony footpath, which approaches the narrows but stops short of the mysteries of the fiord.

Both of the peninsulas flanking Loch Hourn offer superb walking through wild terrain. Knoydart, the

BRIGHT WATER *Sandaig Bay at the seaward end of Loch Hourn is where Gavin Maxwell wrote* Ring of Bright Water. *The beach is where his otters played. The view over the sea to Skye is the one he described in his book.*

southern headland, is especially rugged – there are practically no roads at all, and the map is only pinpricked with human settlement; tiny communities of crofters, foresters and deerstalkers. The peninsula lies between the lochs of darkness and light, for while Hourn derives from the Gaelic root of 'Hell', Nevis, the sunnier loch to the south, comes from 'Heaven'.

Knoydart's peaks of Luinne Bheinn (3,083 ft) and Mealle Buidhe (3,017 ft) are linked by a superbly craggy ridge, while the westernmost summit, Ladhar Bheinn (3,343 ft), has the bare-crested grandeur of a Dolomite peak. The mountain can be climbed by experienced walkers, and the views are stupendous.

But the great masses of rock are also riven by numerous glens, providing less testing ways through the ranges. On the north side of the loch there is a fine track connecting Kinloch Hourn with Corran, by way of the wooded and watery Glen Arnisdale. The whole region is a haven for Highland wildlife; red deer, wildcat and golden eagle haunt the mountains, while seals bask on the shores of the outer loch, Maxwell's place of Bright Water.

Time stands still on this Highland seaboard. The stern, majestic mountains dwarf human ambition, and you can experience a kind of dread among the crags of the tide-lapped inner fiord. Yet it takes only a shaft of sunlight to break the spell: the colours return to hillsides sparkling with innocence, nature's alchemy works on the leaden waters of the inner loch – and the Gaelic Lake of Hell becomes a Viking Valhalla.

THE OLD MAN OF HOY

Orkney

Dunnet Head in Scotland is the northernmost tip of mainland Britain and in winter a place of dark, Wagnerian drama. The mad tides of the Pentland Firth rage with such fury below the 300 ft cliffs that they can hurl pebbles from the shore over the summit to smash the windows of the lighthouse perched on top. But the headland has its own wild beauty. The sun sets here like a slow explosion, streaking the sky with flames of crimson, gold and smoking purple. Looking north across the racing tides you can see the humped back of Hoy in the Orkneys; and there, pointing one dark finger at the sky, is the Old Man – the tallest sea stack in Britain.

Many visitors achieve their only glimpse of the

wonder from the mainland. The island of Hoy is not much frequented, and it takes some effort to get a near view of the Old Man. And yet this astonishing pinnacle more than repays close inspection. Soaring to 445 ft above sea level, the brooding giant is one stratified pillar of rose-pink sandstone. Patches of moss-green vegetation cling to the flat summit and sheer sides, while the seaward face is darkly weathered by the Atlantic. But the Old Man stands ramrod straight, one chin of rock jutting defiance at the onslaught of the elements. Aloof from the cliffs, standing a little offshore, he is the guardian of a colossal rampart.

THE HIGH ISLAND

The island's name evokes its chief characteristic. *Hoy* is an old Norse word which simply means 'High'. (The Orkneys were an ancient bastion of Viking power, the first colonists arriving in the 8th century.) The island is the second largest in the Orcadian group, but is quite unlike its neighbours. For while the typical Orkneys have a skyline of low, undulating hills, Hoy is a sea-girt mountain. Barely 13 miles long, it rises to an imposing 1,565 ft at its highest point, completely dominating the horizon around.

The island can be reached from the Scottish coast by a ferry service which first makes for Stromness on Mainland Orkney. The voyage skirts Hoy's daunting western cliffs, and offers some passing views of the Old Man. The great sea pinnacle is situated between the promontories of Rora Head and St John's Head, but the cliffs here are so huge and precipitous that they dwarf the towering rock stack. St John's Head boasts one of the highest sheer cliff faces in all of Britain – an appalling vertical drop of 1,140 ft. With this mighty sandstone rampart as a backdrop, the Old Man scarcely looks like a record-breaker in his own right; he has the air of a presumptuous pygmy.

Before the Old Man really comes into his own, you have to take the inter-island ferry to Hoy itself. A wild moorland road crosses the isle to reach Rackwick, once a prosperous fishing village but now hauntingly neglected. The road peters out at this bleak hamlet; the western cliffs can only be approached by a steep uphill climb taking half an hour. It is then, when you peer over the edge and a terrifying chasm opens up, that the Old Man reveals himself in all of his grandeur.

A COLUMN OF TIME

No photograph can quite do justice to the impression of height which he generates. To put the stack into perspective you have to focus on a tiny protuberance which rises from the summit like a pimple. That 'pimple' is a cairn of stones erected by the first climbers to achieve an ascent – it is about 6 ft high.

The Old Man was first conquered in 1966, by a team of climbers who took three days to reach the summit. It was a remarkable achievement which passed almost unnoticed by the general public. But the following year, six mountaineers repeated the feat, climbing the sea stack by three different routes. The mass ascent was filmed 'live' by TV cameras and the spectacular documentary reached millions of homes. Almost overnight, the Old Man became a national celebrity.

In structure, he is one, long dizzying column of geological time. Like the cliffs from which he has become detached, the rock stack is composed of layer upon layer of pink sandstone laid down in sedimentary deposits over thousands of years. The base is a dark plinth of basalt, a volcanic rock thickly bedded under cliffs and pinnacle alike and forming a causeway between them.

The giant has been poetically described as 'Orkney's oldest inhabitant'. This is very misleading. As a formation, he should really be known as the Young Man of Hoy, for he was born long after the Norsemen arrived in the Orkneys, and by geological standards he is positively an infant. Once, the stack backed solidly on to the cliffs; the connecting bridge of rock only collapsed some 300 years ago.

Even since he freed himself from the coast, the Old Man has changed dramatically in appearance. At one time he had two 'legs', which were separated by a sea arch at the base. One old print shows a hunchbacked figure striding purposefully into the waves with one limb in advance of the other. The leg and hunch on the landward side crashed down in a massive rockfall; sandstone boulders strewn around the base of the pinnacle include debris of the collapse. Moreover, the stack's eastern face offers clear evidence of its recent exposure to the elements – it is an exceptionally smooth and fresh pink.

THE SLEDGEHAMMER GALES

If the Old Man has changed in a fairly short space of time, it is chiefly due to the savagery of the elements on Hoy's Atlantic coast. The stretch of cliffs leading to St John's Head – and further north to Braebuster – provides one of the finest coastal walks in Britain. It is also among the most dangerous.

The sandstone rampart is subject to constant erosion, and even in calm sunshine it is wise to keep well back from the edge. In winter, gales slam the whole coast with terrifying violence: seaweed, limpets and live fish are tossed up on to the clifftops, and rocks from below even litter the monstrous heights of St John's Head.

On a windy day, the coastal walk should not even be attempted. It is hard to express in words what a 1,140 ft sheer cliff means. Southerners familiar with the sickening chalk drop of Beachy Head must *double* the statistics to approximate the vertiginous height of St John's. In this scale, human figures become as insignificant as the blades of coarse grass which clothe the top – and they are considerably more vulnerable to the wind. The experience of the summit is one which many an intrepid visitor has sensibly funked at the last minute.

But for those with iron resolve and a strong head for heights, calm weather opens up godlike views. Looking north, the whole of Orkney is laid out across the silver-grey sea, with much of Shetland besides. To the south are magnificent panoramas of the Pentland Firth, with the great sweep of the Caithness coastline

spread out beyond. Looking east from the cliffs are the wild and desolate moors, a heathery waste that is the haunt of the rare mountain hare. There are rare alpine flowers too – Hoy is known as the 'botanic treasury' of the Orkneys. Arctic skuas are among the sea-birds which nest on these heights, while alert visitors may even catch a glimpse of a peregrine falcon descending from the heights on its prey in a breathtaking 90 mph dive.

This, of course, is an elusive attraction. The Old Man standing sentinel offshore is a more enduring feature of the scene – though he too is subject to the vagaries of time. Examine the towering sea stack and you can see that it is riven with menacing vertical faults. Sooner or later new rockslips will occur, and the gaunt giant will slim down still further. Eventually, the last skeletal remnant will fall completely to be clawed back for sea burial by the murderous tide.

THE CHALLENGE *In close-up, all humanity vanishes from the Old Man of Hoy, only his colossal size remains – a challenge to man as well as the sea. He still resists the sea, but he was conquered by man in July 1966 when three experienced mountaineers, Rusty Baillie, Chris Bonington and Tom Patey, took three days to inch their way up the east face, right in the picture, to the summit.*

ST GOVAN'S HEAD

Dyfed

The headland faces the full fury of the Atlantic, a limestone anvil for the hammering surf. And the anvil has cracked – for five fantastic miles of clifftop walking, wonder succeeds wonder: Huntsman's Leap, a fearsome chasm riven into the coast; the Devil's Punchbowl, a monstrous blowhole; the Elegug Stacks, jagged rockpiles that bristle with sea-birds; the Green Bridge of Wales, a natural sea arch of incomparable grandeur. Add to these weatherbeaten marvels the tiny 13th-century chapel of St Govan, miraculously wedged in a fissure in the cliffs, and you have a stretch of coastline without parallel in all of Britain.

Pembrokeshire is famed for its glorious seascapes. With rugged peninsulas, whitesand beaches, secluded coves and islands, almost the entire coastline has been designated a national park. A long-distance path offers 170 miles of superlative clifftop walking, but no stretch competes for intensity of interest with that which leads west from St Govan's Head.

The Head itself is the southernmost in Pembrokeshire, and a lonely coastguard station is situated at its furthest extremity. Looking east there are magnificent views across Broad Haven and down the gaping throat of the Bristol Channel. But it is the western aspect which beckons. For beginning at St Govan's Head is a wall of carboniferous limestone cliffs which extends for 10 miles to Linney Head. And the sea has sculpted them with demonic frenzy.

The cliffs are sheer, rising to 150 ft above the waves, and are topped by a perfectly flat plateau. The summit was planed level by the sea itself, at a time when it rose much higher than today. But the squared wall of limestone has been dramatically eroded, and for a very simple reason: the rock is harder in some places than in others. The waves have eaten into the softer zones to gnaw out bays and inlets. In some places they have burrowed into the cliffs to form caves and blowholes. Elsewhere they have bored through promontories from side to side, creating arches. When the arch collapses, a rock stack is left isolated offshore.

The sweep of the limestone coast is wonderfully delineated from the Head – and it invites closer inspection.

ST GOVAN'S CHAPEL

From the coastguard station, the path heads back along the promontory, hugging the cliffs' edge until it reaches a steep gully threaded by a dramatic flight of limestone steps. There are in fact so many steps that it is said that anyone counting them never makes the same total going down as coming up. The flight leads to a tiny medieval chapel perched in a natural amphitheatre of rock.

The chapel itself dates back to the 13th century, but

HIDDEN SANCTUARY *The tiny chapel of St Govan, tucked away in a niche below the cliff, is scarcely bigger than some of the rocks which surround it.*

it was built around a hermit's cell, stone altar and bench which probably date back to the 5th century. This was a time when seafaring Celtic missionaries were travelling in frail coracles around the coast, and set up several small churches in remote locations. The identity of the original hermit is not known, but he is popularly said to have been the Arthurian knight, Sir Gawaine, who became a religious recluse after the death of his king.

Inside, the chapel measures no more than 12 ft by 18 ft, and you can stand in the smooth rock cell behind the altar to turn and make a wish. The little bellcote is empty today, but it is said once to have held a silver bell which was carried off by pirates. Sea nymphs are supposed to have recovered it and hidden it somewhere in the nearby cliffs.

HUNTSMAN'S LEAP TO THE DEVIL'S PUNCHBOWL

From St Govan's Chapel, a short walk along the coast path leads to Bosherston Mere, where the sea has carved out a deep cleft stretching inland. At one point the fissure is especially dramatic, the waves rushing in 130 ft below ground level. This is Huntsman's Leap, so named because a huntsman is said once to have leaped the chasm on horseback; he landed successfully on the other side, but died of shock when he turned back and saw how deep it was.

Iron Age tribesmen knew these cliffs, and their earthen forts cap several of the jutting promontories. Pitted with caves and protected on three sides by the sea, the peninsulas offered outstanding natural defences to those who colonised them. West of Huntsman's Leap, on Buckspool Down, is one little promontory where a blowhole seems to have formed part

of the defences, protecting the landward approach.

But the combination of natural and man-made works is even more spectacular further along the coast path, on a headland jutting from Flimston Bay. Here there is an impressive Iron Age fort with double banks, set on a promontory honeycombed with caves and passages formed by the hungry sea. Within the ancient defence works is a gigantic cauldron where a number of blowholes and caves have come together and collapsed. Known as the Devil's Punchbowl, the awesome abyss has a bridge of rock at its mouth; in high seas the waves are hurled in to thump against the vertical cliff walls and shoot cascades of spray over the old ramparts.

THE ELEGUG STACKS AND THE GREEN BRIDGE

After the Devil's Punchbowl comes drama of a different kind. Two broad limestone pillars rise from the sea just offshore. Seen from the east they look massive enough, but as you walk west they narrow considerably – they look in fact like giant knife-blades cutting into the sea. These are the Elegug Stacks, famed for their birdlife. Only a little to the west of the rock stacks is the Green Bridge of Wales, perhaps the most spectacular of all the sea arches which grace the British coastline. The great bridge stretches out from sheer cliffs, and a thin mantle of green vegetation clings to its summit, accounting for the name. The limestone is warmly tinged with pink marls, and the arch itself is beautifully proportioned; sea-birds gliding through the airy cavity offer a breathtaking spectacle.

At the seaward end there is a low stack which once formed part of the same mass. The bridge itself is formed of thick limestone beds, the roof sustained by one massive joint plane, while the cavity was hollowed by the sea out of thinner layers. The Green Bridge has a look of classical grandeur, as if shaped for eternity – and yet the sea which formed it will one day destroy it too. The great arch will fall eventually, leaving a new knife-edged pinnacle, detached from the cliffs, as company for the neighbouring Elegugs.

The limestone cliffs may be reached from Bosherston, a pleasing village a mile inland, which is famed for its exquisite lily ponds. For nature lovers, visits are probably best made in June, when the birds are nesting on the rock stacks and the lilies are in full bloom. There is parking on the cliffs above St Govan's Chapel, and also on Flimston Down above the Elegugs, but the 3 mile stretch between can only be explored on foot.

There is an irony about this spectacular stretch of coastline. It abuts an area used by the Ministry of Defence for training purposes. When the red flag is flying, the area is out of bounds; you can find out about firing times in advance through the local press, and through the post office at Bosherston.

Restrictions on access to the forbidden coast are at best an annoyance – they have also been called a disgrace. But on the path from St Govan's Head to the Green Bridge there are scenic wonders to spare. Here, the besieging sea has sapped a limestone rampart, and riddled its weak spots with miracles.

THE SEVEN SISTERS

East Sussex

The rolling chalk ridge of the South Downs sweeps seaward from Hampshire in a majestic switchback of swelling domes and swerving flanks. Plunging into four successive river valleys, the hills rise again, surging with confidence, bare-breasted to the sky. And suddenly, hundreds of feet above sea level, the ground falls sheer away. It is as if the downs had been sliced with a knife; there is nothing ahead but a dizzying drop to the sea.

The South Downs end abruptly at a butting head-land of the East Sussex coast, where the Seven Sisters provide the classic panorama of England's white cliffs. Dover in Kent, it is true, boasts famous chalk ramparts on the North Downs, but they do not compete for scenic beauty with the Sussex wonders. Radiant white, the sisters raise immaculate brows above the blue sea. Some gaze serenely across the Channel, others lean slightly towards one another as if in conversation. The green skin of turf is stretched taut over the rolling hillside. The exuberant downs meet the discipline of the sea – and their sudden encounter is breathtaking.

The range of chalk cliffs extends eastwards for some 3 miles between the estuary of the Cuckmere and a cleft in the downs called Birling Gap. The best views are obtained from the west. On the exhilarating clifftop walk from Seaford Head to Cuckmere Haven the rhythmic sweep of the sisters opens up in a scene of unparalleled splendour. Each of the brows has a name, from west to east: Haven Brow, Short Brow, Rough Brow, Brass Point, Flagstaff Point, Baily's Hill and Went Hill Brow. There is in fact an eighth sister nestling among the others, the aptly named Flat Hill. Her modest profile – and the needs of alliteration – have turned her into a Cinderella among the lovely sisters, but she is perfectly delineated from the sea.

ON THE TURF-TOPPED ROLLER-COASTER

Once, this whole stretch of coastline formed part of a single dome of chalk which stretched across to France. Waters streamed from the summit to form the 'blunt, bow-headed, whale-backed downs' which Kipling loved. The centre of the dome was gradually eroded, and the English Channel finally breached the land bridge to expose the white cliffs. At the Seven Sisters, the dips which separate the brows are hanging valleys – the truncated remains of ancient river beds long since dried out.

The Cuckmere, however, still flows through the chalk ridge, albeit at an exceptionally lazy rate. At the Haven it performs fantastic loops through a wide river valley scoured out by a much larger ancestral river. For centuries the meanders of the lower Cuckmere have been quite unnavigable, and the estuary offered anchorage only for smugglers who brought their illicit cargoes up the valley by secret moonlit paths. The river was beautifully useless, which is why the estuary remains unspoiled today.

Crossing the Cuckmere at Exceat Bridge is a section

of the South Downs Way, which runs across the backs of the Seven Sisters. Tread the springy turf of Haven Brow and an experience of unrivalled exhilaration begins. This area comprises part of the Seven Sisters Country Park, bordering water-meadows and the glorious beechwoods of Friston Forest where there are nature trails and hides. But it is the clifftop walk itself which beckons.

At this high edge of southern England, each rolling brow swoops into a hollow only to rise again at the next swelling ridge. Look seaward and the white slashes of chalk streak down to sheets of blue. The brows are sketched with tangles of gorse and in the full blaze of summer, skylarks trill high above while the air is heady with sea breezes mingling with scents of wild thyme. The turf itself seems sprung with elation – lungs pump – and the air invites laughter.

With each ridge, new vistas of down unfold, views of ploughed hills and cornfields, skimmed by chasing shadows. Unquestionably, this is the finest stretch of coast in south-eastern England, remarkable not only for its natural majesty but for its uniquely unspoiled nature. Back to the west lie the unbroken coastal developments of Newhaven and Brighton; ahead are Eastbourne and Hastings. But here the sky is huge and, in the words of the poet Alfred Noyes:

> *The wise turf cloaks the white cliff edge*
> *As when the Romans came.*

No doubt hill tribesmen did once scan the horizon from these heights. There are prehistoric grave mounds on Baily's Hill, and the extraordinary chalk-cut figure of the Long Man of Wilmington lies not far inland. But the ridge of the South Downs is notori-

CHALK WORLD *A rolling sweep of gentle curves leads the eye from Seaford Head to the Seven Sisters.*

CHALK MAN *On the landward slope of the South Downs stands the Long Man of Wilmington, a mysterious 240 ft high figure who is believed to have stood there since pagan times.*

WHITE CLIFFS *Dover has the name for cliffs. But in fact the whitest of English cliffs, and those which typify them all, are the Seven Sisters.*

ously waterless and never invited permanent settlement. Below the sheer chalk walls of the Seven Sisters there are no coves which might have tempted fishermen or provoked exploitation for bathing. In fact, on the sisters themselves, the only significant man-made landmarks commemorate gifts to the National Trust. On Flagstaff Point, for example, there is a plinth and on Baily's Hill a short obelisk. Otherwise, walkers have the freedom and solitude of the downs. The whole stretch of cliffs from Seaford to Eastbourne is protected as part of the Heritage Coast.

AT BIRLING GAP

From Went Hill Brow, the range descends to the cleft of Birling Gap. Humanity at last intrudes in the form of coastguard cottages, a car park and a pub. The dip in the chalk face does not reach right down to the shore; the few fishing boats have to be hauled by a curious contrivance up the vertical cliff. Like Cuckmere Haven, the Gap once offered a breach in the chalk ramparts which smugglers naturally exploited. Steps leading down to the pebbly beach were first cut by Sussex 'owlers' – so called because, like owls, they came out at night – whose contraband passed through the village of East Dean to Jevington further inland (illicit kegs were stored there in the cellars of a co-operative clergyman).

Today the beach at Birling Gap offers a good opportunity to study the sisters' white faces at close quarters. The chalk sediment lies in layer upon layer, formed chiefly from the compressed shell debris of tiny creatures called Foraminifera. It is studded in places by horizontal bands of flints – pebbles composed of almost pure silica. Such nodules litter the downland soil and provided sharp-edged tools for the early hill tribes. They also offer an exceptionally durable building material, widely used along the coast.

The beach is covered with chalk boulders strewn with bright green seaweed. It is easy to see how the sheer faces of the cliffs are formed. The sea pounds at the base of the cliffs, carving out hollows in the rock. Sooner or later the weight of the mass above becomes intolerable. Blocks of chalk crash down along vertical fissures, to be dragged back by the waves and destroyed. A virgin face is exposed – and the sea sets to work again. The process is continuous, and it is dangerous to examine the overhangs too closely.

BEACHY HEAD

East of Birling Gap the headland rises again – and it goes on rising up and up to one of the sacred monsters of the British coastline. This is Beachy Head, the sisters' demented neighbour.

The name has no connection with a beach, but derives from the French *beau chef* (fine head or promontory). Soaring to 536 ft of sheer chalk drop, the great white butt presents the South Downs coast at its grand climax. It can only be seen in full from the sea; it is, supremely, a viewpoint rather than a sight to be viewed. At the top of the headland are car parks and cafeterias.

Approaching the summit from Birling Gap there is little to suggest the scale of the drama which unfolds. Nearing the cliff edge, the sensation of height suddenly becomes indescribable. It is not a question of mere statistics, but the way that the firm earth simply vanishes at your feet. The turf clings desperately to a last rim of rock – and beyond is a hideous emptiness. Far, far below, the white crests of the waves are as thin as cotton thread.

Jackdaws and herring gulls wheel around, riding invisible air currents which swirl up from the cliff. Looking east, the resort of Eastbourne sprawls like a toy town over its sweep of coast. On a clear day, you can see as far as the Isle of Wight – 60 miles to the west. But it is the immediate drop which most

fascinates and appals. One writer has described driving to the summit with an old lady who crawled to the rim on her hands and knees because, she explained, 'gravity is so much stronger at the edge'.

In recent years the Head has attracted hang-gliders whose triangles of brilliant colour enhance the wonder of the upper slopes. But there have been accidents, and a local controversy rages over their continued presence. A more familiar sight is the red-and-white striped lighthouse just off shore. Much photographed, it looks as jaunty as a little stick of seaside rock. Appearances are deceptive; the 142 ft column boasts a beam which can be seen from 20 miles out in the English Channel.

The lighthouse was built quite recently, in 1902, to replace the earlier Belle Tout lighthouse of 1831 which lies a little to the west. The headland has known its tragedies; on October 24, 1853, the East Indiaman *Dalhousie* foundered off the coast and all hands but one were lost. Under the Belle Tout are caves later cut in the chalk so that shipwrecked mariners might find sanctuary from the jaws of the sea.

Beachy Head offers the last glimpses of the Seven Sisters. Beyond, the downs descend steeply to East-bourne. With its villas, shopping centre, one-way systems and seaside pier the resort is a busy, respectable place. It has its promenades and its 'Seaviews'. But the real sea views – of white cliffs and breeze-blown turf, of undulating downside and the huge sky – lie to the west.

CARN MOR DEARG ON BEN NEVIS, HIGHLAND

PEAKS AND PASSES

Foreign visitors are often unaware that Britain possesses mountains. The country's highest ground rises to no more than 4,406 ft, at the summit of Ben Nevis, while Snowdon falls far short of 4,000 ft. Certainly, by the standards of the Alps, the Andes or the Himalayas, quite unremarkable heights. Yet, viewing the majestic pyramidal peak of Snowdon from one of the glacier-gouged passes around, the only appropriate emotion is awe. And then there are the weird, timeworn monoliths of the north-western mainland: Stac Polly, Suilven and the rest, relics as ancient as anything on the planet. The Alps are but infants in comparison. The wonder of Britain's peaks cannot be gauged with measuring rods. It is in the drama of their contours, and the awesome erosions of the sculptor, Time.

BEN NEVIS

Highland

Britain's highest mountain has a habit of defying sightseers. Rising to 4,406 ft above sea level, Ben Nevis is so tall that even when the sky is clear all around, its summit is often obscured by mists; on average the top of the Grampian giant receives no more than two hours of clear sunshine a day. And then, on those precious occasions when the whole mountain is fully unveiled, Ben Nevis disdains easy appraisal.

From its huge rounded shoulders the contours rise to no crowning peak – there is only a summit plateau which falls back into the curved granite mass. The king of the British mountains is, you feel, only slumbering.

The name of the mountain derives from the Gaelic *Beinn Nibheis*, thought to mean 'Hill of Heaven' in tribute to its skyscraping dimensions. And the scale of things in this corner of western Scotland is colossal. With a 24 mile circumference at its base, Ben Nevis looms above the south-western end of the Great Glen, that astonishing 60 mile rip across the face of the Highlands from Fort William to Inverness. Nevis itself is linked by a ridge to its two sister summits of Carn Mór Dearg and Aonach Beag, both topping 4,000 ft.

The Ben's north-eastern cliffs extend for some 2 miles, reaching precipitous heights of 2,000 ft and comprising the tallest rock walls in Britain. Ruggedly gullied and buttressed they are famed as a rock-climber's paradise – a dangerous paradise though, which has tested the best mountaineers. If the long views of Ben Nevis do not always do justice to the grandeur of the mountain, these frost-riven precipices speak of a terrible majesty; Britain's sullen Everest has a savage brow.

AN UNFAILING SNOWBALL ON DEMAND

As befits a sovereign, Ben Nevis has a micro-climate all of its own. Moist air swept to the sub-arctic heights tends to condense in the familiar and persistent clouds of the summit. On the mountain slopes, the damp atmosphere and low evaporation are conducive to typical Highland vegetation – peat and heather moor scattered with rough hair grass. But among the scree and lichens of the colder heights you can find alpine flowers, refugees from the Ice Age, left stranded on the Ben when the climate became milder. It was to study such rarities that the first recorded ascent was made.

The botanist James Robertson climbed Ben Nevis in 1771 to collect specimens for the Edinburgh University Museum. However, he mentioned the feat so casually in his diary that ascents may well have been commonplace already. For although the mountain presents a forbidding face to the north-east, it can be scaled without great difficulty from the west. In 1895 a local hairdresser named William Swan raced up to the summit and back in 2 hours and 41 minutes, starting a craze which has survived to this day.

RARE SIGHT *The fearsome sheer cliffs of Carn Mór Dearg (The Red Cairn), the north-western summit of Ben Nevis are rarely seen, even by mountaineers. For up to 300 days of the year the carn is likely to be shrouded in cloud, and its gullies filled with snow.*

But the mountain has also been climbed for more serious-minded purposes, and in particular for meteorological observation. At the summit of Ben Nevis are the cheerless remains of a once famous weather station, the first mountain-top observatory to be built in Europe. It was in operation from 1883 to 1904, and though closed through lack of funds it was briefly reopened as part of a hotel before falling into its present state of ruin.

The records collected in this squat, flat-roofed building have provided much valuable information on the near-permanent summit snows. Throughout the life of the station, snow persisted on Ben Nevis without interruption, in summer and winter alike; the first complete meltdown did not occur until 1933. In fact, for recreation, the observatory workers were able to ski and toboggan for much of the year round. With a mean monthly temperature of below freezing point, the summit may receive snowfalls at any time, and in winter 100 ft drifts collect in the north-eastern corries. A maximum snowfall of 142 in. was recorded in 1885.

It was said of one 19th-century owner of the mountain that he 'holds his lands by the tenure of an unfailing snowball when demanded'. The man was quite safe until one mild winter was followed by an exceptionally hot summer. Seeing his property literally melting away before his eyes, he set up a tent over the last vital pocket of whiteness – and survived with his lands intact. Today, while it is not quite true to say that the mountain is permanently snow-capped, it still offers a fair chance of making snowballs in August.

ACROSS A SEA OF PEAKS

The recognised way up to the Ben's summit is known as the Tourist Route, a 5 mile pony track first made for the observatory workers. It begins at Achintee Farm in Glen Nevis, some 1½ miles from the resort town of Fort William. A well-marked path climbs steeply up the hillside, crossing the Ben's satellite hill *Meall an t-Suidhe* (Hill of Rest) and rising above the boggy, reed-edged waters of its lochan to approach the summit by a succession of zigzags. No gymnastics are needed; stamina is the essential requirement for the long haul up, with a good pair of walking boots and suitably warm clothing.

The roof of Britain is a bleak, windswept plateau, an altar of rock bared to the sky and strewn with fractured boulders. The rocks of the cliffs and summit are volcanic, bedded into the granite base by an ancient subsidence which locked the upper lavas into the granite while it was still molten. All around are commemorative cairns heaped up from the rocks by human hands, and the summit cairn itself reaches up 12 ft into the ether; it accounts for some discrepancies when the mountain's height is cited (Ben Nevis is sometimes said to rise to 4,418 ft above sea level).

As might be expected, the panoramas from this, Britain's highest viewpoint, are immense. In every direction are seas of peaks and ridges so dwarfed in some cases by the Ben's lofty elevation that they appear no more than dunes of some Highland Sahara, separated by green oases of glen and the glimmer of

their enclosed waters. To the north is the weird rift of the Great Glen with its chain of lochs, while away to the north-east is the broad sweep of Glen Spean. Towering above Glen Coe are the serrated heights of the Aonach Eagach ridge, and the eye travels down the throat of Loch Linnhe to Mull and the triple peaks of the Paps of Jura; on a clear day you can see further south still to the Antrim Mountains of Northern Ireland, 120 miles away.

Across the western hills lie the islands of Rhum, Eigg and Skye girded by cold Atlantic waters, and you look deep into the fastness of the north-western Highlands before the eye is drawn back to the ruler-straight land-rip of the Great Glen.

The awesome chasms of Ben Nevis's north-eastern cliffs are not for too close inspection from the plateau. Gales exceeding 150 mph have been recorded at the summit, and 50 mph gusts are commonplace. In mist, when snow cornices overhang the perimeter ledges,

conditions are especially treacherous. Ben Nevis claims victims with melancholy regularity, and fatalities are not confined to the rock climbers who can be seen in summer and winter alike pitting themselves against the wild gullies and ridges. Ill-dressed and ill-prepared tourists have also perished.

Apart from the Tourist Route, several ascents are possible and a way by the long hanging valley of Allt a' Mhuilinn offers magnificent views of the cliffs, and their climbs: the rock curtain of the North East Buttress, the Castle and Tower ridges and the 700 ft Douglas Boulder, for example. There is a Scottish Mountaineering Club hut shelter, built in 1929, at 2,200 ft which is used as a base for mountaineering – and rescue work. The full route up by Allt a' Mhuilinn is demanding and should be attempted only by experienced Highland walkers, but you only have to go part of the way to obtain staggering views of the Ben's fearsome brow.

THE HIGHEST *The snow-speckled summit of Ben Nevis rears supreme above a mountainous landscape in which peak after peak tops 3,000 ft. Only the bold white peak of Aonach Beag (4,060 ft), to the right, attempts a challenge to Britain's highest mountain. The foreground ridge, Aonach Eagach, which forms the north wall of the pass of Glencoe, has two summits: the left-hand one reaches 3,173 ft, and the right-hand one 3,118 ft.*

For motorists the best views of the summit are from the north; from the Inverness road, for example, or from the Glenfinnan road as it rounds Loch Eil at Corpach. To the south and west the mountain is bounded by the Highland valley which bears its name – Glen Nevis, one of the most beautiful glens in Scotland. A minor road reaches some 7 miles into the valley, terminating at a car park – and a wonder. To the left is an astonishing waterslide, the Allt Coire Eoghainn, which flashes white as it hurtles down the steep back of Ben Nevis in a 1,250 ft rock chute.

If you follow the footpath further into the glen you enter a magnificent gorge, carved by the tumultuous Water of Nevis between the flanking heights of the Ben Nevis massif and the Mamore range to the south. The craggy gullies here are lined with pine, oak, birch and rowan, and echo to the thunder of the waters as they crash and churn over huge misshapen boulders. It is a place of dark magic frequented, it is not hard to imagine, by the shade of Cailleach Bheur (the blue hag), a fearsome witch of Gaelic legend who is said to have kept a lovely maiden prisoner in her abode on the mountain.

But as the footpath winds its way through to the head of the gorge you suddenly enter a more serene landscape. The valley broadens to floors of green meadowland, and to the right is the splendid cascade of the Steall waterfall. Dropping in misty white plumes down the 350 ft cliffs of Sgurr a' Mhàim, this is a scenic wonder in its own right. Throwing caution to the wind, the National Trust for Scotland has called it the best waterfall of its kind in Scotland.

The Glen Nevis Gorge and its waters offer a fitting hinterland for the king of the mountains. It would be hard to find a glen more majestically contoured by nature. And its bare northern slopes just rise and rise, up to the slumbering giant which is monarch of the glen as it is sovereign of the whole British landscape.

THE BEN NEVIS RACE

An ascent of Ben Nevis requires no mountaineering skills; lungs may pump, the pulse race and calves may ache, but you can take the recognised route at your own pace.

The gruelling Ben Nevis race dates from 1895, when William Swan, a Fort William hairdresser, ran up to the summit and back from the old post office in the town's high street.

The distance to the summit and back is roughly 14 miles, but about four of those can be saved by cutting out zigzags. The record is held by David Cannon, a Gateshead man, who ran the course in 1976 in an extraordinary 1 hour, 26 minutes and 55 seconds. The women's record, set in 1978 by Ros Coates, a local woman, is 1 hour 53 minutes and 23 seconds.

A motor car was first driven to the summit in 1911 – a feat repeated many times since.

WAYS UP *Runners in the annual Ben Nevis race (top). The first car at the summit in 1911 (above).*

THE BLACK MOUNTAIN

Dyfed

A dark mass as sombre as its name, the Black Mountain heaves from the South Wales landscape as a huge tilted platform of layered rock. Purple moors cloak its smooth southern flanks, seamed with dark peaty dips and scattered with ruined farmsteads. This is a derelict landscape, abandoned by generations of crofters driven from their homes by whipping winds and lean soil. And yet it has an aura of wild magic. From the crest of the scarp rise the burial cairns of Bronze Age peoples, and Celtic legends of a lake maiden linger about the shadowed waters of one of its glacial lakes. The sullen massif is a place of mystery, and its dark brow looks into the heartland of ancient Wales.

In spite of its name the Black Mountain comprises a whole range of summits rather than a single one. Sloping up from the south-west, the great wedge of sandstone broadens to reach its highest points in the north-east, where the ground falls away in a dramatically contoured escarpment.

It lies to the west of the Brecon Beacons, and forms part of the same spectacular landscape. The smooth-backed mountains with their swooping northern scarps were formed by the tilting of Old Red Sandstone rocks laid down over 300 million years ago. Ice Age glaciers gouged out the concave, north-facing cliffs leaving pockets of meltwater to form isolated lakes and cwms, dammed up behind moraine – debris swept up by the moving ice. The Black Mountain has two such crescent pools: *Llyn y Fan fach* (Little Lake of the Top) and *Llyn y Fan fawr* (Big Lake of the Top).

THE HAUNTED SILENCES

Today the uplands form a vast expanse of common grazing land whose coarse grasses are clipped by hardy mountain sheep. Their bleating, carried by sudden winds, is about all that disturbs the long, haunted silences. The sheep far outnumber the human inhabitants, and many shepherds cover the desolate acres on horseback; perhaps the finest way to explore this wilderness is by pony-trekking.

But the Black Mountain also offers magnificent walking country, and the most spectacular route follows the contours of the precipitous north-eastern ridge. The walk begins at the hamlet of Llanddeusant, nestling among foothills below the cliffs. A stony track winds for 2½ miles up the little valley of the River Sawdde until it reaches the waters of Llyn y Fan fach, shadowed by an enclosing amphitheatre of sheer rock. The cliffs soar to 500 ft and the rock is thinly

GLOWING HEIGHTS *Save under the darkest skies of winter, the Black Mountain glows with any colour but black – from the green of fresh spring grass to the purple of autumn heather. Its blackness is that of magic, mystery and the unknown.*

LLYN Y FAN FACH

veiled with a verdant green, producing a striking backdrop for the dark waters. The cwm holds today a reservoir with a tiny dam at one end, but it in no way diminishes the strange loveliness of the setting.

THE MAIDEN OF THE LAKE

It is said that Llyn y Fan fach was once the home of a beautiful water maiden. A poor farmer named Rhiwallon fell in love with the fairy girl and courted her with humble offerings of bread. She eventually agreed to marry him on condition that he would never touch her with iron. They lived together in perfect happiness – until by accident the pledge was broken. Three times cold iron touched her skin, and the fairy returned to her lake, taking her rich dowry of oxen, sheep and goats with her.

The legend is one of the most famous – and enigmatic – in all Welsh folklore. It is said that the fairy left three sons behind, but met them again to teach them secret herbal arts which allowed them to become great physicians. The sons healed at the village of Myddfai, 6 miles to the north, and so began a long line of doctors who continued to practise there over many generations. In fact, Myddfai was long famed as a centre of healing, and its church commemorates several descendants of the famous line of physicians (the last was a certain Dr C. Rice Williams, who lived in Aberystwyth and died in 1842).

What is the meaning of the tale? The story dates from the Middle Ages, but it is believed to embody a much older folk memory. Some scholars maintain that it recalls an ancient culture clash between the Bronze Age communities who once inhabited the Black Mountain, and the more sophisticated Iron Age Celts who later settled in the hills around. Carn Goch, the largest Iron Age hill-fort in Wales, is only a few miles to the north. Perhaps some Celtic youth did once fall in love with a mountain princess by Llyn y Fan fach, and perhaps their love was blighted by tribal suspicions which found expression in the taboo on iron.

From the haunted waters of Llyn y Fan fach the route rises to the ridge of the Black Mountain's northeastern escarpment. It follows the crest for some 6 miles of glorious walking which takes in the peak of Bannau Sir Gaer (2,460 ft), the jutting snout of Fan Foel and its summit at Bannau Breicheiniog (2,630 ft) – the highest point on the mountain. Broad-winged buzzards may sometimes be seen circling the upland moors, and on the windblown crest the views are immense. To the west you can see for 40 miles, as far as the Prescelly Mountains; to the north as far as Cader Idris, more than 50 miles away. While 50 miles to the south, on a clear day, the views extend across the Bristol Channel to the uplands of Exmoor.

In closer focus, below the wild, ledged scarp, are the green valleys of the Sawdde, Usk and Tawe. Under Bannau Breicheiniog a path descends steeply to Llyn y Fan fawr, the Black Mountain's other glacial lake. Although somewhat sunnier than its mysterious northern counterpart, it is curiously bereft of fish. It seems that fish have never been able to survive in the lake – their absence was noted by a 17th-century writer who

observed that even when introduced artificially: 'as soon as they have tasted of this water turne up there Silver Bellies and dey'.

The cwm feeds a tributary of the River Tawe, and by following the stream downhill you come at last to an artery of modern life – the road from Craig-y-nos to Defynnog. But to prolong the exhilaration of the upland walk, the descent can be made by way of the astonishing ridge of *Fan Hir* (Long Top).

This is an extraordinary example of glacial sculpture. Almost ruler straight, the ridge runs along the eastern face of cliffs which seem to have been planed away with geometrical precision. At the foot of the scarp is a curious long mound which runs for three-quarters of a mile, a snow scree formed of sandstone blocks which tumbled from the heights as the ancient glacier retreated.

THE MOUNTAIN ROAD

The heights of the Black Mountain can only be explored on foot or on horseback. But west of the wild summits the massif descends for some 15 miles to the tip of the wedge at Ammanford. The western slopes were once heavily worked for stone, and are scattered with long-abandoned quarries and strewn rock debris. Today, the road from Brynamman to Llandovery winds its way over the centre of the range, following the route of an 18th-century turnpike road. For motorists reluctant to face the rigours of the summits, the pass offers superb views of the heights and also (looking north) of the cairn-capped ridge of Trichrug. There is a car park and a marked viewpoint near the highest spot on the road (1,618 ft).

George Borrow, author of *Wild Wales*, crossed the Black Mountain by this route in 1854, and considered the road one of the wildest he encountered. The Welsh uplands are notorious for their rains and mists, and the flanks of the Black Mountain are especially exposed to wet westerly winds. Borrow made his crossing in atrocious weather – he got 'drenched to the skin, nay through the skin, by the mist'. When it started to rain, too, he did not bother to put up his umbrella as he could not get any wetter.

West of the mountain road are a number of minor roads and lanes which swerve down among banked hedgerows to green fields and copses of ash and yew. And a new vision opens up – one of the most spectacular sights in all of Wales. This is Carreg Cennen, a fairytale castle perched 300 ft above the valley which separates it from the mountain.

Built of limestone and perched on a limestone crag, the 12th-century ruins seem to grow organically from the landscape. In full sunlight the crumbling walls and towers shine with a radiant whiteness; at sunset the western face is bathed in a luminous pink. The vision provides a fitting climax to a tour of the Black Mountain. Like the brooding mass which it overlooks, Carreg Cennen has an unforgettable air of secrecy and isolation; no town or village ever grew up below those pale cliffs. Castle and mountain share the same subtle fascination – the bewitching aura of abandoned splendour.

THE CUILLINS

Highland

Romance clings to the blue sickle of peaks like the mists which so often veil their contours. Seen from the mainland of Scotland, the Cuillins of Skye can seem dreamy and unreal, cloud fantasies of the western horizon. Bonnie Prince Charlie, who went 'over the sea to Skye' must often have held them in his gaze in his flight from the Battle of Culloden. And when the net tightened around him on the island itself, the fugitive found sanctuary in a cave below the Cuillins' spires.

By geological reckoning these are young mountains – a 'mere' 50 million years old. Soaring in triumph, the peaks appear turbulent with youthful emotions. But in close focus the heights are austere and the wild cliffs hideously precipitous. Mountaineers know the Cuillins' darker aspects and have written of a malignant stillness.

The Cuillins offer a range of chameleon moods, but their magic is undisputed. Cloud castles or infernal crags, the Cuillins are unforgettable – and by general consent they make up the finest mountain range in Britain.

THE RED AND THE BLACK

Seen on the map, Skye is a scribbled mass almost 50 miles long, riven by deep sea lochs and trailing huge peninsulas. It does not, in fact, take much more than ten minutes to get over the sea to Skye. The island almost touches the Scottish seaboard at Kyleakin, where the narrow strait is crossed by a car ferry from Kyle of Lochalsh. Girdled by water, Skye is by no means inaccessible, and it has a long history of human settlement.

Viking blood is deeply grafted on to the Gaelic stock of the people, and the Norse presence is reflected in place names. Skye, for example, is thought to derive from the Norse *skuy* meaning 'cloud', while the Cuillins are Norse *kjölen* (high rocks). It has to be admitted though that both roots have been contested by those favouring Gaelic derivations. Skye has also been traced to the Gaels' *sgiath* (winged) and the Cuillins to their legendary hero Cuchullain.

Whatever the origin of the names, Skye's structure is not controversial. The island is volcanic in origin, formed by great laval eruptions which took place about 50 million years ago and gradually built up a massive basalt plateau which recurs throughout much of the Hebrides. The basalt underlies most of north Skye, but the mountain core of the centre belongs to a later stage of volcanic activity. Masses of molten rock intruded the basalt from below – and it cooled to form two strikingly different mountain ranges.

ISLAND GIANTS *The Black Cuillins of Skye loom darkly across the slate-blue waters of Loch Scavaig. The mountains are well named. In good light, the gabbro of which they are formed warms to grey. But when the sun is obscured they turn to black.*

LOCH CORUISK

MOUNTAIN GEM *Loch Coruisk (see previous page) lies like a jewel at the heart of the Black Cuillins. Its setting is the mountains themselves which surround the loch in three linked ridges forming a gigantic sickle that includes 20 peaks over 3,000 ft.*

The majestic Cuillins are fashioned of gabbro, a compacted and immensely hard rock which is practically impervious to weathering. The colour is a dark grey; the mountains are sometimes known as the Black Cuillins. The neighbouring Red Hills of Skye emerged slightly later, and consist of granite – more prone to erosion despite its reputation for hardness.

The Ice Age stripped away great swathes of the basalt, and erosion acted on the gabbro and granite in different ways. The beautiful Red Hills emerged with low, rounded contours, while the Cuillins survived as lofty, defiant peaks.

The Cuillin range is barely 8 miles long, yet it boasts 20 peaks which reach more than 3,000 ft. The mass is grouped in a jagged horseshoe around Loch Coruisk, lying in an ice-carved corrie of sublime grandeur. This is the very shrine of the mountains, and distils the essence of their romance.

The sliver of water reaches over a mile into the dark heart of the range, and its glacier-gouged trough is more than 100 ft deep. From the glimmering, mysterious sheet, the eye travels up colossal walls of rock flanking Sgurr Alasdair, at 3,309 ft the highest of the Cuillin peaks, and around the whole amphitheatre of wonders. Sir Walter Scott, who did much to open Skye's beauties to the public, evoked the scene in stanzas of *The Lord of the Isles*, while Turner sketched it to illustrate the writer's works.

A DANGEROUS BEAUTY

The Romantics turned Skye into a 'must' for Victorian sightseers, and today once-secret Loch Coruisk is no stranger to tourists. Yet it has retained its character of isolation. No road comes anywhere near it, and the only overland approaches involve some splendid but strenuous walking; by the hill and glen path from Sligachan to the north, or by skirting the sea loch, Scavaig, to the south.

It is across Loch Scavaig that many visitors arrive – by boat from the hamlet of Elgol. Nestling at the tip of its peninsula, Elgol has a shingle beach which is one of the most magnificent viewpoints for the Cuillins. To the south is the cave where in 1746 the fugitive Bonnie Prince Charlie hid before leaving Skye.

With a price of £30,000 on his head, beleaguered by troops and government spies, it is unlikely that the Young Chevalier enjoyed Elgol's incomparable views. Besides, until the Romantics wrought delight out of wild scenery, the mountains' tops were considered hellish and forbidding places. By Gaelic tradition, the lonely screes of the Cuillins are the haunt of the *glaistig*, a hag-like she-devil capable of assuming goat's form; and the *uruisg*, a water goblin.

Even today, most of the summits are accessible only to experienced mountaineers, for the Cuillins have a dangerous beauty. There is scarcely a peak on the range which does not require at least some hand-gripping for ascent. The conditions, moreover, are changeable – the famous mists, rising from the encircling sea, can blanket the landmarks in no time. Magnetic compasses often prove unreliable, bewitched by magnetic properties in the rock. Even the

cautious walker may wind up a blind alley suitable only for equipped rock climbers.

THE PEAK OF THE YOUNG MEN

The easiest of the Cuillin peaks is Bruach na Frithe (3,143 ft), whose name means 'ridge of the forest' and which is attained by a four-hour trek up its north-west ridge; a very narrow stretch near the summit can be avoided by dipping off the crest for the last few hundred feet and coming up a little to the right.

The most popular peak, though, is Sgurr nan Gillean (3,167 ft), the most prominent of the northern summits, whose name means 'peak of the young men'. The route begins at the Sligachan Hotel, a famous mountaineering base from which the Victorian pioneers of rock climbing began their assaults on the Cuillins. The ascent takes about four hours, and begins along a marked path over the heathery moorland, crossing the Red Burn, and rising up the rugged corrie of nan Allt nan Clachan Geala through a waste of grey scree and boulders.

The ridge walk which follows is steep – so steep that you have to scramble off repeatedly to avoid the worst stretches, and use your hands incessantly to steady and gain purchase. The last stretch is particu-

ROSE OF THE MOUNTAINS

One of the least-known plants in Britain is the mountain avens – not because it is particularly rare, but because it grows in places normally visited only by climbers and mountain walkers. It occurs on the mountains of northern England and Scotland, including Skye, where it sometimes forms large mats on the thinnest of soils. Its short-stemmed white flowers, which appear from May to August, look like wild roses.

Mountain avens
Dryas octopetala

larly awkward. There is a gap where the cliffs fall vertiginously away. Although it is sometimes tackled by unwary tourists, Sgurr nan Gillean is best left to experienced hill-walkers and climbers.

'I HAVE SEEN WORSE PLACES'

It is unlikely that anyone stood on a Cuillin summit before the advent of mountaineering in the 19th century. Sgurr nan Gillean was in fact the first peak to have been scaled; it was conquered in 1836 by an Edinburgh geologist, J. D. Forbes. From that time on, one after another, Skye's forbidding summits were conquered, and many today bear the names of the climbers who mastered them.

The spire of Sgurr Alasdair, the highest, was for example first scaled in 1873 by the ebullient Sheriff Alexander Nicolson (*Alasdair* being the Gaelicised form of Alexander). The Sheriff was a local man, born near Dunvegan, who threw himself at the Cuillins' challenges with immense gusto. He was cheerfully offhand about his most famous achievement, writing 'one or two places were somewhat trying, requiring a good grip of hands and feet, but on the whole I have seen worse places'.

Another important event was the conquest of the Inaccessible Pinnacle in 1880. This astonishing obelisk crowns the summit of Sgurr Dearg, adding an additional 20 ft to the mountain's accepted height of 3,234 ft. (The rock spire owes its name to the Victorian Ordnance Map which had it marked simply as 'Inaccessible Pinnacle' when the Pilkington brothers, its conquerors, first decided to tackle it.)

But perhaps the most impressive achievement was the first traverse of the entire Cuillin ridge, accomplished in 1911 by two climbers, L. G. Shadbolt and A. C. McLaren. From Gars bheinn to Sgurr nan Gillean, the ordeal takes in some 10,000 ft of rock climbing and was accomplished in 15 hours. The feat has since been repeated many times, and the so-called Greater Traverse, which takes in the Cuillins' outlier of Blaven (Bla Bheinn), was first accomplished by F. G. Charleson and W. E. Ford in 1939. Adding 3,000 ft of climbing to the total, this has become the great marathon of British mountaineering.

The severest rock-climbing ordeals tempt few of Skye's visitors, and you do not have to make a single ascent to appreciate the Cuillins' grandeur. From beach, loch, moor or glen those dancing peaks seem to jostle the sky – and bring something of heaven to the landscape.

IN THE GLOAMING *With their jagged cliffs and corries hidden in the shade cast by the setting sun, the Cuillins assume a deceptively gentle air. This is the distant romantic view, experienced by the traveller who goes over the sea to Skye. To the climbers seeking foot and handholds on the naked rock, the Cuillins offer a challenge unrivalled in Britain.*

THE GREAT GABLE

Cumbria

Wast Water is the deepest of Cumbria's famous lakes, reaching down 258 ft into the incised valley of Wasdale. And its blue-grey waters are flanked by the highest mountains in England – Scafell Pike (3,210 ft) and Sca Fell (3,162 ft) which rise to the south. But the glory of Lakeland does not consist in mere dimensions, and the profiles of the highest mountains are not easily discerned from below. If you stand at the foot of Wast Water, the mountains sloping down on both sides form a swooping V-shape at its head, and in the background there rises an exultant pyramid to complete the scene. That immense, harmonising upthrust is the Great Gable, the shapeliest mountain in England.

The view is perhaps the most famous in the Lake District, made familiar through innumerable postcards. Often, the mountain is photographed in October, when the green-baize slopes are sketched with the copper of bracken, and the autumn tones are diversified by mosaics of cloud shadow. Vividly coloured, the masses of lake, mountain and slope are so finely balanced that the scene might have been composed by an artist.

The Gable is in fact only the seventh highest peak in Lakeland and at 2,949 ft it just fails to reach the magical 3,000 ft mark. But its architectural grandeur has a majesty denied to many loftier summits. Its name evokes its appearance; recalling the triangular gable of a mansion, it looks down from the volcanic roof of England.

THE CLOUD-CATCHING PEAK

The Great Gable is situated in the central massif of the Lake District, a region formed some 500 million years ago by the ash and lava of a prodigious volcanic eruption. The mountain itself might be mistaken for the isolated cone of a single volcano, but this is an illusion. Ice Age glaciers contoured its slopes and they scoured out the valleys which radiate from south-west to north-east: Borrowdale, Buttermere, Ennerdale and Wasdale.

From the summit a fantastic view down the long trough of Wasdale provides a textbook example of a U-shaped glacial valley. The flat bottom is quilted with fields and lit by the shining sheet of the lake, while the rugged fellside rises steeply to left and right. In Borrowdale, meanwhile, is a staggering example of the sheer motive power of ice; this is the famous Bowder Stone, a 2,000 ton boulder left there like a pebble by the Ice Age glacier which carried it south from Scotland.

But if the core of Lakeland was shaped by titanic

SHAPELY PEAK *The gable-end of the roof of England displays the symmetry for which it is named in this view from Lingmell Crag. To the right of the Gable is a rare glimpse of Styhead Tarn – the wettest place in Britain, it is usually obscured by rain or cloud.*

WASDALE AND WAST WATER

forces of fire and ice, the landscape has been textured by milder forces. The mountains are not far from the Cumbrian coast, and moisture-bearing air moving in from the west is swept upward by the rising ground to cool as cloud and break in persistent rainfall over the region's peaks and fells. The Great Gable is especially exposed, for Wasdale forms an air tunnel leading from the coast; clouds catch on the peak of the mountain and burst in torrents on the lee side.

The mountain may not be the highest in England, but it does have its statistical boasts. Styhead Tarn on the eastern side is the wettest place in the United Kingdom, recording a mean annual rainfall of 172.9 in. Not to be outclassed, neighbouring Sprinkling Tarn has notched up the UK's highest ever rainfall over a 12 month period – an astonishing 257 in. in 1954.

These moist superlatives might seem to contribute little to the appeal of the wonder, and yet the weather is intimately connected with the Lakeland landscape. The rains have gloved bare fists of rock with green to create what the poet Thomas Gray (1716–71), called 'a little unsuspected paradise'; the caprice and drama of the weather is part of its enchantment. On the Gable rain falls often in sheeting downpours of exhilarating intensity, drilling into the backs of scurrying fell-walkers. But the swirling air currents can clear the skies just as quickly to leave the landscape sparkling with freshness. Water gurgles from the countless becks and gills, pearls of rain hang from bracken fronds and the air itself is deliciously scented with wet matgrass.

Most characteristically, the dales around are seen in dappled light, with moving shadows bringing only partial showers to the hillsides. In weatherman's jargon, 'unsettled' is the term which comes readily to mind. Wordsworth, poet laureate of the Lake District, was more elaborate, likening the fleeting patterns of light and shade to 'finely interwoven passages of gay and sad music'.

FROM WASDALE HEAD

From the foot of Wast Water you can approach the Gable by a winding lakeside road, and as you draw closer the scenery becomes more and more spectacular. To the right, the famous screes plunge straight down to the water, and you begin to see why the shapely pyramid ahead has long attracted mountaineers. The green slopes give way to fearsome crags at the top; what has seemed sublime, becomes something huge and forbidding.

At the end of the lake is the little village of Wasdale Head, the geographical centre of Lakeland and a shrine among mountaineers for generations. The Wastwater Hotel (formerly the Huntsman Inn) here was once owned by Will Ritson, one of Cumbria's most colourful characters. Sportsman, wag and source

TWO VIEWS *From Great Gable (see previous page) the view looks down Wasdale to Wast Water with the hump of Yewbarrow on the right. Almost the same view in reverse (this page) looks up Wasdale from Yewbarrow to Great Gable on the left and Scafell Pike.*

ENGLAND'S ROOF *Looking south from Great Gable, the north-facing cliff of Sca Fell (3,162 ft) peers over the summit of Lingmell Crag. To the left of Sca Fell, and in this view looking slightly lower, is the highest mountain in England, Scafell Pike (3,206 ft).*

of innumerable legends, Auld Will made his inn a meeting place for the English Alpine Club, encouraging the Victorian pioneers of mountaineering worldwide. Men who tested themselves on the climbs of the Gable and the Scafell Pikes went on to explore the Matterhorn and the Himalayas.

The tiny 17th-century church at Wasdale Head is one of the smallest in England – it has but three windows and eight pews. And its churchyard bears witness to the hazards of the fells, in the gravestones of climbers who perished up above. Looking up at the Gable, you can see the challenge of the crags. Beneath the summit, somewhat to the right, are the celebrated White Napes and Great Napes ridges. Here is the famous Eagle's Nest Ridge, a horribly steep and exposed rock wall, first scaled in 1892 and still testing climbers today. Here, too, is the fang of Napes Needle, a pinnacle whose ascent was pioneered in 1886 by Haskett Smith, the 'father of English rock climbing'. Near by is the Climbers' Traverse, a dizzying ledge riven across the cliff face, and not far away is the Innominate Crack, a forbidding vertical fissure.

Running up to the summit is the long grassy ridge of Gavel Neese, which provides one route from the dale to the top. It is, however, best tackled only by experienced climbers, for the upper reaches are steep and gruelling. Though the way is marked, it is very easy to lose your direction among the strewn boulders and scree, and some very strenuous rock scram-

NAPES NEEDLE

The event which marked the beginning of rock climbing as a serious sport was the first ascent of Napes Needle, on Great Gable, by Walter Haskett Smith in 1886. The needle is a pillar of sheer rock capped with a separate block of stone. Haskett Smith, by example, and through his book *Climbing in the British Isles, England*, published in 1894, became known as the 'father of English rock climbing'. There were rock climbers before Haskett Smith, but until his time the Lake District crags were largely for looking at, not climbing. Early 19th-century writers were suitably awed by sheer rock faces and gaunt pillars of stone, but they saw no challenge in them. Then came Haskett Smith. Since his first ascent thousands of climbers have mastered Napes Needle – and a host of other Lakeland crags.

THE LAST LAP *High above Wast Water a climber surveys the overhang that he has to negotiate to reach the top of Napes Needle.*

bling is required. Though Wasdale offers the finest views of the Gable, its ascent is best made from elsewhere.

ACROSS WINDY GAP

The most direct route to the Gable's summit is from Sty Head Pass to the south-east. There are spectacular views on the way up, but the track has been badly eroded by climbers' boots – the loose stones are no friends to the ankles.

The easiest, and most sheerly pleasurable approach is from Honister Pass to the north. There is a car park at the top of the pass (1,100 ft) and an undulating walk of some 3 miles takes you over the Gable's sister peaks – Grey Knotts (2,287 ft), Brandreth (2,344 ft) and Green Gable (2,603 ft) – before reaching the summit itself. The path begins by following the sleepers of an old slate-miners' tramway track, but soon takes you up on to an exhilarating ridge walk with superb views on both sides. To the right are the beautiful green dales enclosing Buttermere, Crummock Water and Ennerdale Water; to the left is the sterner valley of Gillercomb, while all around are the sinuous ridges and peaks, opening to the eye with ever increasing grandeur.

Beyond the Green Gable is a dip known as Windy (or Wind) Gap, a depression scoured by southwesterlies eddying from the windbreaking summit of the Great Gable. Lying at the intersection of a number of high-level routes, the top has been called a Piccadilly Circus of fell-walkers. From it there is a steepish climb to the summit of the Great Gable, which appears more of a humped dome than a pyramid from this angle.

On a rock near the summit cairn is a bronze plaque commemorating men who died in the First World War, and recording the gift of the mountain to the National Trust by the Fell and Rock Climbing Club. It is engraved with a relief map of the neighbouring peaks. The views from this rock-strewn summit are among the finest in all of Lakeland – and much more impressive than those from the crag-locked heights of the Scafell group, which can be seen rising above Lingmell to the south.

The Gable's apex is airy all around. To the east is the long ridge of the Helvellyn and High Street ranges, with hints of the Yorkshire fells beyond. Looking back to the north you can see down the whole length of Borrowdale to Skiddaw and Blencathra towering above. As you turn westward, the eye encounters the mighty Pillar Rock set against the heights of the Pillar Mountain. And then, to the south-west, is the breathtaking plunge into Wasdale, with its lake framed by the screes to the left and Red Pike and Yewbarrow to the right. The eye travels down the valley as far as the coast – and beyond to the Isle of Man smudged in the seas which usher the wind.

The views from the Great Gable take in a whole galaxy of Lakeland stars, and statistics mean little at this height. You are looking across England's scenic paradise – and it is hard to imagine getting much closer to heaven.

THE LAIRIG GHRU

Grampian

The Cairngorms make up the largest area of high mountains in Britain. Stretching for 160 sq. miles between the valleys of the rivers Dee and Spey, the immense granite mass includes nine peaks of over 4,000 ft and a dozen more topping 3,000 ft. The climate at the summits is sub-arctic – for seven months of the year the mean temperature remains below freezing point – and the range provides an Alpine-style playground for lovers of winter sports.

Snow and ice, so prized by holidaymakers today, also helped to shape the landscape. The great clan of domed summits is riven by steep-sided glens scoured by glacial action some 10,000 years ago. And the most astonishing feature of the range is not a mountain but a mountain pass – the Lairig Ghru – a tribute to the titanic musculature of ice.

One-thousand feet deep, the gigantic glacial trough runs right through the Cairngorms, cleaving them into two great masses, east and west. The vistas opened up are huge and stern, of plunging cliff, cauldron-like corrie and ice-cold mountain tarn. *Lairig Ghru* is the Gaelic for 'Gloomy Pass', a name which evokes its terrible austerity. And yet the granite screes can glow red in the sun, conferring a wild splendour on the setting.

The proportions are colossal. So immense are the mountains around that even the floor of the trough rises to loftier heights than many a British peak. The Lairig Ghru's drama though is not solely of rock, but of rock ripped away – the wonder is defined by an absence.

IN THE PATH OF GLACIERS

The rock of the Cairngorms was formed when seething molten granite cooled and then weathered in a high rolling plateau. The presence of pink felspar in the rock accounts for the reddish glow in sunlight; the old name for the Cairngorms is *Monadh Ruadh* (Red Mountains).

During the Ice Age a vast sheet of ice ground its way across the mass in a north-easterly direction. Often the glacial masses drained along dips in the plateau, simply deepening the existing troughs as they passed. Sometimes, however, they met a granite wall head on; and the rampart of rock was sundered.

This was the origin of the Lairig Ghru. Unimaginable volumes of grinding ice collected and compacted in what is now Glen Dee, filling the valley with its frozen mass. Moving northwards and finding no natural outlet, the glacial agglomeration simply ploughed straight through the granite ahead, leaving a mighty furrow in its wake.

Although the Lairig Ghru may be walked in either direction, it is best accomplished from south to north, following the path of the ancient glaciers; this approach offers the sunlight illuminating the mountains ahead. The full classic walk is a 27 mile route from Braemar on Deeside to Aviemore on Speyside, a true

RETURN OF THE REINDEER

Reindeer lived wild in Scotland until hunted to extinction in the 12th and 13th centuries. Then, in 1952, a group of domesticated reindeer were introduced to the Cairngorms. They soon flourished, and a sizeable herd now roams the Glen More Forest area, close to the northern end of the Lairig Ghru. They keep to the high ground where they feed on lichens and mosses. Reindeer, *Rangifer tarandus*, are about the same size as red deer – 4 ft high at the shoulder.

GREAT DIVIDE *A moment's sunshine strikes blue from the waters of the infant River Dee and shades of green and purple from the hillsides, giving the lie to the name Lairig Ghru – which means 'Gloomy Pass'. An Ice Age glacier carved the pass, a trench 1,000 ft deep which splits Britain's mightiest mountains, the Cairngorms, in two.*

60

HIGH POINT *The last stretch up to the summit of the Lairig Ghru is reached after 19 miles hard walking north from Braemar. At 2,733 ft, the summit, which is marked by a cairn, is higher than many mountains in Britain.*

traverse of the Cairngorms from one valley boundary to another.

Both ends of the walk are important tourist centres: Aviemore is a popular resort for winter sports, while the village of Braemar is celebrated for its annual Highland Gathering (with events including tossing the caber). And from Braemar the path sets out through some of the most beautiful scenery in Scotland.

The route first leads to the famous Linn of Dee, where the turbulent river hurtles through a rocky chasm narrowing to just 4 ft in places. A track leads on up Glen Lui to Derry Lodge, the furthest point accessible to vehicles. Beyond is a tramp up round the steep slopes of Carn a' Mhaim (3,329 ft); as you enter Glen Dee you approach the Lairig Ghru proper.

You do not see the pass immediately when you enter Glen Dee. Rearing up ahead is the majestic bulk of the Devil's Point (3,303 ft), which as you continue soars to a superb craggy pyramid on the opposite side of the glen. As the immense mass of Cairn Toul (4,242 ft) emerges behind it, the great rift of the Lairig Ghru opens up, gaping its promise of a passage.

The track keeps to the east side of the Dee for several miles of rough but level walking, with astonishing views across to the glacier-mauled cliffs to the

west. Between Cairn Toul and Braeriach (4,248 ft) are 2 miles of plunging precipice which ring the mighty amphitheatre of An Garbh Choire. This is one of the wildest corries in Scotland. The infant Dee falls over the rim of the cauldron, dropping from Braeriach's flat summit as a thin thread of white, barely discernible in the desolate grandeur of the setting.

HAUNTED SUMMIT

Up to the right looms the giant Ben Macdhui (4,296 ft), loftiest of all the Cairngorm mountains and the second highest in Britain – it is surpassed by Ben Nevis by a mere 110 ft. The bare summit of Ben Macdhui is said to be haunted by a phantasmal Big Grey Man, whose existence was attested to in the 19th century by Professor Collie, a member of the Royal Society. Reaching the top in 1891, the eminent scientist heard a persistent, eerie crunch of footsteps behind him. He fled in panic from the mountain, later writing: 'Whatever you make of it I do not know, but there is something very queer about the top of Ben Macdhui and I will not go there again by myself I know.'

As you tramp on up the Lairig Ghru track, the pass becomes darker and narrower, and it is not hard to

hints of green valley, and these grow to huge vistas of woodland. At last you reach trees at the edge of Rothiemurchus Forest, and it is worth pausing here to look back.

AMONG ANCIENT PINES

Seen from the north, the Lairig Ghru is at its most awesome; the great cleft looks as if it has been chopped out with a giant's axe. In fact what happened here was that the creaking volumes of Ice Age glacier at last found release, voiding vast quantities of shattered granite on the landscape. The soil, in consequence, is coarse and poor – but sufficiently well drained to support both pine and birch.

Rothiemurchus is one of Scotland's loveliest forests, an ancient, natural woodland scattered with clearings where the heather and blaeberry (bilberry) grow thickly. From the haunt of the ptarmigan you enter the domain of woodpecker, crossbill and the rare crested tit. Among the gnarled old Caledonian pines, red squirrels are withstanding the advance of their grey cousins. The air is resinous, and if you are lucky you may hear the tinkling of reindeer bells.

The woodland track leads to an iron footbridge, erected in 1912 by the Cairngorm Club. Just beyond it, the path forks. The quickest way to civilisation is to keep straight ahead for Coylumbridge, whence Aviemore can be reached by a 2 mile walk along a metalled road. But for those with spare ounces of energy, a slightly longer route to Aviemore branches to the left and skirts the shores of Loch an Eilein. This is a beautiful water, almost enclosed by pines and with the romantic ruins of an island castle rising off shore. Ospreys used to nest in the castle until the beginning of this century. They have gone (though others now nest at Loch Garten, north-east of Aviemore), but the setting is superb, and there is a nature trail and a small crofter's house renovated as a visitor centre.

Already you will have rejoined humanity; the loch is a popular beauty spot. But you must summon up energy for a last 3½ miles before Aviemore is reached.

Walking the Lairig Ghru requires no rock-climbing skills, but it does need immense stamina. The full route involves some 12 hours of hard slogging, and many curtail it by using the closest convenient points of access by car: the Linn of Dee and Coylumbridge. But the minimum walking distance is still 19 miles, and there are no houses along the way. For emergencies, two lonely refuge huts are situated at the extremities of the pass: one below Devil's Point and the other under Lurcher's Crag.

The passage should not be attempted alone. Despite its fame, the Lairig Ghru will not guarantee you the company of other walkers. You should be fit, properly clad, shod and equipped, for although the way is safe the weather can deteriorate very quickly.

In all, the walk is a test of endurance, and one of the most challenging one-day traverses in Scotland. But its marvels match its proportions. For when Ice Age glaciers ploughed this furrow, they ripped a range apart – and trailed scenic glory in their wake.

see how it acquired its title of 'gloomy'. Now and again you may hear sudden disquieting cries from above; these are the calls of the cock ptarmigan, a refugee from the Ice Age.

Skirting the chill tarns of the Pools of Dee, the track finally approaches the top of the pass – at 2,733 ft above sea level, higher than many British mountains. The summit reaches are crowded with boulders which once had to be cleared by drovers. Improbable as it may seem to weary walkers, the Lairig Ghru once served as an important cattle track over which herds were driven to cattle fairs in the Lowlands.

The Lairig Ghru survived as a drovers' road until the end of the 19th century. But apart from the summit cairn, you have no sense of man modifying the landscape in any way. All around are brutal immensities of rock. If you have tramped here from Braemar you have covered 19 miles, and a 2,000 ft descent lies ahead.

The track continues for another mile through the steeply walled glacial trough, picking up the stream of the Allt Druidh as it descends. Looming to the right is the Lurcher's Crag (3,448 ft), standing sentinel over the northern end of the pass. Beyond it the views slowly broaden out. Across the rocky waste there are

BIRD OF THE MOUNTAINS

The Cairngorms is one of the few places in Britain where the ptarmigan *Lagopus mutus* lives and breeds. It occurs only at altitudes above 2,500 ft, and can be seen along the higher reaches of the Lairig Ghru and on the surrounding heights where it feeds on the leaves and fruits of bilberry, cranberry and heather. The ptarmigan is an arctic species, and like several other arctic birds it changes colour with the seasons – the only British bird to do so. Its summer plumage, which is mottled brown above with white underparts and wings, becomes completely white in winter except for the tail.

Speckled upper plumage camouflages the hen and her chicks among the summer herbage.

Female in winter plumage (above) Male in summer plumage (below)

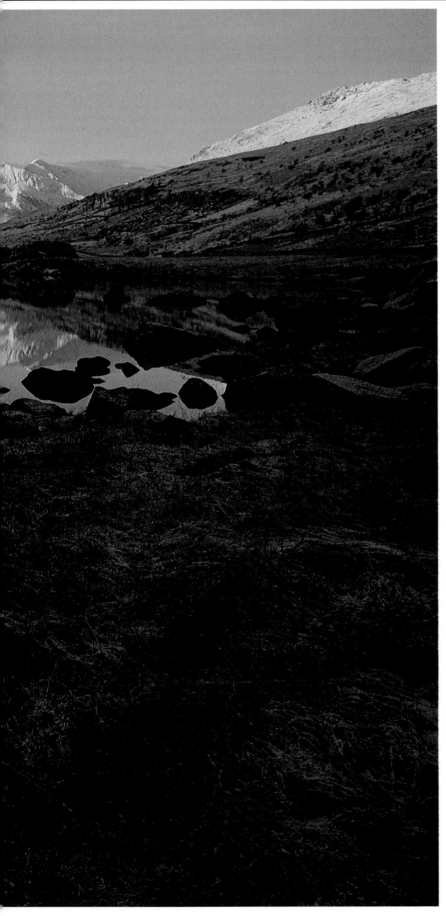

SNOWDON

Gwynedd

Here is a titan that looks the part. Rising to 3,560 ft at its summit, Snowdon is the highest mountain in both Wales and England, a cathedral of glacier-carved rock wrought from its massif by the grandiose sculpture of the Ice Age. Buttressed by knife-edge ridges radiating from the peak, its flanks swoop to vast cupped chasms whose black shadows serve only to enhance the upward thrust of the sharp, pyramidal spire.

Long before its exact height was calculated, people knew it to be the sovereign of all the Welsh mountains. Legends cling to its rugged slopes, and for centuries the wild heights were the mountain fastness of a whole nation. In reality, Snowdon is just one of a whole range of peaks situated in the north-west corner of Wales – it tops its closest competitor by only 75 ft. But Snowdon is isolated from the other mountains by its three famous passes: Llanberis, Nantgwynant and Nant y Betws. These deep valleys open up a host of spectacular views from below, conferring on the colossus an almost Himalayan grandeur.

ON A CLEAR DAY...

If a crow were to fly due south from the summit it would meet no higher mountain until it reached the Pyrenees. Snowdon's lofty elevation, combined with the way that the ground falls away on all sides, have made the apex the finest 180 degree viewpoint in all of Britain. Some have made still bolder claims – an 18th-century visitor wrote: 'It is doubted whether there is another circular prospect so extensive in any part of the terraqueous globe.'

You can look deep into four countries from the summit: Wales, England, Ireland and Scotland. But the familiar prelude 'On a clear day you can see...' has a special relevance to Snowdon. More often than not, the mountain is wreathed in grey vapours, and even when the sky is clear at the summit, clouds may blanket the views below. Wordsworth, who climbed to the top by moonlight in 1793, looked down on a 'silent sea of hoary mist' stretching:

In headlands, tongues and promontory shapes
Into the main Atlantic.

And yet when blessed with fine weather (as in April especially) the views are quite extraordinary. Looking west across the mountain tops and far beyond the sweep of Caernarfon Bay you can see the Wicklow Mountains of Eire descend to the suburbs of Dublin. Turn east and the views extend 100 miles to the Peak District of Derbyshire. To the south the long arm of the Cambrian peaks stretches for nearly 100 miles.

SUN ON SNOWDON *Lit by a rising winter sun, and reflected in the waters of Llynnau Mymbyr, the great horseshoe of Snowdon curves round to the summit. It is to these snow-capped peaks that Yr Wyddfa owes its English name, originally* Snawdun (Snow Hill).

THE LONG VIEW *Even with the landscape under a canopy of cloud, Snowdon lives up to its reputation as the finest viewpoint in Britain. Here the white sands near Llandudno on the Conwy Estuary, 20 miles to the north-east, are clearly visible from the mountain slopes.*

Look north and you can see as far into Scotland as Kirkcudbrightshire, where Merrick Head is the farthest point visible – it is a staggering 144 miles away.

The immense compass takes in two of the upland wonders described in this book: the Black Mountain is visible some 82 miles to the south, while the Great Gable in Cumbria presents a distinct silhouette over 100 miles to the north.

Of course, the weather is not often sympathetic to the longest views. But even when mists lick the summit and the far distances are lost, the immediate foreground presents scenes of superb and craggy majesty. Snowdon's summit is braced by three particularly sharp ridges which plunge to awesome abysses. Thomas Pennant, an 18th-century visitor, described the prospect as he approached the summit as being disclosed 'like the gradual drawing up of a curtain at a theatre'.

THE PLACE OF EAGLES

Snowdon's wild vistas were shaped by those great scene-shifters of the Ice Age – the glaciers. The massif is one mighty fold of volcanic rock, grits and shales which were raised up more than 300 million years ago. Monstrous downward-moving rivers of ice and snow bulldozed their way through the range to hollow out U-shaped troughs and leave pinnacle ridges between.

The effects are nowhere more dramatic than on Snowdon's eastern face, where the three glacial lakes of Llyn Teyrn, Llyn Llydaw and Glaslyn were left as pockets of meltwater. They are enclosed by the two razor-edged reefs of Crib-goch (the Red Comb) and Lliwedd, which between them form what is known as the Snowdon Horseshoe. Above mile-long Llyn Llydaw, the Lliwedd cliffs drop some 1,500 ft to the water. Today, ice and frost are continuing to cut back the hollows, sharpening the rock blades still further.

Winter gave the mountain its name – the term Snowdon seems first to have been applied by Saxon invaders, seeing the summit under its seasonal white mantle. For centuries people continued to believe that the mountain was white-capped all the year round. In fact, the last patches of snow rarely survive later than the end of May.

The Welsh name for the mountain is *Yr Wyddfa* or 'The Burial Place', for its summit is said to be the tomb of Rhita Fawr, a giant slain by King Arthur. Arthur himself is supposed to have died at a dip in the Lliwedd ridge known as the Pass of Arrows – his knights are alleged to be sleeping in a nearby cave, awaiting their sovereign's summons to rise again.

Snowdon has also been known as *Eryri* or 'The Place of Eagles' after the birds which once haunted its heights. The eagles are gone today, like the rebels and outlaws who once took refuge in the mountain fastness; Snowdon sheltered Owain Glyndŵr among others. And Llewelyn II was besieged there by the English until forced by hunger to surrender in 1277.

When Wales fell definitively to the English, the mystique of the mountain endured. To this day, for example, local tradition asserts that the turquoise

---

THE SNOWDON LILY

One of the rarest flowers in Britain grows only on the slopes of Snowdon and two neighbouring mountains. It owes its common name, Snowdon lily, to the place where it is found, and its scientific name, *Lloydia serotina*, to the man who first described it, the 17th-century Welsh botanist Edward Lloyd.

The Snowdon lily grows 2–6 in. and flowers in June.

THE WAY UP *The Miners'
Track is one of the easier
routes to Snowdon's
summit, and scenically
one of the best. Much of it
was originally a cart track
down which was carried
copper ore mined from the
mountain.*

waters of Glaslyn hold the corpse of the Monster of
Conwy, a beast which terrorised villagers until pitched
into the lake from the cliffs. The extraordinary colour
of the water, though, is susceptible to rational explanation. It was stained peacock blue by copper ore
seeping in from mines dug on its banks. Snowdon has
been probed for its minerals for centuries, and
workings around Glaslyn and Llydaw were in operation from the 18th century until the First World War.

The people have been coming for centuries now,
and for all the untamed splendour of the scenery,
Snowdon has a notoriously humanised peak.

The first recorded ascent was made by one Thomas
Johnson in 1639. He was a botanist, and since he was
escorted by a brace of guides it can be assumed that
others had reached the summit before. Throughout
the 18th century, processions of scientists and gentle-
manly adventurers began to appear on the mountain
in ever increasing numbers. Particular interest was
aroused in 1781, with the publication of Thomas
Pennant's *Journey to Snowdon*. Pennant made ascents
by several different routes, even spending a night at
the top to watch the sunrise.

In the Victorian era, guides offered pony rides up
the mountain, and shacks were built at the peak. For a
price, they offered bed, breakfast – and a view of the
sun coming up. By 1896, when the famous rack-and-
pinion railway was built, Snowdon's aura of isolation
had already gone. The summit station today is an
unsightly affair, and the 'cairn' at the peak serves
basically as a huge viewing platform. Even if you
ignore the steam-assisted ascent, there are places
where rock which withstood the mauling of Ice Age
glaciers has been seriously eroded by human feet.

THE BEATEN TRACKS

There are six main paths to the top of Snowdon.
Each offers superb scenery and a good, testing walk of
varying degrees of difficulty. None, however, provides
solitude.

Taking the routes clockwise, starting from the
north, the Llanberis Path is the easiest and it runs
roughly parallel to the railway. At 5 miles in length it is
also the longest approach and, some would say, the
least rewarding despite the fine views of Clogwyn du'r
Arddu, the most daunting rock wall in Wales.

The shortest route is the Pyg Track to the east. It
begins at the Pass of Llanberis (1,170 ft) and there are
splendid views of the Glyders from the outset. As you
climb you look down on the glacial lakes cupped in
the Snowdon Horseshoe. The Miners' Track begins at
the same point but skirts the lakes themselves before
climbing to rejoin the Pyg Track above Glaslyn. This is
perhaps the most scenically appealing route.

The southern approach by the Watkin Path is
gruelling, but it also has its devotees. The track is
named after Sir Edwin Watkin, the Victorian railway
engineer who pioneered it. The opening in 1892 was
a grand affair attended by the prime minister, Mr
Gladstone. Aged 83, the premier walked up as far as
what is called today the Gladstone Rock, from which
he delivered an address. The full walk involves an
ascent of 3,300 ft, starting not far above sea level amid
oakwoods and rhododendrons. It rises up the middle
of a hollow, passing waterfalls and old mine workings
before ascending scree-strewn heights in a succession
of zigzags.

The Rhyd-Ddu Path offers a quick way up, but it has
its moments of hazard. It follows the Llechog ridge up

THE WAY THROUGH *Carved
by an Ice Age glacier, the
narrow pass of Llanberis
divides Snowdon from its
neighbouring peaks, the
Glyders, and provides a
way through the
mountains to Caernarfon.
Three of the six main paths
to the summit of Snowdon
start from the pass.*

THE EASY WAY UP

All walkers toiling up the approaches to Snowdon's summit share the ironic knowledge that there is a simpler way of reaching the top – the Snowdon Mountain Railway, which was opened in 1896.

The track is some 4½ miles long. It starts just outside Llanberis and reaches to within 67 ft of Snowdon's summit, and it is the only mountain railway in Britain to work on the rack-and-pinion principle. It still uses the original steam-engines, which were made in Switzerland.

to the top, and there are some narrow stretches. With lovely views westward it is a favoured way of descent, for you have the setting sun in your face.

The north-western Snowdon Ranger Path completes the circuit of routes, reaching the Llanberis railway track near the top. It is named after an early guide named Evan Roberts, who lived in what is now the Pen-y-Pass Youth Hostel at the start. Styling himself the Snowdon Ranger, Roberts was a colourful character who spared his charges the worst rigours of the climb – his route is short and easy.

WALKING THE KNIFE EDGE

None of the paths, however well trodden, should be taken lightly. The weather on Snowdon is notoriously changeable, and suitable boots and clothing are essential. The National Park authorities also advise a map, compass, whistle, torch, spare food and first-aid kit. An alarming number of accidents do occur; you need sure footing on the narrows of the Rhyd-Ddu, for example, and stamina on the Watkins zigzags.

These qualities are especially necessary on the famous Snowdon Horseshoe, which is by far the best way to experience the mountain's grandeur. The 8 mile route follows the great Crib-goch and Lliwedd crests of the eastern face, taking in the summit between. It is not for beginners or young children, though, since some stretches require rock-climbing skills – or at least a willingness to use hands as well as feet. Above all, you need a head for heights.

The route climbs the coxcomb crest of Crib-goch, with a knife-edge ahead so narrow that it has sometimes been negotiated by dizzy visitors edging along astraddle. Hideous chasms yawn on either side, and there are some famous pinnacles ahead. From the summit, the way descends by the Arthurian Pass of Arrows. The majestic Lliwedd ridge rises to fine peaks of its own, and you have to climb spires as you descend.

The whole route takes some six to eight hours, and the going can be very rough. But there are staggering views of sheer cliff overhanging green, winding valley. You follow the ice-scoured rim of a whole cauldron of wonders – it is the best ridge walk in Britain.

THE HARD WAY UP *Sheer cliffs, ice-covered slopes, knife-edge ridges – these are the ramparts which defend Snowdon's crown (left). They also offer the most spectacular and exhilarating route to the summit – for the experienced climber. The way up follows the ridge of Crib-goch (right), as it runs in front of the peak of Crib Ddysl and along the skyline to Snowdon's summit.*

STAC POLLY

Highland

Its name may mislead, suggesting something caged and slightly comical. But there is nothing tame about this ancient mountain. Stac Polly in fact derives from the Gaelic *Stac Pollaidh* (Rock of the Watery Pools), evoking the wild, flooded landscape from which the weird ridge rises. Situated in the remote Coigach district of north-western Scotland, Stac Polly is frankly outrageous in appearance. Bristling with rock pinnacles, the mountain has commonly been likened to a porcupine – if a giant were to caress its spine, you feel, those needle-sharp quills would draw blood.

In reality, no image drawn from the present-day animal kingdom quite does justice to the immense age of the sandstone mass. If a likeness must be found, then Stac Polly is a dinosaur among mountains, for it is 1,000 million years old and squats on a rock bed which is older still, belonging to the planet's original crust.

It is not alone on its ancient plateau. To the north are other primordial relics: Cul Mor, Canisp and the Sphinx-like monolith of Suilven. Eerie formations left stranded by the ages, each is a disquieting presence. But what time has done to Stac Polly amounts to more than the normal ravages; it seems almost an act of atrocity.

OUT OF ANCIENT CATACLYSM

The north-western Highlands of Scotland are Britain's emptiest place. Stac Polly, on the edge of the former county of Ross and Cromarty, looks into the wilderness of Sutherland, the least populated region in the nation with only 12,000 inhabitants for an area of over a million acres. The solitudes can be as grim as the district's history; the whole region was cruelly depopulated during the Highland Clearances of the last century, when landlords drove thousands from their homes to make space for sheep and deer. The terrain reflects the mood of its past; it is spectacular, certainly, but forbidding too, as if indifferent to the human scale of things.

And it is old – almost unbelievably old. The real dinosaurs had not come into existence when Coigach's landscape was formed. The sandstone mountains rise from a petrified sea of Lewisian Gneiss, the most ancient rock in the British Isles and one of the oldest known anywhere in the world. Estimated to date back an astonishing 2,800 million years it is a metamorphic rock, formed by cataclysmic earth forces of such heat and pressure that its component mineral deposits were, so to speak, welded into alternating bands of crystals including quartz, felspar and mica,

SPLINTERED SPLENDOUR *Stac Polly's central ridge of crumbling pinnacles gives it an outline unique among Britain's mountains. Rearing up from the riven landscape of Coigach, it creates an atmosphere of awe out of all proportion to its size.*

DYING MOUNTAIN *The bristling ramparts of Stac Polly are a reminder that the spectacular fortress mountain is slowly yielding to the assault of ice, rain and wind. In contrast, the smooth bulk of Cùl Beag, rising (left) above Loch Lurgainn, resists erosion – thanks to a cap of hard quartzite which its crumbling neighbour lacks. Cùl Beag will still be there long after Stac Polly has vanished.*

for example, intruded by granite and pegmatite.

About 1,800 million years ago, this hard bed lay at the bottom of a primeval sea. And following that time massive sedimentary deposits of plum-coloured Torridonian sandstone were laid down. Later outpourings from the earth's core capped the sandstone with a layer of tough quartzite. Aeons after the sea had receded, Ice Age rivers and glaciers wrought havoc with the landscape, scouring away great masses of the sandstone and carving even into the implacable gneissian bed to leave it pitted with countless dips and troughs in which waters have collected. All that survived of the Torridonian rock were a few lone outcrops – Stac Polly and the rest – rearing in strange, isolated westward-running ridges above the waste.

Suilven (2,399 ft) to the north presents a magnificent example of a residual ridge. Seen from east or west it appears to soar like a column from the bare horizon (its name derives from a Norse-Gaelic root meaning Pillar Hill). Only when you look at it from the north or south can you see its long ridge formation.

Stac Polly (2,009 ft) shares the same characteristic. Look at the ancient mountain from the coast road to the west and it seems a graceful pyramid. But approach it from the south and the monster bares its shark's teeth.

Stac Polly is unique among its neighbouring mountains for its wildly splintered appearance. The reason is simple; while Suilven and the rest have retained their blunt caps of hard quartzite, erosion has stripped Stac Polly of its protective covering. Ice, rain and wind have been able to insinuate themselves into the softer sandstone below, working down the vertical joints to quarry out gullies and chimneys, leaving forests of isolated stacks.

The process of erosion is continuous. One of the mountain's most famous sights used to be a slender cleft pinnacle, situated to the south of one of the central gullies. Known as the Lobster's Claw, it was capped by a wonderfully lifelike notched pincer of rock, clearly shown in photographs taken this century. But the claw first lost its pincer, and has now been amputated by erosion.

JACK THE RIPPER AND OTHERS

Hosts of bizarre formations have survived though, providing mountaineers with some of the most exciting climbs in Scotland. Tom Patey, pioneer of the Old Man of Hoy, was among those who took up their challenge. In 1968 he achieved the first free-climbing ascent of The Forefinger, a startling rock spire which stabs at the sky from the south-western slopes of the main mass. The Enigma Groove, the Virgin Pinnacle –

the names given to the stacks and fissures are as fittingly off-beat as the features they describe; one of the toughest climbs is a 500 ft ascent by a route known as Jack the Ripper.

ON THE PORCUPINE'S BACK

You do not have to be a mountaineer to experience Stac Polly's wonders. The ridge is fairly accessible, and can be reached from the main road from Ullapool to Lochinver by taking a minor road which runs left to the shore of Loch Lurgainn. A mile-long walk from the road, across open moorland dotted with scrubby trees or by marked path, leads up to the foot of Stac Polly which at first shows none of its bristles. It is, rather, a looming rock castle, a palace of dreams – or of nightmares.

A direct approach from the south presents the whole fantastic ridge in full view. The conspicuous features are easy enough to make out. To the left is the hulking mass of the Summit Buttress, with a second buttress beside it. From those heights, the eye travels down into the crazy central zigzag of turrets and spires which make up what is known as the Pinnacle Basin. There is then a dip into an open 'saddle' in the mass, before the skyline rises again to the two eastern hunks of the Keep and East Buttress.

Cleaving the ridge are a number of gullies, and you have only to scramble up the scree-strewn slopes to gain access to them. One recognised way up the 45 degree slopes is to make for the open saddle, but you can reach the foot of the raw rock ridge at a number of different points. Several tracks lead along to the western summit, which should not be attempted unless you are an experienced and properly equipped rock climber.

For the climber who reaches the summit there are extraordinary views of the weird terrain around. Two large loch systems, north and south of the ridge, seem almost to encircle the mountain with a straggling moat, while innumerable small dips in the gneissian plateau also flash with confusions of water. The landscape, you feel, is half-drowned.

Away to the north-east, across Loch Sionascaig, is the crouching form of Suilven whose whole unforgettable silhouette is clearly delineated. The shapely peak to the right is Canisp (2,779 ft). In closer focus as you turn east are the twin cones of Cul Mor arching up to their caps of quartzite. Next comes the heathery hump of Cùl Beag (2,523 ft), while south across Loch Lurgainn is the steep buttress of The Fiddler on Ben Mor Coigach (2,438 ft). To the west, where Stac Polly's jagged slabs of sandstone drop steeply away, you can see the mouth of Loch Broom, with its broken string of islands stretching out to sea.

The summit views are splendid, but you do not have to make a full ascent to take in the eerie landscape. Stac Polly is so curiously isolated that even its slopes offer superb, open vistas, and many visitors will be content to walk or scramble among the maze of paths and gullies at the lower levels. The East Buttress particularly offers some safe but exhilarating scrambles from ledge to ledge, where the uninitiated

may make cautious experiments with rock climbing. But however you explore Stac Polly, take a camera. The gnarled and fissured rock forms are wonderfully photogenic in themselves, and provide startling foregrounds for the long views beyond.

FLORA OF THE SHATTERED ROCKS

Stac Polly lies in the Inverpolly Nature Reserve, a wild and remote area of loch-strewn moorland, scree-slope and bog. Covering 26,827 acres it is the second largest reserve in Britain (after the Cairngorms) and its rugged acres provide a refuge for all manner of flowers and wildlife.

The naturalist James Fisher has written of the 'truly Alpine' character of Stac Polly's flora. By no means a high mountain, it nonetheless shelters an extraordinary variety of plants. On the ridge itself you may find dwarf azalea and starry saxifrage, cowberry, and alpine forms of club-moss, lichen and fern. Studding the shattered rocks at a slightly lower level are sea pinks, rock speedwell and alpine hawkweed. The islands of Loch Sionascaig, clearly seen from Stac Polly, contain remnants of primeval birch and hazel woodland untouched by man, while red and roe deer abound in the dark grove of Doire Dhubh under Cùl Beag.

There is a rich bird life too. This is one of the few places in Scotland where you are genuinely likely to see a golden eagle in flight. Quartering the land with slow but powerful wing-beats, size alone makes the king of birds an unforgettable sight. While the eagle hunts over land, the black-throated diver patrols the endless pattern of lochs, its eerie wail echoing from the mountains before it plunges underwater in search of fish.

The reserve is a paradise for geologists. Above the Ullapool road to the east is a dark cliff, about a mile long, which provides a classic example of thrust faulting in a landscape. This is the Knockan Cliff, where a break in the earth's crust known as the Moine Thrust is exposed to view.

Some 400 million years ago, a whole chunk of country was forced out of place by titanic earth movements and slid bodily over the landscape to overlie the surface rock. The so-called Moine schists, thrust here from a distance of some 12 miles away, can be seen lying on their beds of quartzite and limestone. The cliff is now a nature trail, splendidly maintained by the Nature Conservancy Council with an Information Centre, and 17 marked observation points illustrating the geology, flora and fauna of the region.

Knockan Cliff is a magnificent viewpoint for Stac Polly, and a place which evokes the ancient forces which have shaped the landscape: plutonic upheavals and grinding collisions, the slow laying of foundations and the vandal ravages of erosion. Creased with age, the splintered mass of Stac Polly looms up in mute witness to an epic of endurance played out in a time-scale beyond human comprehension. You are not aware of its secret plant life from this distance. What you see is a dying mountain whose weird, tall sheaves are waiting on the Reaper.

HUNTER OF THE HIGHLANDS

The wild reaches of the Inverpolly Nature Reserve provide an ideal habitat for that elusive Highland predator, the wildcat.

Wildcats are larger than domestic tabbies. Weighing up to 13 lb, they have a yellowish coat striped black and a long bushy tail. They hunt on open ground at night, stalking voles, hares or game birds.

Wildcat
Felis sylvestris

75

HAWESWATER AND KIDSTY PIKE, CUMBRIA

WHERE WATERS SPARKLE

It brings completeness to a landscape. Awesome in wrath, bewitching in tranquillity, water has nourished the soil of Britain and shaped the pattern of human settlement. And perhaps that elemental purpose has shaped its scenic appeal. At the Swallow Falls, the water roars in foaming cataracts down the steps of a jagged rockbed. At Symonds Yat it glides and curves in mature glory between wooded bank and meadow. At Hickling Broad the water lies still, a reed-edged mirror for the wide Norfolk sky. And above all in the Lake District where the attraction of water in all its moods is doubled by the reflected glory of the mountains above. But whatever character the water assumes, its effect remains compelling, a liquid magnetism which binds viewer to the view.

Swallowtail butterfly
Papilio machaon

HICKLING BROAD
Norfolk

There is drama in the flat horizon. Come to East Anglia's open spaces from almost any other part of the country and you sense a startling absence. There is nothing where the hills ought to be; instead, the sky is everywhere, falling sheer to the ground for as far as the eye can see. You feel curiously bereft – even disquieted – and experience solitude intensely. That lonely aura is part of the east country's magic; here you are intimate with immensities of space.

In Norfolk's Broadland, especially, empty space is a strange and deceptive presence. Lying between Norwich and the coast the area is an extensive wedge of flat country which contains some 30 wide, shallow lakes. The 'Broads' as they are known are linked by a complex network of rivers and dykes which provide a paradise for yachtsmen and pleasure-cruisers. But the waterways lie slightly below the level of the land and are often quite invisible until you are upon them. It is a common and unsettling experience to gaze over the fields and see a disembodied sail drift across the landscape.

Hickling is the largest of Norfolk's broads, and also its least spoiled. With its satellite waters of Heigham Sound and White Slea it covers an area some 3 miles long and 1 mile wide at its greatest. The open waters are well known to boating enthusiasts and the margins of reed-bed, willow and alder provide a haven for wildlife. Above all, though, Hickling embodies the attraction of Broadland, where the sky and the landscape are wide.

MYSTERY OF THE BROADS

Three eastward-flowing rivers water the broads: the Bure, Yare and Waveney, which seem once to have formed an open estuary. From about Roman times, however, the estuary silted up to produce a swampland on which thick layers of peat accumulated. A slight rise in the land surface allowed the peat to dry out, producing the essential substructure of the flatlands known today.

What then of the broads? Until recently, it was assumed that they must have been freak effects of the estuary's silting up. Research in the last 20 years, however, has indicated a quite different origin. It is now known that they are accidental human creations – flooded medieval peat diggings.

Peat was widely used as a fuel in the Middle Ages, and Norwich was a major market for it. The peat from many thousands of acres was extracted between the 11th and 13th centuries, but later, when the sea level rose slightly, the workings were inundated and left as watery lagoons.

The Broadland scene is ever changing; some broads have silted up since the first Ordnance Survey maps were produced, and others are contracting. Hickling itself is one of the shallowest – it is nowhere much more than 6 ft deep. With its mixed habitat of fen, grazing marsh and open water it lies close to the North Sea coast and its water is slightly brackish. These factors have contributed to a rich and unusually varied wildlife. Today, the Hickling Broad National Nature Reserve covers 1,400 acres, and is known internationally for its marshland birds and butterflies.

'YON GOES A HEN HARRIER'

Miss Emma Turner, an early bird photographer, was among many who have loved Hickling's reedy solitudes. She first visited Broadland in 1902, and came upon another enthusiast who greeted her with the words: 'I am Alfred Nudd. Yon goes a hen harrier'. Encouraged by Nudd and other local naturalists, the indefatigable photographer spent much time at Hickling, in a houseboat moored against an island in the broad. That island is still known as Miss Turner's Island.

Hen harriers are no longer a feature of the Broadland scene, though marsh harriers are occasionally sighted. Among Emma Turner's achievements, however, was the discovery of the first young bittern to have been seen in Norfolk for decades. A rare species of heron, the bittern had ceased to breed in Britain around the mid-19th century, because of the drainage of the marshes. It re-established itself in Broadland at the beginning of this century, and remains a haunting presence at Hickling. Bitterns are known especially for their eerie booming call and their habit of 'freezing' when startled; the neck is thrust upwards so that the streaked brown plumage blends with the perpendicular lines of the reeds.

At Hickling, the bitterns keep company among the reeds with sedge warblers, reed buntings and bearded reedlings. The broad is also the home of the beautiful swallowtail butterfly – the largest butterfly in Britain. The reed-beds are a precious asset for naturalists, and the reserve authorities keep them cut regularly to prevent them from being invaded by trees and shrubs. Reed-cutting, of course, is scarcely an innovation; it has been practised for centuries to provide material for the traditional skill of thatching, which in Norfolk has been elevated to an art.

Besides protecting the reed-beds, the reserve authorities also maintain hides and wader pools, carefully regulating their water levels to prevent drying out in summer. These have encouraged such rarities as the black tern, spotted redshank and spoonbill to frequent the broad. The aptly named spoonbill is an especially fascinating wader, related to the heron. It may be seen from April to September arriving as a visitor from Holland.

Lying so close to the coast, Hickling is a stopping-off point for many species of migrating birds, and the rarities are not the only memorable sights. Visit the broad on a late summer evening and you may see clouds of starlings darken the sky, descending on the reed-beds to settle for the night in flocks of thousands.

Sometimes, as you explore the lake's edge at dusk, you may glimpse a huge, dark shape plunge into the water; this is the coypu, Broadland's weirdest resident. A native of South America, which was introduced to

East Anglia in the 1930s, the coypu is a rat-like creature, at 2 ft long as big as a dog. They were farmed for their fur, but many escaped and colonised the river banks, becoming a considerable menace to farmers. They feed on sugar beet and bulbs, also using their webbed back feet to swim in search of mussels and the roots of aquatic plants. They are not to be interfered with, for they have sharp teeth and claws which they use if provoked.

HAUNT OF THE BEARDED REEDLING

Hickling Broad lies a mile south of the village which shares its name. It is best approached from Hickling Staithe, a quay where the Pleasure Boat Inn is a noted meeting-place for boating enthusiasts. The huge expanse of water is screened off at this inlet, however, by trees and reed-beds. To experience the wonder of the broad, you really have to take to the open water; vessels can be hired at the boatyard facing the inn, and a 4 mile water trail can be followed in a boat which plies the lake in summer.

Though popular, Hickling Broad is rarely overcrowded. It is at the north-eastern extremity of Broadland, and remote from the most frequented waters. It is big enough, too, to shelter many secluded inlets; anglers know the quiet places abounding with bream and rudd. The pike fishing is the best in Norfolk; a 31 lb specimen was once drawn from the waters of Hickling.

For a sense of seclusion, the most rewarding route leads down the mile-long Meadow Dike which runs north-east to Horsey Mere. This tranquil water, scattered with tiny islets, is now owned by the National Trust. The reed-beds are a specially favoured breeding site of the bearded reedling. It is also known as the bearded tit and the reed pheasant because it resembles a miniature version of the game bird, with a long tail which streaks out behind in flight. At Horsey Mere you become intensely aware of the sea, which is not much more than a mile to the east. Breezes which ruffle its waters bring with them salt air, and you can make out sandhills in the distance.

Hickling's landscape provides no dramatic natural viewpoints. The most distinctive man-made structures are the windmills: there are examples on the north and south shores of the main broad, while a mile west of Hickling village is the tallest windmill in the country. This is the nine-storey Sutton mill, built in 1787 and recently restored. From it there are magnificent views of flat farmland, marsh and water. Space and distance seem curiously enlarged as you scan the low-lying Norfolk landscape. The eye travels towards the horizon through a vast emptiness magnified, as it were, by the lens of the sky.

PRINCE OF THATCH

For more than 2,500 years, men have been using reeds, rushes and heather to put a warm, dry roof over their heads. With thatching back in fashion, Norfolk reed is in demand these days, because it is long-lasting, as well as handsome. Traditionally, harvesting was by hand – cruel work since the reeds cannot be harvested until the first hard frosts.

The reed-cutter's scythe needs constant sharpening.

FAR HORIZONS *With its blue skies, drifting clouds and golden reed-beds, Hickling Broad is one of the most tranquil corners of a tranquil county. These marshlands, where the land shades almost imperceptibly into the water, are a paradise for bird-lovers, with shy bitterns sheltering in the reeds, along with reed buntings, sedge warblers and stately Bewick's swans.*

LOCH NESS

Highland

To newspaper readers the world over, the name means one thing alone. Loch Ness is the home of the Monster, an elusive creature which has excited Press attention for over half a century. Thousands have come to the loch for no other purpose than to try to catch a glimpse of the beast, and though Nessie may disappoint through failing to appear, the scenery provides ample compensation. For stripped of its folklore, Loch Ness remains one of Scotland's most magnificent inland waters.

The setting is strange and compelling. Over 24 miles long by about a mile wide, the loch runs dead straight through rugged mountains. The depth of the slaty-blue waters is astonishing. The most recent soundings suggest that they attain 975 ft – deeper than any part of the North Sea.

Though surpassed for surface area by Loch Lomond, Loch Ness is the longest continuous body of still water in Britain and holds by far the greatest volume. Its own statistics, however, only hint at the scale of the drama which shaped it. For Loch Ness is a part of something more immense still; the most stupendous geological feature in the British Isles. This is the Great Glen, a land-rip torn across the face of a nation.

THE CATACLYSMIC SLIDE

If you look at a relief map of Britain, you can see that the 100 mile diagonal gash of the Great Glen – *Glen Mor* in Gaelic – splits Scotland in two, running ruler straight from the Moray Firth to Loch Linnhe. About 350 million years ago, cataclysmic earth movements caused the crust to tear, and the whole of northern Scotland slipped some 60 miles to the southwest. Seas vanished in this violent wrench whose vibrations have still not quite died. Faint earth tremors continue to be recorded along the fault line.

The initial cataclysm left a gutter which was deepened during the Ice Age. The biggest glaciers in the Highlands descended into the trough to gouge out the basins of the three main lochs: Loch Ness, Loch Oich and Loch Lochy. The land rose slowly after the glaciers' retreat, elevating the surface of Loch Ness some 50 ft above sea level. Rains streaming from the heights around contributed to the drowning of the trough, but the final separation of northern from southern Scotland was completed as recently as 1822. In that year the great Caledonian Canal was opened, connecting the lochs with each other and the seas to east and west, to provide a coast-to-coast waterway. Today northern Scotland is, in effect, an island.

IS ANYTHING DOWN THERE? *From Fort Augustus, Loch Ness stretches for more than 20 compellingly beautiful miles along the line of the Great Glen. The legend of a monster in the loch goes back at least as far as the 5th century, when St Columba is said to have rescued a monk from 'Nessie'.*

Loch Ness is both the biggest and most remarkable of the Great Glen's lochs. The depth and volume of water are such that its temperature varies little with the seasons. At a fairly constant 42°F, it is cold but never freezes over. The mysterious chasms of its bed are far too difficult for divers to attain and are cloudy with peaty silt brought down from the mountains. Even the most sophisticated underwater cameras have revealed little more than ill-defined shadows in the murky depths.

It is not known exactly what goes on at the lowest levels. However, the waterlogged trunks of ancient pine trees may sometimes be brought to the surface by the escaping gases of decayed matter. Breaking to view in aerated cauldrons of foam, they may account for some, at least, of the mysterious sightings. The blackened trunks would, of course, sink as soon as the bubbles were spent.

ALONG THE FLOODED TRENCH

The road from Inverness to Fort Augustus follows the whole western shore of Loch Ness and provides a scenic drive through the great Highland fault. There are no islands in the loch and it has no wildly scribbled skyline of peaks. In general the mountains on either side are of fairly even height, rising abruptly to some 1,500 ft and mantled at the water's edge with woodlands of oak, birch, ash and, above all, of pine. The loch is most majestic when autumn daubs its banks with the variegated tones of gold, indigo and olive which are mirrored in the surface. To watch the western sun set fire to the sheet is a sublime experience.

The road itself is well used but less overburdened with traffic than it becomes when it reaches Loch Lomond, far to the south. Those 'bonnie banks' are justly famed for their loveliness – but lie perilously close to Glasgow. Loch Ness, in contrast, has an aura of unspoiled emptiness. Away across the water rise the lonely Monadhliaths – literally Grey Mountains – where there are miles of fine walking through wild country. Ahead, as you drive, is the romantic silhouette of Urquhart Castle, jutting into the water on a promontory at Strone.

Here there is a rare break in the straight shoreline, where the rivers Enrick and Coiltie come down from the moors to form a sweeping horseshoe bay. Urquhart Castle, commanding the southern entrance to the inlet, is a haunting ruin fought over through centuries of turmoil. You can see why the soldiery wanted it. The views from the promontory are superb and command practically the full length of the water. Look back down the loch and you can see almost as far as Inverness; ahead the eye travels towards Fort Augustus.

Up above, on the Coiltie, are the woodland Falls of Divach – a famous beauty spot – and the walk up provides some of the best high-level views of the loch. J. M. Barrie wrote *Peter Pan* in a lodge overlooking the falls, but for lovers of fantasy the Urquhart area has a stronger fascination. In the waters off the Bay are the deepest reaches of the loch – and it is here that the Monster has most often been 'sighted'.

For all its aura of mystery, Loch Ness is a practicable waterway, and Urquhart has melancholy associations with modern times. A cairn there commemorates the racing driver John Cobb who died on Loch Ness in 1952, trying to break the world water-speed record.

From the Bay, the road resumes its straight course, looping round the mouth of Glen Moriston, before reaching Fort Augustus at the south-western extremity. The Caledonian Canal issues into Loch Ness down a staircase of locks running through the village. By the canal is a Great Glen Exhibition which illustrates the story of the landscape (and has a room devoted to the Monster).

THE GENERAL'S ROAD

The village is a historic one which owes its name to a fort built here by General Wade in 1729 and dedicated to William Augustus, Duke of Cumberland. Its purpose was to protect the general's famous road through the Highlands; Wade's men laid down 250 miles of roads and bridges to assist troop movements and keep down unruly Jacobite clans.

The general's military road ran the length of Loch Ness on the eastern side, and is the route used by motorists today. It climbs steep gradients out of Fort Augustus to level out on high, open moorland where the heather grows thick. Off the road are a number of delightful little lochans, more intimate than the wide sheet below. Among them is reed-edged Loch nan Lann, reached by way of Knockie Lodge, whose waters stream down through a steeply wooded gorge to feed the Monster loch.

The road itself returns to the lochside at the village of Foyers, the site of one of Scotland's grand spectaculars. Here, through a forest ravine, the peaty waters of the River Foyers crash down some 400 ft in little over a mile, forming two thunderous cascades of 40 and 90 ft. Dr Johnson, no faint-heart, had to turn his eyes from their 'dreadful depth', while the poet Robert Burns commemorated them in verse (sadly the lines are by general consent among the worst which he ever penned). The tremendous power of the water has been harnessed for hydroelectricity since 1896, and a generating station is still maintained – it does little to detract from the grandeur of the falls or the natural beauty of the surroundings.

Across the water rises the hump of Meall Fuarmhonaidh (2,284 ft), the most prominent of the loch's mountains and a noted haunt of the golden eagle. From Foyers, General Wade's road runs for 10 miles along the wooded lochside, passing the hamlet of Inverfarigaig at the mouth of a narrow and bewitching pass where a Forest Trail has been laid out. As you drive on, Urquhart Castle comes into clear focus across the water and, finally, at Dores, the loch and road part. While the general's way keeps straight ahead, Loch Ness narrows into the River Ness and the approaches of the Caledonian Canal.

BIRTH OF A LEGEND

It would be unfair to leave Loch Ness without

THE SECRET OF THE LOCH

It's a fish. It's a hoax. It's an otter at play. It's a floating log. It's rotting vegetation, rising up from the bottom of the loch. It's a monster from the days of the dinosaurs. All of these theories and more have been put forward to explain the mystery that lurks in Loch Ness.

A monster? Pictures taken in 1960 (top) and 1934.

sketching the origins of its lore. The Monster's pedigree is impeccable; the first reported sighting was made by none other than St Columba, the 6th-century Irish missionary who brought Christianity to Scotland.

The incident is recorded by St Adamnan, the missionary's biographer, in a *Life* of about AD 700. It seems that a water monster attacked and killed a ferryman on Loch Ness. Undaunted, St Columba determined to cross the water and sent one of his followers to swim after the ferryman's boat. The Monster rose again from its depths, jaws gaping with anticipation. But St Columba firmly rebuked it with the words: 'Thou shalt go no further nor touch the man; go back with all speed.' The Monster meekly obliged.

Sporadic reports of Nessie persisted until the 20th century. Daniel Defoe, for example, reported 'leviathans' disturbing soldiers at Loch Ness in 1716. The frenzied interest of the Press dates only from April 1933, when an Inverness couple, Mr and Mrs John Mackay, filed a detailed story which appeared in the *Inverness Courier*. Sober citizens, they described a creature which 'disported itself, rolling and plunging

for fully a minute, its body resembling that of a whale, and the water cascading and churning like a simmering cauldron'.

Throughout that summer the national papers carried reports of new sightings, and blurred photographs which seemed to confirm Nessie's existence.

The story – and the sightings – have persisted ever since. Sonar, infra-red cameras and other devices have been used to probe the waters – in 1982, a patent was taken out for a new scheme involving pressure-sensitive cameras attached to trained dolphins. Innumerable theories have been advanced, ranging from a stranded colony of prehistoric plesiosaurs to giant eels and schools of otters.

Fascinating as the unsolved problem remains, Loch Ness has other attractions. By this long, majestic water you are always aware of a strangeness. It is in the curiously straight shorelines, the banked mountains to either side, and the sheet which extends like a broad, immobile river as far as the eye can see. The views inspire a wonder independent of the folklore. The true mystery of Loch Ness is in its landscape, and the titanic forces which shaped its weird geometry.

PROUD TOWER *The Great Glen provides a ready-made invasion route through the Highlands, and the site of Urquhart Castle has been fortified since Pictish times. A castle built there in the 12th century changed hands at least 16 times during the two centuries of bloodshed that followed. One of its holders was Robert Bruce. The battle-scarred site was repaired in 1509, but in 1692 William of Orange had the castle blown up to prevent it from falling into Jacobite hands.*

PONT CYSYLLTE

Clwyd

When the foaming salmon waters of the River Dee come down from the mountains of Gwynedd they enter one of the loveliest landscapes in Wales. This is the green Vale of Llangollen. Looming to the north is the ancient hill-fort of Castell Dinas Bran; to the south is the windswept mass of the Berwyn Mountains. But between the heights, the valley offers much gentler views, Arcadian vistas of rolling meadow and woodland slope. And the Dee is accompanied by a delightful neighbour as it threads its way through the vale – the Llangollen Canal, a sleepy man-made waterway.

For some 7 miles, river and canal run parallel to one another, never more than half a mile apart. At Pont Cysyllte, however, the artificial waterway connects with the Shropshire Union Canal and turns abruptly south. Gliding over the Dee at a breathtaking height, it is sustained by a scenic miracle of engineering. When the great aqueduct was first opened, people called it the 'stream in the sky'.

Pont Cysyllte is counted as one of the Seven Wonders of the Waterways. Opened in 1805, the majestic structure boasts 18 slender piers which soar to 127 ft over the Dee, spanned by a cast-iron channel extending 1,007 ft across the vale. This is a supremely functional piece of architecture; the water is contained in a trough of flanged plates bolted together almost 200 years ago, and today they are not leaking a drop. But it is also a thing of beauty. Seen from below, the massive tonnage of iron and stone seems airy, almost weightless. No classical colonnade more graces a landscape, or more successfully combines elegance with grandeur. It is rare for an item of industrial architecture to be protected as an Ancient Monument, but Pont Cysyllte has won that distinction.

THE MASTER BUILDER

The Pont Cysyllte aqueduct was the work of Thomas Telford, born in Scotland in 1757 and a giant among the engineers of the great age of canal building. Although the aqueduct was not his first project to reach completion, it was the one which made his reputation.

North of Pont Cysyllte there used to be important limestone quarries, collieries and smelting works. The Shropshire Union Canal was planned to bring coal, iron and lime down from the Welsh uplands to the Cheshire plain, while the Llangollen Canal was conceived as a feeder to serve the larger waterway. To bear their combined waters over the vale, an aqueduct was needed.

The first experiments with iron aqueducts were just being made when Telford started work, in 1795, and he became fired with enthusiasm for the material. The advantages of iron were manifold; structures would not need to be so massive, and units could be prefabricated at a much lower cost than masonry blocks. Telford set to work with visionary flair.

CANAL WITH A VIEW *Crossing Pont Cysyllte in a boat offers a remarkable view of the Dee below, but is not an experience for those prone to vertigo.*

He began by working on plans for a seven-arch aqueduct, the remainder of the span to be raised by embankment. But earthworks were obtrusive, and he radically reduced the need for them by increasing the number of arches to 19. There were to be 18 piers, or squared pillars, each solid up to 70 ft and then left hollow but braced by internal cross-walls. The iron was cast at the Plas Kynaston ironworks just north of the vale, and the trough was composed of plates shaped in 11 different patterns. Bolted together they comprised a long mosaic of wedges forming a watertight gutter.

Pont Cysyllte gained its name from a hamlet on the north bank of the site. The aqueduct took over eight years to complete, and the cost was exactly £47,018. The structure was officially opened on November 26, 1805 to a salute of cannon fired by infantrymen of the Shropshire Volunteers. A huge crowd gathered to witness the event, and gaped as a file of boats floated in majestic procession over the vale, including one craft carrying a band playing martial music. There must have been talk among the onlookers of the progress of the war against Napoleon: 1805 was the year of Trafalgar. But Telford took some pride in his own logistic struggle – among his army of labourers, only one life had been lost.

A FRAME FOR THE SKY

Today, an inscribed stone under one of the arches records the initiation of the building work. A little upstream of the aqueduct is the much older Bont Bridge, dating back to Roman times, which offers one of the best views of Telford's work. The effects are magical. Eighteenth-century landscape artists sometimes erected folly bridges purely to delight the eye – they never achieved anything like this. Like many great works of architecture, it is an essentially bold and simple design: a range of towering verticals, a spanning horizontal, and a set of delicate arches to unite them. For all its massive strength, the sense of air and space is overwhelming. The sky *between* the arched piers absorbs the eye as much as the aqueduct itself.

To enjoy a full view of the whole span, it is best to climb up from the river and walk across the aqueduct itself. The towpath can be reached from both sides of the vale; on Pont Cysyllte it does not run alongside the canal but is cantilevered over it. The towpath protrudes nearly 5 ft over the trough of water, leaving a space 7 ft 2 in. wide for boats to pass along. There is a railing along the outer edge of the towpath, but on the other there is nothing at all. Boats touch the very rim of the trough, and passengers look over their gunwales straight into the chasm – a hair-raising experience. If you stand on the towpath as a pleasure craft crosses the aqueduct, you are likely to hear squeals from the deck.

The tree-tops are some distance below, and the boisterous Dee sparkles like tinsel through the tracery of leaves. Looking west, Bont Bridge has suddenly become very small, and the few buildings beyond are like dolls' houses. In the far distance, the rounded hills fade into mists of blue.

Pont Cysyllte might have been erected for sheer pleasure as an artificial viewpoint, but of course it was not. Telford made every provision for the practical maintenance of the aqueduct. The bed of the trough is cleaned simply by pulling out a plug in the bottom.

Keeping to the towpath and heading north from the aqueduct is a wonderful walk back up the Vale of Llangollen to the end of the canal. The path winds through woods and meadows, skirting the slopes of Castell Dinas Bran, and offering fine views of the Dee. The towpath passes under canal bridges built by Telford and eventually terminates at the head of the vale where another of his works can be seen. This is the Horseshoe Falls, an exquisitely curved weir where a flat sheet of water drained from the Dee drops only 18 in. to feed the canal.

There is a particularly pleasing fitness about the towpath walk, following the works of the master builder from the Horseshoe Falls, past the sturdy bridges with which he spanned the infant canal to the vale's broad mouth where he carried it high over the mother river. After building Pont Cysyllte, Telford went on to create many marvels of Britain's inland waterways. But he never surpassed his great Welsh masterpiece for scenic wonder – and no successor has matched it since. For many, the Vale of Llangollen remains Telford's valley, a landscape of natural beauty enhanced by the vision of genius.

WATER OVER WATER *Carrying the Llangollen Canal over the River Dee on graceful arches, Telford's Pont Cysyllte aqueduct is as watertight today as the day it was built, at the dawn of the 19th century. Originally, an all-stone aqueduct was planned, with locks at either end. But Telford fell in love with a new building material – cast iron.*

RIEVAULX

North Yorkshire

The first glimpse can stop you dead in your tracks. Half hidden in the valley of the Rye, the silver-grey arches of Rievaulx Abbey soar in magnificent tiers against the background of wooded hills. Seen from the tree-shadowed bowers, the ruins have an unearthly quality of tranquillity. Shafts of sunlight stream through the great open roof and bays to cast luminous pools over smooth lawns of emerald green. This is a place of reverie. The Yorkshire writer James Herriot has called it the most beautiful monastic ruin in England, and he is not alone in his judgment. Turner attempted to capture its magic in paint, while the poet William Cowper wished to live within sight of the abbey forever. Rievaulx is a hymn in stone, and its serene grandeur can shock through sheer loveliness.

THE WOODED DALE

Ryedale is among the most pleasing of all Yorkshire's upland valleys. Winding its way through the North York Moors, the River Rye itself is only 25 miles long from its source in the Cleveland Hills to its confluence with the Derwent. And yet it encompasses in miniature all that is distinctive about the dales. It rises in wild country to tumble down across Snilesworth Moor and descend into a pastoral landscape of hill, field and greystone farm. The bare moorlands continue to dominate the skyline, but as the river enters the dale its banks become deeply wooded.

The steep escarpment, clustered with oak, sycamore and ash, offers a number of superb river views. From the edge of Hazel Head Wood on the east bank, for example, are splendid panoramas across the river to the tawny heights of Arden Great Moor. Another viewpoint, also on the east bank, overlooks the spot where the River Seph runs into the Rye from Blisdale. The confluence is dominated by two delightfully hummocked limestone hills called Hawnby Nab and Easterside.

Not far downstream from this beauty spot, enfolded by tree-girt hills, is Rievaulx itself.

THE AUSTERE BROTHERHOOD

The tremendous ruin stands on a shelf of land above the Rye, and green water-meadows extend for some distance below before meeting the river banks. The abbey owes its name to the river – Rievaulx is Norman-French for 'Rye Valley'. The monks who named it would have pronounced it 'Reevo', but in local parlance it emerges as something like 'Rivers'.

The abbey was founded in 1131 by Walter l'Espec, a great and pious soldier, as a mission centre for the Cistercians. It was the first among many Cistercian abbeys which were to be established in the North of England and whose riverside ruins today are the glories of the Yorkshire dales: Fountains in Skeldale, for example, and Bolton Priory in Wharfedale.

The Cistercians were an austere monastic order who deliberately sought out remote places to set up their communities. In the 12th century the Rye valley was certainly wilder than today, and a contemporary chronicler called Rievaulx 'a horrible and solitary place'. Yet it is hard to believe that a sense of its beauty played no part in the monks' choice of site. It was not ideal from the practical point of view, and in one respect demanded a radical departure from hallowed tradition.

Convention required that a church should be aligned on an east-west axis. But the shelf at Rievaulx slopes markedly in this direction. Instead of looking elsewhere, the brothers broke the rules. They built their church to run north and south, roughly parallel with the river.

The cruciform church itself is the most imposing part of the ruin, its huge unroofed walls offering the vision which quickens the pulse. Not much remains of the original nave to the north, dating to the 12th century and built in the plain style of the order's Rule. Rievaulx's crowning glories are the superb choir and presbytery to the south, which were added in about 1230. Here the builders abandoned all thought of simplicity to produce one of the finest surviving examples of English Gothic architecture. Three splendid tiers of arcading form the east and west-facing walls, with a double tier of three arches in the wall facing south. At the north end, a majestic stone bridge arches ethereally above; this once helped to support a central tower which, like the roof, has been lost.

It is hard to conceive the original impact of the whole, but today the church's very ruin contributes to its enchantment. Below, on the river side of the green shelf, are the remains of the chapter house, cloister, kitchen, warming house, dormitory and refectory. They are in various stages of decay, but testify to the size of the community in its prime. Rievaulx once

supported 140 monks and 500 lay brothers, and it was written that the church 'swarmed with them like a hive of bees'.

The brethren colonised vast tracts of the surrounding wilderness, clearing fields for crops, but most important of all tending huge flocks of sheep on the hills above. It was the wool from these sheep which provided the wealth that allowed them to build on such a magnificent scale. Among their most impressive works was to deflect the course of the Rye itself. In the 12th century the river flowed on the east side of the dale, immediately below the abbey. To provide themselves with some valuable meadowland, the monks cut a new channel for the river on the west side of the valley. The work was completed early in the 13th century, and if today the Rye snugly embraces the contours of Ashberry Hill, it is because the brethren put it there.

THE RIEVAULX WALKS

Gazing at the noble ruin, it is difficult to imagine its builders as frontiersmen. The abbey seems to belong to some vast cathedral city rather than a secluded dale. And, in fact, the scale of the brethren's ambitions took its toll. They fell badly into debt. A decline set in, hastened by the depredations of the Scots and the ravages of the Black Death. When Henry VIII dissolved the monasteries in 1538, Rievaulx was already a shell, supporting a community of only 22 monks.

Today, the ruin stands near the little village of Rievaulx, whose parish church is built on the foundations of the abbey gate chapel. A fine old stone bridge spans the river a little downstream; it was erected to replace the monks' original bridge which was washed away by flooding in 1754.

This stretch of the river offers some lovely walks, and one of the most attractive starts from the village of Old Byland, on the other side of the Rye. Old Byland used to have its own abbey, which was abandoned as being too close to Rievaulx for comfort. The monks on each side of the river could hear each other's bells, and the incessant ringing was 'not fitting and could by no means be endured'. The walk from Old Byland encompasses Ashberry Hill, with some entrancing views over to Rievaulx, seen through dappled glades.

Another approach can be made from Helmsley, a market town south of the abbey. Helmsley is the starting point of the Cleveland Way, a long-distance footpath leading right around the North York Moors National Park as far as the east coast. Rievaulx lies just off the Way, and the route to it is by a marked footpath.

But perhaps the finest views of the abbey are obtained from Rievaulx Terrace, situated on a wooded escarpment to the south. This superb embankment was landscaped in the 18th century, with Grecian-style temples at either end. It winds for half a mile above the river, with vistas cut through the hanging woods to reveal one glimpse after another of the abbey far below.

It would be hard to find a more imaginative example of landscaping than this. The setting is one of classical elegance, and looks down on ruins haunted with sublime Romantic enchantment.

THE GLORY OF RIEVAULX *The handsome nave of Rievaulx Abbey church leads the eye to the majestic windows beyond the high altar. Because the church was built in a narrow valley, it could not be aligned in the traditional way, with the altar at the east end. Instead, it is set on a north-south axis.*

TEMPLES ON THE TERRACE

High above the wooded banks of the Rye, Rievaulx Terrace was created specifically to offer views of the ruined abbey below. The splendid lawns and temples were laid out in the 1750s by Thomas Duncombe, who lived at Duncombe Park about a mile downstream.

The terrace follows the sinuous contours of its tree-clad escarpment. Gaps were cut through the foliage to provide thrilling vistas of the ruin from different angles. A Neoclassical temple stands at each end of the terrace: a Doric rotunda to the south-east and a rectangular Ionic temple at the north-west.

The Ionic temple. It was used as a palatial dining-room

The Doric rotunda, based on classical Greek designs

SWALLOW FALLS

Gwynedd

Wales is a land of waterfalls, its splendid cascades varying in character from the awesome might of the Mynach to the curtained grace of the Mellte and the shadowed enchantment of the countless lesser cataracts which thread the woodlands of, for example, the Dinas and Talybont forests. At 240 ft, Pistyll Rhaeadr in Powys has the highest drop of them all, but even this magnificent natural showpiece is rivalled for fame by the Swallow Falls in Snowdonia.

Here, rushing down from the mountains, the River Llugwy does everything that you could ask of moving water. It plummets, spouts and seethes, swirling and bending among the broken fangs of its rock-bed in a roaring chaos of foam. From certain angles the falls have an air of exquisite grace, as if the very fabric of the river had been unravelled into a delightful confusion of white skeins and threads. From others it is a wild thing, the very spirit of tormented energy, and a lash for the agonised ghost which is supposed to lie wailing below.

In essence, the Llugwy drops in three stepped falls, though each is so fractured by jagged rocks that the overall impression is of a multitude. George Borrow, the 19th-century author of *Wild Wales*, gave an account which remains true to what is there today:

'First there are a number of little foaming torrents, bursting through rocks about twenty yards above the promontory, on which I stood. Then come two beautiful rolls of white water, dashing into a pool a little way above the promontory; then there is a swirl of water round its corner into a pool below on its right, black as death and seemingly of great depth; then a rush through a very narrow outlet into another pool, from which the water clamours away down the glen ...'

THE RIVER OF LIGHT

Borrow called the Llugwy valley a 'region of fairy beauty and of wild grandeur'. And although the river's course is followed today by the tourist artery of the London to Holyhead road, the setting has lost none of its majesty. The scenery all around is near alpine in character, the main road running through spectacular mountain country backed by the Glyders, the Carnedds, Moel Siabod and Snowdon itself.

The name *Llugwy* in Welsh means 'light' or 'bright', a tribute to the many falls and rapids which irradiate the river's course. Rising high on Carnedd Llewelyn, the stream tumbles into its valley, swollen by the inflow of countless small torrents as it rushes down pine-clad slopes and through oakwood gorges.

FOAMING FALLS *Churning and thundering, the waters of the river Llugwy plunge over Swallow Falls in Snowdonia. The name of the falls has no connection with swallows, but is derived from the Welsh* Rhaeadr Ewynnol, *'Fall of foam'.*

LEGEND OF THE FALLS *As if the excitement of thundering waters were not enough, Swallow Falls (facing page) has its own legend, too. The spirit of the wicked baronet Sir John Wynn is said to lie beneath the falls, tormented by the waters in death for the misdeeds of a shameful life.*

THE UGLY HOUSE

There is no bridge across the Llugwy at the Swallow Falls; the nearest way of crossing the river is Ty Hyll Bridge, about three-quarters of a mile upstream. *Ty Hyll* in Welsh means 'Ugly House', and takes its name from an extraordinary cottage on the north bank. Squat and bulbous in appearance, it is built of huge, uncemented boulders. The building is thought to date back to about 1470, and is said to have served both as a bandit's den and a shelter for cattle drovers.

The cottage may originally have been built by night. There is a local tradition that if a person managed to erect a chimney and fireplace – and have the fire going – on a landowner's estate between sunset and sunrise, he could claim the plot for his own. The custom further permitted the builder to stand at the front door and throw an axe north, south, east and west, claiming for himself all the ground covered. It is said that some brothers built Ty Hyll in precisely this fashion.

Ugly House

The Swallow Falls lie between Capel Curig and Betws-y-Coed, and long before a tarmac road opened up the beauty of the region to motorised travellers the grandeur of the cataract had been known. In the 18th century, for example, the author Thomas Pennant described how the Llugwy hurls itself into the chasm of the falls: 'The river runs along a straight stony channel for a considerable way, amidst narrow meadows bounded by majestic alpine scenery; then falls into an amazing hollow. The bottom is difficult of access; but, when arrived at, exhibits a wonderful scene of mountain and precipice, shaded with trees.'

George Borrow believed that the falls' name derived from the speed with which the waters rush and skip along, resembling the beautifully erratic flight of the swallow. It is a pleasing notion, which many present-day visitors have probably shared. In reality, though, the name is a corruption of the original Welsh *Rhaeadr Ewynnol*, meaning 'Fall of foam'. Through careless popular usage this became *Rhaeadr y-Wennol*– 'Fall of the swallow'.

THE GHOST OF THE FALLS

At the bottom of the Swallow Falls, the waters emit a tremendous roar. It is said locally that the noise is not an entirely natural phenomenon, but incorporates the howling of a soul in purgatory.

For centuries, the falls themselves, and the land all about, were owned by the Gwydyr estate of the Wynn family, one of the great historic dynasties of North Wales. Their memory survives in, among other things, the name of the Gwydyr Forest which flanks the Llugwy above Betws-y-Coed. The family's tumultuous early history was written by a member named Sir John Wynn (1554–1627), who is remembered as more than a historian of note. He was also, it seems, known locally as a grasping oppressor. After his death, a superstition evolved that the old tyrant's shade lay under the Swallow Falls, 'there to be punished, purged, spouted upon, and purified from the foul deeds done in his days of nature'.

At the beginning of this century, a blind harpist named Arthur Owen, of Trawsafon, used to regale visitors at the falls with songs of Sir John and his wickedness.

Today, the rocky spur on which George Borrow stood is hard by the main road, equipped with railed steps and observation platforms at three different levels. An admission fee is payable, but no one could begrudge the modest charge. The view from the top platform is magnificent, showing the initial downward plunge; and from the lowest platform the impression is even more spectacular.

FROM THE SANCTUARY IN THE WOOD

The cascade is generally reached by the main road from Betws-y-Coed, a tiny, beautifully situated town which is justly famed for its picturesque charm. Besides the Llugwy running through the village, Betws-y-Coed is also positioned at its confluence with the Conwy and Lledr. With three rivers coming together in one place, you are never far from the

sound of rushing water. You are never far from a bridge either. There are two fine old stone bridges and, in addition, Thomas Telford's cast-iron Waterloo Bridge, built in 1815 to span the Conwy. Elaborately worked with motifs of rose, thistle and shamrock, it was its designer's pride and joy. 'When you reach Waterloo Bridge,' wrote Telford, 'I must insist that you leave your carriage and examine the work fully. It is the best cast-iron bridge yet constructed.'

Betws-y-Coed means 'Sanctuary in the Wood', and there is no finer centre for experiencing the delight of Wales's forest waters. Walks to the south, for example, lead to the Conwy and Machno falls, to the Beaver's Pool and Fairy Glen. Cupped in the mountain slopes around are countless woodland lakes and reservoirs, among which is the lovely Llyn Elsi, south-west of the village.

But the Swallow Falls are the grand attraction, and they too may be approached on foot, rather than by car, from the village. The path crosses Pont y Pair bridge, a fine 15th-century stone affair leading over to the north bank of the Llugwy. The way then runs for some 2½ miles through woods and meadows. In the hills north of Betws are a number of abandoned lead mines, and en route for the falls you can make your way down to the old Miner's Bridge, a curious wooden structure which spans the Llugwy at an angle. The top end is supported by rocks, and it runs like a ladder down to the opposite bank. The bridge was built as a short cut for the miners of Pentre-du, the little village on the south bank of the river.

Returning to the upper path, the walk leads on to fine views of the Swallow Falls which are seen streaming white far below. You can also, by taking some care, make your way down to a spot which presents the whole length of the cascade in full view.

IN GWYDYR FOREST

Nature trails have been laid out in Gwydyr Forest on both sides of the falls. They wind among pines and more traditional woodlands of oak, birch and mountain ash. Take one of these routes and you walk almost immediately into a world far from the bustle of traffic.

Polecats are often sighted in these quiet places and the bird life is especially rich, varying with the nature of the woods. Among the broadleaved trees, for example, are wood warblers, blackcaps, pied flycatchers and redstarts. Enter the dense plantations of young conifers and you have as companion the coal tit, jay and tiny goldcrest. Among the mature pines, meanwhile, are members of the finch tribe – siskin, redpoll and the rare crossbill which uses its scissored beak to extract seeds from pine cones. There are delights for the botanist too; on the spoil-heaps of overgrown lead workings you may find such rarities as forked spleenwort and alpine pennycress.

But it is the water all around that lends a unique character to these woods: the tranquil lakelets glimmering among the trees, the streams which feed the river, and the cataracts which climax at the Swallow Falls, where the shade of Sir John howls eternally under the white scourge of the Llugwy's wrath.

SYMONDS YAT

Hereford & Worcester

It is a classically serene river view. Looking north-east from the summit of Symonds Yat Rock, the silken Wye winds its long course between woodland slope and water-meadow, disappearing at last into a scalloped landscape of hedged fields. Up to the right is the shaggy hump of Coppett Hill, a green mound whose bracken flanks glow ember red in autumn. Beyond can be seen the spires of Goodrich and Ross and, in the far distance, a line of hazed blue hills. Come to Symonds Yat and the prospect is yours for as long as you choose to linger.

A viewing platform has been cut from the gnarled rocky top of the Yat, offering not one view, but many. Lean against its north-eastern parapet and there is a vertiginous drop at your elbow; over the wall the ground plunges sheer for hundreds of feet into a forested abyss. Look back to the south-east, for example, and the Wye can be seen approaching in a lazy curve under the pale cliffs of Coldwell Rocks. A few paces across the viewing platform leads to the north-western prospect where the river, having been compelled to perform a 4 mile loop around Huntsham Hill to the north, sweeps back among wooded slopes dotted with cottages. A fourth angle, to the south-west, shows the Wye sliding away under the clifftopped rim of its limestone gorge.

In reality, Symonds Yat offers a whole panorama of Wye views, fragmented by hill crest and tree-tops. The high rock is almost an island, moated by the loveliest river in Britain.

RELICS OF A TURBULENT PAST

Few could deny the Wye the superlatives which have been lavished on it. Rising in the Plynlimon mountains of eastern Wales, the salmon-rich water extends for 130 miles to its confluence with the Severn near Chepstow.

This is the country of the English-Welsh borders, and scattered along the Wye's banks are a number of timeworn relics of a turbulent past. The river winds serenely past the magnificent ruins of Goodrich Castle, for example, a 12th-century border fort laid waste by Cromwell's cannon. It flows under the splendid gatehouse bridge at Monmouth, and on to the massive castle at Chepstow.

But besides such romantic historical sites there is a natural beauty in the river's course. Flowing broad and level among high wooded hills, the Wye bends, curves and loops in a series of wonderful meanders combining grandeur with pure fantasy.

Symonds Yat, between Ross and Monmouth, is easily reached from the old forest mining centre of

POET'S RIVER *Seen from Symonds Yat, the River Wye curves lazily through meadows and wooded slopes. This was the valley, and this the kind of scene, that led William Wordsworth to muse on thoughts that 'connect the landscape with the quiet of the sky'.*

Coleford, or by a narrow road which crosses the river by a single-track bridge from Goodrich and climbs steeply to the summit.

THE DEEP MEANDERS

A slow drama of the ancient landscape shaped Symonds Yat's imposing scenery. Some 2 million years ago the Wye was probably flowing across a broad and level plain, having little effect on its underlying rock bed but meandering slowly, rather like an estuarial river. Then, during succeeding Ice Ages, the sea level gradually fell. The river quickened in consequence, cutting with some force into its winding bed as it flowed more swiftly, to shear away the steep cliffs which remain exposed today.

Technically, the results are known as incised meanders, and at the Yat they begin at Coldwell Rocks, about 4 miles upstream from Monmouth. Here, the river meets a hard type of limestone known as Lower Dolomite – the rock of the Yat itself – which tends to form impressive vertical cliffs. The river at first escapes on its looping northern detour, but returns to re-enter limestone country where it carves the majestically contoured Wye Gorge.

The wonders of this stretch of the river have been known to tourists from 1745, when a local vicar had a pleasure boat built to escort his friends down the Wye. It was not long before the Wye Tour, a popular two-day cruise from Ross to Chepstow, was being run. William Wordsworth described the landscape in verse with his *Lines Composed a Few Miles Above Tintern Abbey*, and the opening passage well evokes the scenery of Symonds Yat with its reference to:

> … *steep and lofty cliffs*
> *That on a wild secluded scene impress*
> *Thoughts of more deep seclusion; and connect*
> *The Landscape with the quiet of the sky.*

Yat Rock knew human presence long before the Romantics came to admire it. Five parallel lines of ancient earthwork fortification run across the neck of the spur. They are thought to be Iron Age in origin, but were also incorporated much later into Offa's Dyke, the 8th-century earthwork rampart built by the Saxon King Offa to mark the boundary between his Mercian kingdom and the lands of the Welsh to the west.

The name 'Symonds Yat' in fact derives from a pass through the earthworks; a *yat* in Old English was an opening or gateway, while the Symonds was probably Robert Symonds, a 17th-century High Sheriff of Herefordshire.

Highmeadow Woods, which backs on to the Yat, formed part of the original Forest of Dean, an ancient royal hunting ground. It survives today as one of the largest areas of ancient woodland in Britain. Though diversified with conifers today, the woods have retained their aura of ancient mystery through the oak, ash, beach, yew, hazel and holly which abound. Yews from the Forest of Dean supplied Agincourt archers with their bows; oaks served the Tudor fleets.

A maze of woodland footpaths leads off from the

viewpoint. One, for example, runs down to the western bank of the Yat where a hand-drawn ferry, resembling a punt, plies to the other side of the river. There, you can walk downstream through the gorge by a footpath banked shoulder-high in summer with wands of purple loosestrife and rosebay willowherb. Dragonflies skim the water's edge, and there are rapids where canoeists may be seen manoeuvring among boulders fallen from the gaunt cliffs above.

The overhanging cliffs are pinnacled, fissured and pitted with shadowy caves, and the footpath leads eventually to the spectacular Seven Sisters Rocks, commanding tremendous views of the river. A little above is King Arthur's Cave, discovered in 1870. Though the association with England's legendary monarch is somewhat suspect, there is no question of the cave's long use by man. For in this rock shelter, archaeologists excavated the flint tools of Stone Age men. They date back some 60,000 years, and with them were found the bones of bears, beavers, mammoths, reindeers, elks, woolly rhinoceroses and hyenas. They were the denizens of the true primeval woodland; the forest's ancient aura is no romance.

ECHOES ACROSS THE WATER

A light suspension footbridge, strung across the river at a spot known as the Biblins, provides a way back to Highmeadow Woods. A path here leads up to an ecological reserve, where the trees have been allowed to grow entirely in their natural state. There are fallow deer in the forest, and foxes and badgers abound, though you do not often see them.

There are wonders aplenty. Close by the reserve is the Suck Stone, said to be the largest detached boulder in the kingdom and whose weight has been estimated as 14,000 tons. Not far away are the Near and Far Hearkening Rocks, both masses of conglomerate rock with extraordinary acoustic properties. Gamekeepers, listening on the opposite side of the river, used to use them to detect the rustle of poachers, preying on the king's deer. And they really do act as amplifiers – the sound of a man chopping wood, for example, echoes back across the river like gunshot.

The Forestry Commission has laid out a 10 mile circular walk through Highmeadow Woods, taking in the Buck Stone, a logan, or rocking stone, perched at 915 ft with fine long-distance views to the Black Mountains; and the weird Staunton Long Stone, an ancient tribal mustering point which is said to bleed if pricked at midnight on a certain night of the year.

But you do not have to accomplish the full circuit to enjoy the wonders of woodland walking or the delights of the riverbank. You can pick out shorter walks for yourself, finding your own spots to rest by the river and trail weary feet in its silken water.

Loiter by the Wye and the river becomes a mesmerising presence, ever changing with the play of light on streaking currents, but timeless too in its unceasing green sweep, the certainty of its broad curves. The minutes pass, as the centuries have passed, to the murmur of endlessly moving water.

WINGED DAGGER OF THE WYE

Walking the quieter footpaths of the Wye as it meanders round Symonds Yat, you may be startled by a flash of iridescent blue darting across your field of vision. This is the flash of the kingfisher – and it is often as no more than a radiant blue streak, moving a few feet above the water, that the bird is seen. Plunging headlong after a fish, it moves like a winged dagger.

One of the kingfisher's haunts at Symonds Yat is St Martin's Pool, below the Seven Sisters Rocks, which is believed to be the deepest part of the Wye. Here, if you are lucky, you may get a chance to observe the birds more closely, perched above the water with their eyes fixed steadily on their prey.

Kingfisher
Alcedo atthis

ULLSWATER

Cumbria

Craggy mountains, level waters, tumbling becks and fellside fields – diversity is the essence of Lakeland's appeal. The landscape seems to ripple with delicate harmonies, and though the proportions are not colossal they are concentrated. Comparing the district's enchantment with the more widely spaced wonders of the Scottish Highlands, the poet Coleridge wrote of 'a cabinet of beauties'.

Each of the 16 main lakes has its own individual charm, deriving from the character of the surrounding fells. Wast Water is stern and Windermere open, Coniston wood-fringed and Buttermere bare. Many of the waters are rich in literary associations, for this, supremely, is the landscape of the Romantics. Tiny Rydal Water and Grasmere, especially, are associated with the poet William Wordsworth who lived and worked by their banks; they embody the wonder of Lakeland in miniature. Yet even Wordsworth was moved to judge one lake supreme among all of its neighbours. At Ullswater he saw 'the happiest combination of beauty and grandeur, which any of the lakes affords'.

THE BENDING WATERS

Seven miles long and almost a mile wide at its broadest, Ullswater is the second largest of the lakes (after Windermere) and unique for its serpentine form. Roughly resembling the letter Z in its shape, it winds from a low, placid landscape at its foot deep into high mountains at its head. The curvature of the waters is such that at no point, on fell-top or lakeside, can the eye take in their full sweep. From wherever you look down the silken sheet, the waters disappear somewhere from sight.

Ullswater's formation derives, like that of the other lakes, from the Ice Age. Glaciers descending from a central dome of the mountains carved deep paths down from the summit. When the ice rivers melted, watercourses remained and created lakes trapped behind dams of moraine. In most cases, the glacial troughs were more or less straight, radiating, in Wordsworth's oft-quoted image, like spokes of a wheel from the hub of the mountains. At Ullswater, however, the descending glaciers met two different consistencies of rock which contributed to the distortion of the lake's form.

The mountain core of Lakeland is a mass of rocks known as the Borrowdale volcanics, forged by eruption 450 million years ago. This is the substance of Sca Fell and the Great Gable – and Helvellyn towering above Ullswater. It is a hard rock which ice and erosion have shaped in dramatic fashion.

Above Ullswater the glaciers began by cutting through the volcanics, but as they pushed north they met a bed of older and softer rocks. These are the so-called Skiddaw slates, which date back 500 million years. They were formed of compacted sediment which once lay under the sea. Earth movements

BESIDE THE LAKE It was in the spring of 1804 that the banks of Ullswater gave Wordsworth the inspiration for Daffodils. *But the lake is surpassingly lovely at any time of year. The spring flowers have vanished from Glencoyne Wood, 2 miles or so along the shore from where the poet saw his dancing daffodils, but the russets of autumn have a charm of their own.*

buckled the bed upwards, exposing it to ice and the elements. The slates have weathered smoothly and evenly.

Today, retracing the path of the glaciers from Ullswater's foot to its head, you can see both geological zones quite distinctly. You begin among the sylvan flanks of the smooth-backed Skiddaws – then bend into a crag-locked landscape.

THE DAFFODIL BANKS

The present-day road from Penrith to Windermere follows Ullswater's northern shore into the Lake District mountains. Since ancient times, the route has provided an important artery of communication, climbing beyond the lake's head to Kirkstone Pass and giving access to Windermere beyond. The Romans knew the route well, and the Vikings left their mark on the neighbourhood. The Norsemen arrived in Cumbria during the 10th century and their memory has survived in countless place names throughout the Lake District. The word Fell, for example, comes from the Norse *fjall* (hill), Dale from *dalr* (valley), Beck from *bekkr* (stream) and Gill from *gil* (ravine). Ullswater itself has its root in Ulfr's Water, after a local Norse lord. (He is also recalled in the name of Lyulph's Tower, an 18th-century folly on the north shore of the lake, which was built on the site of the early Norseman's home.)

Dramatic scenery has not always inspired appreciation. When Daniel Defoe visited the southern Lake District in the early 18th century he called it 'a country eminent only for being the wildest, most barren and frightful of any that I have passed over in England, or even in Wales ...' But in later decades, travellers seeking refuge from the increasing pressures of civilisation began to discover the appeal of untamed solitudes. The poet Gray visited Lakeland in 1769, and his *Journal of a Tour of the Lakes* introduced it to a wide public. Later, Wordsworth and his sister Dorothy (who were natives of the district) settled there for life and encouraged others to experience its charm: Coleridge, Southey and De Quincey among them. By 1817, a whole 'Lake School' of poetry had evolved.

What the Romantics found in the district was more than picturesque scenery; for them it was a place where people could refresh themselves spiritually through intimacy with nature. Perhaps no celebration of innocence in the Creation is better known than Wordsworth's poem *Daffodils*. Composed in 1804, it was inspired by a visit to Ullswater on whose banks, the poet's sister wrote, the flowers 'seemed as if verily they laughed with the wind':

> *I wandered lonely as a cloud*
> *That floats on high o'er vales and hills,*
> *When all at once I saw a crowd,*
> *A host of golden daffodils;*
> *Beside the lake, beneath the trees,*
> *Fluttering and dancing in the breeze.*

Specifically, the scene of the poet's meditation was the northern shore of Ullswater, in the beautiful woodland area of Gowbarrow Park, now owned by the National Trust. Daffodils still grow wild at the margin of the lake, while Aira Force, a tremendous waterfall also frequented by Wordsworth, can be heard as distant thunder in the background.

The road along the north shore of Ullswater provides a splendid lakeside drive which should be approached from Pooley Bridge at the northern foot of the water. Beginning modestly enough, it presents the unfolding drama of the landscape with ever-increasing grandeur, ending at the headwater villages of Glenridding and Patterdale, where the mountains loom awesome above.

For walkers, however, the south bank provides an even finer experience. It was recommended by Wordsworth himself, who wrote: 'In order to see the lower part of the lake to advantage, it is necessary to go round by Pooley Bridge, and to ride at least three miles along the Westmorland side of the water, towards Martindale. The views, especially if you ascend from the road into the fields, are magnificent.'

Magnificent indeed; if you follow Wordsworth's advice you come to the village of Howtown, and the slopes of Hallin Fell – one of Lakeland's classic viewpoints. The minor lakeside road turns away from the water here, and to explore its course further you must go on foot.

AT HALLIN FELL

Hallin Fell is a wooded hump of a hill which elbows its way into the lake, narrowing its course at the point where it makes its first dramatic change of direction. At 1,271 ft it has by no means a lofty elevation, but its position opens up a huge panorama. The top is reached by a broad grassy path which starts opposite Martindale church; the turf here is so luxuriously soft that it is said you can climb up in bare feet.

At the summit is a fine drystone cairn, and you have to pause for some time to take in the scenic feast. Across the blue waters are the craggy heights of Gowbarrow Fell, with the great Skiddaw range beyond. Look down the lake as it sweeps into the mountains and your eye meets Helvellyn above. Turn to the south and you look on the dusky tops of the Martindale Fells, one of Lakeland's quietest regions. Shadows play over the glacier-carved valleys of Boredale, Bannerdale and Ramps Gill, floored with green fields and drystone walling. Their becks are just a few of the streams which flow into the lake, uniting Ullswater with its surrounding heights.

TO THE HEAD OF THE WATER

From Hallin Fell there is a fine 5 mile walk along the lake's edge as it curves round the huge, wild bulk of Place Fell (2,154 ft). The paths are lined with beech, sycamore and oak, with lovely views through foreground shade to the glimmering waters beyond. If the air seems intoxicating it is perhaps because of the juniper scrub above – a gin-scented evergreen, it produces berries from which the flavouring of the liquor is distilled.

Approaching the very head of the water by the old stone quarry at Blowick, the vistas of the mountains

WINTER HOME FOR WILDFOWL

In winter Ullswater becomes a feeding ground for large numbers of migrant wildfowl which fly in from their breeding grounds in Scandinavia and eastern Europe. Included among them is the goldeneye, which has the curious habit for a duck of nesting in trees. Another duck with an unusual habit is the wigeon: it often grazes on grass like a goose. A few hundred pairs breed in Britain, but their main breeding grounds are in northern and eastern Europe. The pochard is a common visitor to Britain and some breed here.

Goldeneye
Bucephala clangula

Pochard
Aythya ferina

Wigeon
Anas penelope

grouped around become tremendous. The skyline is dominated by the noble summit of St Sunday Crag (2,756 ft), the monarch of Ullswater's mountains, whose north-eastern ridge provides one of the finest views of the lake. East of the crag, framed by the dip of Grisedale, is Dollywaggon Pike (2,810 ft) with Eagle Crag and Striding Edge rising to Helvellyn (3,113 ft) in the distance. In the foreground, the skyline dips again into the valley of Glenridding, overlooked by the brow of Birkhouse Moor (2,318 ft) and the tree-fringed nab of Glenridding Dodd (1,400 ft).

Patterdale, the village at the head of the lake, is an excellent base for exploring the mountains, and you can make the lakeside walk circular by returning to Howtown round the back of Place Fell. To get back at a more leisurely pace, though, there is a lake steamer.

Ullswater is not one of the most crowded lakes in the district. With no sizeable settlements it is under less pressure from tourism than, for example, Winder-mere or Derwent Water. For a sense of real solitude it is of course best visited out of season; in winter, especially, it is a place of great quietness where gulls come to roost in huge numbers and wintering ducks such as goldeneye, pochard and wigeon may be seen patrolling the waters. It is then, too, that Aira Force can often be seen to best advantage, flooded with rain-water to produce the deafening experience which Wordsworth knew.

Even in summer, the surrounding fells offer many secluded walks by woodland track and crystal beck twinkling with butterwort and tormentil. Like its serpentine form, the lake's inflowing streams contri-bute to its attraction – the sense of an extra, hidden dimension.

LAKELAND DAWN *The light of the rising sun strikes gold from the mirror-like surface of Ullswater where the reflection of the surrounding hills seems almost more tangible than the land itself, whose substance is diffused by the fragile morning mist.*

BRITAIN'S LAST WILDERNESS

Wilderness Britain offers more than miles of fine walking through lonely, rugged country. Piercing the lean soil of the moors are a host of astonishing rock formations – at Brimham, and at High Cup Nick, for example. There are human relics to marvel at, too. Hadrian's Wall, amid the Northumbrian moors, is a wonder not only of Britain but of the world. The tawny vastness of Dartmoor is strewn with relics of much more ancient origin still; and under the brooding rockpile of Hound Tor the remains of a lost medieval village have been found. In reality, the wilderness is a living thing, inhabited not only by its familiar denizens of curlew, buzzard and grouse, but by the ancestral shades of peoples long forgotten.

BRIMHAM ROCKS

North Yorkshire

The huge, eroded boulders cover some 60 acres of moorland, ranged there like the playthings of giants. The Rhinoceros, The Indian's Head, Baboon and Yoke of Oxen – these are just some of the exhibits on display. Clefts, basins and pinnacles, tubular cannon and rocking stones ... what freaks of geology cannot be found on these strange acres? Even their fanciful names do not quite capture the essential weirdness of the setting. Brimham Moor is an alien world – a Yorkshire moonscape.

Millstone grit underlies much of Yorkshire's Pennine moorlands. The coarse sandstone is composed of layers of hard grit interspersed with beds of weaker shales. Great swathes of the rock have shaped a dour landscape, and Brimham is in many respects characteristic. Rising to 950 ft above Nidderdale, the tableland is tufted with rough vegetation: heather, bilberries and bracken from which rise clumps of birch scrub and mountain ash. Typically, too, the gritstone pierces the summit in outcrops of raw rock. But at Brimham the great slabs have been eroded and weathered in truly spectacular fashion. Nowhere else in Britain is there quite such a dense concentration of crazy effects.

Well over 50 named monstrosities people the moor, and a brief litany must suffice to introduce the menagerie: Oyster Shell, Boar's Head, Wishing Rock, Sleeping Hare, Primeval Tank, Mushroom Rock, Brimham Monster, Needle's Eye, Roaring Lion, Eagle's Beak, The Crocodiles and Henry VIII. Not long ago, people believed that the whole fantastic assemblage was shaped by pagan hands, and they named several formations accordingly – there is a host of Druid stones: the Druid's Bedroom, Druid's Parlour, Druid's Cave and Druid's Kissing Chair, for example.

Many of the names were first applied by gaping Victorian visitors. But not all of the boulders have such a pedigree. There is one particularly notable 20th-century addition; a rock which has been christened Donald Duck.

THE LIVING DESERT

Violent earth upheaval brought Brimham's gritstone to the surface. It was wrenched up in Carboniferous times, and what had once been a sea-bed was exposed to fire and ice. Frosts splintered the joints and bedding planes, savaging especially the weaker shales. The ledged outcrops were scoured by searing winds and abrasive grains of rock, which acted on them like a natural sandblast to smooth and round the contours. Many look like warped pepperpots or pawns.

A FANTASY OF NATURE *Deep among the rocks at Brimham, with the weird formations looming starkly up on every side, it takes an effort of will not to see them in the same light as earlier generations – as the work of Druids or other ancient wonder workers.*

MOORLAND SENTINELS *The outer rocks at Brimham stand like a ring of sentinels defending the untamed moorland from the encroaching discipline of the farmland advancing from the valley below.*

While the rocks were being sculpted, Brimham was a desert. Only when the climate became milder did moorland vegetation begin to clothe the slopes, leaving the bizarre statuary arrayed around the summit. And although not all of the exhibits quite live up to their names, many really are remarkably lifelike.

The Dancing Bear is unmistakable with his jutting snout and rounded brow. He looks as if he is wearing a studded collar and extending a paw in expectation of reward. He stands in the same group as the Lover's Leap, a rocky cleft arched by a keystone and complete with local legend. It is said that two benighted sweethearts named Edwin and Julia once jumped from the top to seal a suicide pact. The story has a happy ending however – they landed safely and were later reconciled with their parents.

The largest of the boulders is estimated to weigh some 500 tons, but perhaps the most impressive is the Idol Rock. This 200 ton monster rests on a stem of rock barely 12 in. in diameter. Mounted on its tiny pedestal it looks like some grotesque totem of womanhood; headless but with swelling hips and torso.

One day, the idol's tiny plinth will collapse and it will become a logan, or rocking stone. There are four of these grouped together north of the Oyster Shell.

The biggest of the rocking stones is 13 ft long by 7 ft wide, but so delicately poised that a child can tilt it. Erosion has created a natural basin in the top of this stone, and of its neighbour to the west. Between the logans is a curious formation known as the Druid's Coffin.

South of the main group is a fifth rocking stone which, though nameless, is the largest of them all, weighing 100 tons. It is situated near the Cannon Rocks, boulders some 20 ft long, which have circular holes running through their entire length. One of these is called the Druid's Telescope.

Brimham Rocks can be seen from some distance around, and there is one particularly prominent outcrop, a logan isolated on the moor's southern heights. It is known as the White Rocking Stone, for it was at one time lime-washed as a landmark. Even without its white coat it remains quite distinctive. On a clear day it can be seen from Harrogate, 9 miles away.

A STRANGELY FANTASTIC SCENE

Below the rock-strewn heights is a section of an old Monks' Wall. Brimham once belonged to the monks of Fountains Abbey, and it is easy to imagine that the weird boulders must have inspired nightmares in the brethren, disturbing their piety and toil. Certainly, many 18th-century visitors came to·the site believing that they were viewing a pagan temple. In 1786 a certain Major Rooke even presented a formal paper to the Antiquarian Society describing the rocks as Druidical Monuments. The mistake is understandable. There is, for example, one pillar known as the Noonday Stone which stands somewhat apart from the main group of rocks, in such a position that its shadow falls across an adjacent stone exactly at midday. Who would not, on first discovering the phenomenon, picture rites of tribal sacrifice?

Victorian travellers were advised to come to the moor at dusk when 'the whole scene is more strangely fantastic than any other that can be found on this side of Saxon Switzerland'. The site was much visited, and on one occasion sermons were delivered from the rocks to a congregation of 3,000 Wesleyans.

In the present century, Brimham Moor has lost none of its fascination. It is easily reached, lying 3 miles east of Pateley Bridge, a small town set among beautiful green hills and formed, like the Rocks, of gritstone. Once important for lead-mining, it is today an excellent centre for moorland walking, with a particularly testing climb over into Wharfedale by way of Greenhow Hill, a desolate upland village which is one of the highest in England.

From Pateley Bridge, Brimham is reached by well-marked minor roads. At one time people used to drive up to the moor and park where they liked among the boulders. Some damage and much litter was the result. But since 1970 the site has been carefully maintained by the National Trust. It is open at all times, and there is a car park and an information centre at Brimham House with maps which chart the formations.

Some of the rocks are steeply faced, and one is used as a training centre for mountaineers. Most, however, are easy enough to scramble up and they offer splendid viewpoints. On a clear day you can see some 40 miles to the north-east across the Vale of York to the North York Moors beyond – and, looking south-east, it is quite possible to make out the spires of York Minster.

Brimham is an all-weather wonder. Come in sunshine and you have the sweeping panoramas seen from a fantastic giant's playground. Explore the heights when a mist is rising from the moor and the views are gone – but the site gains in eerie fascination. Inanimate boulders seem to come alive, those outlandish snouts to snuffle. Much photographed, much visited, Brimham becomes a disquieting place where you may feel the prickle of raw fear.

LOOKOUT POINT *Towering among the trees, the rocks at Brimham are not only a sight to be seen in their own right – they also provide a magnificent viewpoint over the surrounding countryside. Most of the rocks are easy enough to climb and, this done, they offer wide views in all directions. In particular, the views to the east and south-east extend over 40 miles or more of the broad acres of Yorkshire.*

HIGH CUP NICK

Cumbria

Hills or mountains? The Pennines defy easy classification. Known as the 'backbone of England', the long upland mass extends from the River Trent in the south to the Cheviot Hills in the north, rising to 2,930 ft at rugged Cross Fell – a respectable height for an English mountain. Yet few Pennine high points have a clear identity of their own – they are lumps which swell from the mass. In reality, if you follow the 250 mile footpath of the Pennine Way, you traverse an immense, fragmented moorland.

The heights are as wild and remote as anywhere in England; soot-black with peat, treacherous with bog-mosses, and tufted with heather and moor grasses. Yet here and there a ridge or outcrop may open up tremendous views down to the flanking limestone dales, lush with green vegetation. Such contrasts only enhance the loneliness of the uplands, and to experience their solitude there is no more awesome site than High Cup Nick. It is a place of heart-stopping drama.

THE WHIN SILL

The High Cup is a horseshoe chasm chewed from the Pennines by the teeth of Ice Age glaciers. Situated in eastern Cumbria, near the border with Durham, its summit edge is some 2,000 ft above sea level. Strictly speaking, the ravine itself is the High Cup Gill, while the 'Nick' is a cleft in its cliffs. Buttressing the crescent with sheer rock walls of 80 ft and more, the cliffs form a dark amphitheatre round the void.

The views are both terrifying and sublime. Look over the edge of the High Cup and your eye plunges 1,000 ft into a moorland abyss strewn with rock debris and threaded by the thin stream of its beck. Beyond are the beautiful meadowlands of the Vale of Eden, with a blue horizon of Lakeland Fells in the far distance.

It is the foreground frame of stark columnar rocks which gives the High Cup its extraordinary grandeur. The cliffs form part of the Great Whin Sill, a swathe of quartz dolerite which has scattered the north country with wonders. It emerged through volcanic action in late Carboniferous times, extending from the Pennines to the Farne Islands. Hard and dark blue-grey in colour, the Great Whin Sill intrudes abruptly into the landscape, conferring its magic on a whole clutch of marvels from Hadrian's Wall to Beblowe Crag on Lindisfarne.

At High Cup Nick, a half-moon chunk was eaten from the dolerite sheet by glacial erosion. The cliffs drop with razored suddenness from the moor's edge in a forest of perpendicular columns. Here and there, individual pillars stab upwards in partial isolation, and on the moors behind the High Cup is one particularly prominent plinth. It is known as Nichol's Chair after a local cobbler who, it is said, once mended a pair of boots on top of it.

High Cup Nick is backed by the sombre masses of the Dufton and Murton Fells. The closest point of access for motorists, though, is a delightful place – the village of Dufton, 4 miles west in the Vale of Eden. With lime-washed cottages, a tree-lined main street and spacious village green it is dominated by the pleasingly conical hill of Dufton Pike.

The village's summertime charm, however, belies the storms of the colder months. Cross Fell, the Pennine high point, is only 6 miles to the north, and from its desolate, domed plateau a fierce local wind descends in winter. Known as the Helm, it blows with such savagery around Dufton that roofs may be ripped from barns.

The walk up to High Cup Nick is by the Pennine Way, leading from farmland to moor, and rounding the shoulder of Peeping Hill (1,651 ft) where it turns into the ravine. It reaches the edge of the High Cup cliffs under the crag of Narrowgate Beacon (2,153 ft), where fires used to be lit to warn valley folk of the approach of invading Scots. The Pennine Way follows the perilous northern ledge of the cliffs and caution is, of course, essential.

THE MOORLAND FALLS

The climb from Dufton, though steep, is manageable. For experienced walkers, however, the High Cup's views are best attained as the grand climax to the moorland walk from Teesdale to the east. It is by no means for families or casual strollers, but it takes in the wonder of amazing moorland falls, and an excursion through the Pennine wilderness.

Tributaries of Durham's 70 mile River Tees rise in the fells behind High Cup Nick, tumbling eastwards to the valley of Teesdale. The name of the Tees is thought to mean 'boiling or surging river' and certainly, if you drive through Teesdale, halting at the High Force Hotel, you will quickly discover why. A short walk along a marked footpath leads to the most majestically proportioned falls in England.

At the High Force – *force* is an old Norse word

NATURE'S WALL *The vertical ramparts of the Whin Sill thrust up through the earth's crust to form a natural wall across a large stretch of northern England. It was a barrier that the Romans knew and appreciated – since they incorporated long stretches of it into Hadrian's Wall.*

IN THE NICK *Ice-shattered rocks frame the view down from a 2,000 ft high perch in the cleft of High Cup Nick (far left). A thousand feet below, a tiny beck tumbles down beside drystone walls in High Cup Gill to the very edge of the Pennines before joining the River Eden in the valley beyond.*

FURIOUS WATERS *Hissing and seething in one long chaos of foam, the furious waters of the River Tees rush in full spate to the brink of High Force. There they plunge 70 ft into a boiling cauldron carved from the volcanic rock of the Whin Sill.*

meaning 'waterfall' – the Tees has carved a deep gorge through massive beds of the Whin Sill and drops some 70 ft down into a seething pool below. The falls are an astonishing sight, particularly after heavy rainfall.

Drive on up the road for 2½ miles to the little village of Langdon Beck and an altogether tougher experience awaits. For it is at this point that the 13 mile, six-hour traverse to Dufton begins, a classic Pennine crossing.

You reach the Tees by a rough farm track amid pasturelands frowned on by dark fells to either side. After some 3 miles of walking, the way becomes strewn with boulders fallen from the Falcon Clints above. These are jagged cliffs of the Whin Sill whose name evokes their elusive denizens – the rare peregrine falcon is known to nest among the rocks. And rounding the scree slopes you come to a fork in the river. Up to the right, the Tees crashes in fury over the fractured Whin Sill, to produce the 200 ft cascade of Caldron Snout – the highest waterfall in England.

Crossing the Tees by a bridge at the falls, the route strikes out by its tributary, the Maize Beck. Now the really rough walking begins. The Pennine Way passes Birkdale, known as the loneliest farm in England, and beyond is a featureless Nowhereland. The Countryside Commission's official handbook calls this stretch 'the wildest and loneliest crossing in the whole length of the Pennines', and few walkers could disagree.

Apart from the 'Moss Shop', a derelict lead-miners' settlement, there are no significant landmarks. The horizons are hemmed by shaggy masses of peat and heather, and after an hour's tramping through the wilderness, with nowhere behind and nowhere ahead, stark fear can come upon you. The eye scans feverishly for the few rough cairns which mark the route, and an exit from the wasteland.

Another hour's tramping brings you to the Maize Beck again, in a landscape somewhat softened by limestone. The moorland stream can flood dangerously when in spate, and though several fording points are safe in dry weather the wise course is to follow its north bank until you reach a footbridge. You then strike south-west for a short distance over a level plain – and suddenly High Cup Nick gapes ahead.

Whether approached from east or west, the High Cup must be treated with respect. The route from Teesdale is unthinkable without proper footwear, clothing, rations, map and compass. You should never stray knowingly from the Pennine Way, and remember that the weather conditions are hazardous. The fierce Helm wind is not the sole peril of Dufton's high abyss; fog and snow descend on the cliffs throughout the winter, while mist and rain are all-season risks. Often, vapours coil around the rim of the void, masking both its views and its perils.

But in fine weather, to come upon the chasm from out of the waste is an unforgettable experience. The green vale and blue distances are unbelievably sweet to the eye – it is as if you really were looking through to an Eden, cupped from the wilderness edge.

HOUND TOR

Devon

The granite outcrop looms like a derelict fortress on Dartmoor's horizon. Weathered grey stacks stab at the sky, forbidding turrets shaped by nature and scoured by the erosions of time. Approach the tor and you seem to see gargoyles in the rock, the profiles of dogs and men which leer and grimace across the moors. The wind howls through jagged battlements to produce an eerie baying sound. People have sensed a canine menace in the site from the earliest times; it features in the Domesday Book as *Hundatorra* – the ancient root of 'Hound Tor'.

Dartmoor is a granite landscape, and the obdurate rock underlies its desolate acres of tufted moor and boggy mire. The bare upland plateau was formed nearly 300 million years ago when a mountain of molten granite heaved up from under a crust of sedimentary rock. As the granite cooled it hardened and crystallised. Although the moor is cloaked with vegetation, outcrops of the raw granite can be seen piercing the hills at their summits in natural rock castles known as tors.

There are about 170 tors on Dartmoor, each weathered into its own distinctive shape. The highest peaks are in the north-west, where High Willhays and Yes Tor top the 2,000 ft level. But the most dramatic outcrops lie in the eastern section of the moor: Haytor Rocks, for example, a monstrous hunchback crouching on the horizon; Bowerman's Nose, a single pinnacle which oddly resembles a man in a cloth cap; and Hound Tor itself.

THE RAVAGED BATTLEMENTS

At Hound Tor, wind and weather have created savage effects. The heart of the rockpile looks as if it has been blasted out by cannon; the foot of the tor is littered with debris known as 'clitter', which suggests just such a cataclysm. In fact, the outcrop was eroded over millions of years, as seasonal rains entered the vertical joints, freezing to form fingers of ice which prised masses apart. As the ice thawed, fragments of rock loosened and whole boulders crashed from the tor to leave new cavities for the ice to maul.

Seen from close to, the granite mass appears stratified, as if it had been laid down in beds parallel to the ground. This 'layering' actually resulted from the contraction of the oozing granite as it cooled. But the horizontal thrusts are very marked, and have created the illusion of profiles in the rock: chins, lips, noses and brows which jut from the mass. Some of the faces are striking – one Dartmoor writer, Vian Smith, has discerned a clear portrait of the film actor Finlay Currie in one rock. (He played the Dartmoor convict Abel Magwitch in a screen version of Dickens's *Great Expectations* – a fitting profile for the setting.)

Daunting as Hound Tor's gargoyled battlements appear, they can be climbed without difficulty, and the highest turret offers one of the finest viewpoints in all of Dartmoor. To the west are the tawny moors, but looking east the ground swoops gloriously down to the delectable valley of the River Bovey, with the gentle hills of the Teign Valley beyond. Dartmoor is the source of no fewer than 14 rivers, and their green wooded banks relieve the sombre russets and olives of the bare uplands.

Looking south from Hound Tor you can see the humped mass of Haytor Rocks, another splendid viewpoint, whose stone was once quarried to provide granite for the British Museum and London Bridge. The urban associations are curiously inappropriate on this windswept plateau. From Hound Tor, Haytor looks like a second ruined castle, a sister fortress strung out along the moorland ridge.

WALKING THE MOORS

The tors, of course, are natural creations, weird fantasies of granite in a desolate landscape. Dartmoor covers some 330 sq. miles in all, and nowhere else in England generates quite such a sense of solitude. Its notorious mists can blanket even the closest landmarks in a matter of seconds. For walkers who stray off the beaten tracks, warm clothes, a map, compass and whistle are indispensable aids.

Luckily, Hound Tor is one of the most accessible of the moor's granite outcrops. It is only a quarter of a mile from a minor road which runs between Manaton and Widecombe-in-the-Moor (famed for the folksong of its Fair), and there are safe walks in every direction. One well-trodden path leads down into the little valley to the east and up again to Haytor Down and south to Haytor Rocks.

A longer walk leads north-west from Hound Tor following the road for a few hundred yards to Jay's Grave. The little green mound, with stones at head

ALIEN GIANT *Looking like the statue of an alien giant, from Easter Island perhaps, Bowerman's Nose is the most human-looking of the many weird rock formations scattered on Dartmoor's tors. But in fact, like all the others, it is the work of nature not man – a granite outcrop left standing after softer surrounding rocks had been worn away by wind, rain and frost.*

HOUND TOR

THE BROODING MOOR *From the decaying granite ramparts of Hound Tor (previous page) the view extends across the brooding Dartmoor landscape to Haytor, looming with menace on the skyline. Each of the 170 or so tors on the moor has its own character; created by the action of the weather over thousands of years.*

and foot, is the burial place of an 18th-century workhouse girl named Kitty Jay. She hanged herself at nearby Canna Farm and, being denied Christian burial as a suicide, was interred in an unmarked grave at the crossroads below Hound Tor. The grave has been secretly tended with flowers by nameless mourners ever since.

From Jay's Grave, a bridleway leads around the head of the Webburn river to a celebrated Bronze Age camp at Grimspound, a 4 acre tract containing the remains of some 20 stone huts.

THE LOST VILLAGE

Dartmoor might seem the most inhospitable terrain for human settlement. And yet it has known habitation from prehistoric times. Long ago, the uplands were not quite so bare, they offered a generous expanse of lightly forested land which was well supplied with water. Prehistoric tribes congregated here in huge numbers, and the moor is scattered with countless relics of their presence: burial chambers, standing stones and hut circles. On the south-western slope of Hound Tor itself, just short of the summit, is a prehistoric burial cist, or stone coffin, surrounded by a ring of stones.

But Hound Tor's most remarkable relic is the ruins of a lost medieval village. It is situated south of the summit, and just above a line of springs. The walls have been excavated and stand today about 2 ft above ground level. They are best seen in early spring, for later in the year the tall bracken almost obscures them from view.

The settlement seems to have been founded in Saxon times, and at first comprised a dozen or so rectangular longhouses built of turf and wattle. There was a hearth and living area in the south end of each hut, and a cattle shelter in the north. Situated at 1,100 ft above sea level and exposed to Dartmoor's biting north-easterly winds, it must always have been something of a frontier settlement. This was the Hundatorra of the Domesday Book, its skyline dominated by the canine crags above.

STONE BUILDINGS

In around 1200, Hundatorra's buildings were remade of stone, corn-drying barns were erected to serve small tracts of farmed land, and a two-roomed manor house made its appearance. It seems that the village continued to prosper until the mid-14th century. Then something happened: the manor became a farmhouse, and the longhouses were mostly converted to barns. By 1400 the site was abandoned.

What caused the village to die? The Black Death of 1349 may well have been the key factor, but there are other possibilities. The climate became harsher in the 14th century, and there was something of a tin boom on Dartmoor. Perhaps the rugged crofters were tempted from their wind-blown homesteads by the promise of an easier life elsewhere. In all events, the site became derelict. Whatever killed the village, the moors encroached with their swirling mists and buried it under a mantle of turf and bracken.

By local tradition, Hound Tor is the lair of the dogs of night who come out under cover of darkness to ravage sheep and cattle. Legends of such spectral creatures are not unique to Dartmoor, but there is one famous Hellhound with whom the site has become particularly associated.

In 1901, Sir Arthur Conan Doyle, creator of Sherlock Holmes, was told a wonderfully gruesome Dartmoor legend by a West Country friend named Fletcher Robinson. It concerned a real-life blackguard, the 17th-century Sir Richard Cabell of Brook Manor. As Robinson told it, Cabell falsely accused his young bride of adultery and stabbed her to death with a hunting knife as she fled across the moors. The lady's devoted hound flew at the murderer and ripped out

BRACKEN ON THE MARCH

If any plant can be described as aggressive, then bracken is that plant. It will grow anywhere below the tree-line, but thrives particularly on light acid soils like those of Dartmoor, where, if left unchecked, it will take over from rough grassland and heather. Its success depends on a dual method of reproduction. It is a fern, and so reproduces from minute spores which are shed in millions then spread by the wind. In addition, bracken sends out root-like rhizomes which spread underground, sending up new plants.

Bracken
Pteridium aquilinum

his throat in avenging fury. The hound died during the struggle, but its phantom continued to prowl Dartmoor, baying lugubriously in the black of night and returning to haunt successive generations of Cabells.

Conan Doyle was riveted by the tale, and placed it at the heart of his most famous Sherlock Holmes adventure, *The Hound of the Baskervilles*. While plotting the story he visited Dartmoor to seek out atmospheric material; the surname of 'Baskerville' was that of Robinson's coachman who drove Conan Doyle around the moors.

The novel's action is set within a few miles of Dartmoor prison at Princetown, and Conan Doyle had to tamper with geography to meet the story's needs. His 'Grimpen Mire', for example, is based partly on

Fox Tor Mire, but the prehistoric dwellings in which Holmes camped out are the famous huts of Grimspound. 'Baskerville Hall' is based partly on Brook Manor near Buckfastleigh, but its two sinister towers were drawn from Conan Doyle's old school – Stonyhurst in Lancashire – which the novelist detested.

Brooding tors dominate the novel's horizons, as they do the Dartmoor skyline. Watson's first glimpse of the moor, from a railway carriage, is of 'a strange jagged summit, dim and vague in the distance'. Hound Tor is not referred to directly in the text – but Conan Doyle had done his research. If any site lurks at the very heart of the novel it is surely that fanged granite rockpile, scoured by baying winds and haunted by the dogs of night.

BELOW THE MOOR *Wooded combes and neatly hedged green fields reach out to the edge of the moor below Hound Tor, marking the limit of man's penetration of the wilderness.*

HOUSESTEADS

Northumberland

One of the bleakest areas in all of Britain extends between the Pennine foothills of Northumbria and the Cheviots further north. For mile upon mile, open moorland extends as far as the eye can see, a heaving ocean of low hills and ridges which swell like waves to long crests but rarely break in climactic peaks. It is a dour, inhospitable landscape whose vast expanses of coarse grass, heather and bracken are scoured by sudden winds and drizzle. And yet rising from the moors is the finest Roman monument in Britain, a stupendous man-made barrier which once walled the landscape from coast to coast with a daunting screen of stone. This is Hadrian's Wall, and today its most impressive remains survive at the fort of Housesteads.

No one should visit the site expecting a turreted castle. What exists today is only the ground plan, with unroofed walls rarely rising more than 6 ft above the ground. But it is the best preserved Roman fort in Europe. To east and west run some of the finest sections of the rampart itself, in a setting of exceptional drama.

Housesteads lies in the central sector of the ancient Wall. On this stretch, the rampart follows the Whin Sill, a precipitous ridge of quartz dolerite which offers rare moments of grandeur in the featureless landscape. Apart from its historical fascination, Housesteads is a superb viewpoint. Looking south there are fine vistas of the South Tyne valley. To the north, a cluster of small, dark lakes lie in marshlands below the cliffs: Greenlee Lough, Broomlee Lough and lesser waters. Beyond their reed-fringed banks are the rugged moors, extending as far as the Cheviots which smudge the distant horizon. Scanning the desolate landscape it is not hard to imagine the loneliness of the Roman sentinels on this wild frontier – cold, often homesick and always alert for the tribesmen from the north.

BY DECREE OF THE EMPEROR

The emperor Hadrian ordered the Wall to be built in about AD 122. It was an amazing undertaking, designed to separate the semi-civilised peoples of Roman Britain from the unruly tribes to the north. The rampart ran for a distance of 73 miles (80 Roman miles) from Tyneside to the Solway Firth, and marked the northernmost frontier of the empire. Statistics do little justice to the scale of the enterprise; it has been estimated, however, that 25 million stones were used to face the completed Wall – each stone was uniform in shape, tapering slightly at the back so that it held firm in the core of clay and rubble.

FRONTIER OF AN EMPIRE *Hadrian's Wall, near Housesteads. For more than 200 years, Roman Britain lay secure behind the sea-to-sea Wall. But in AD 367, Scottish tribesmen swept through the Wall – a foretaste of the collapse that was to come.*

Fine sections survive at Housesteads, but they are barely one-fifth the height of the original rampart. Hadrian's Wall was 15 ft high, with a parapet of some 6 ft above that. Nor was the Wall itself the only defence. To the north of the barrier, a V-shaped ditch was dug 9 ft deep as an additional protective measure. It ran the whole length of the Wall except, as at sections near Housesteads, where steep cliffs made a trench unnecessary.

On the south side of the Wall, a flat-bottomed ditch known as the Vallum was later added. Flanked by earthen mounds, its purpose remains controversial. Since it ran on the southern or 'home' side of the Wall it cannot have been dug to deter alien aggression. Probably it acted as a demarcation line separating the military frontier zone from the civilian province. Some experts, however, have suggested that it may have been dug to deter surprise attack from the rear, or even that it was designed to keep people *in*. Like an ancient Berlin Wall, the Vallum may have acted as an obstacle to would-be escapers – conscript labourers and disgruntled tribesmen hankering for the freedom which lay beyond.

At every mile along the Wall was a small fort called a milecastle, and between every two milecastles was a pair of watchtowers spaced at even intervals. The system guaranteed a vantage point for every stretch of ground, and meant that messages could be flashed from coast to coast in a matter of minutes – simply by shouting along the Wall. In addition, a number of larger garrison forts were built near key strategic points. They were installed some years after the Wall was built because the tribes to the north proved more hostile than originally anticipated. Ultimately, 17 garrison forts were set up, and some came to support flourishing civil settlements. Housesteads was one of these.

THE CLIFFTOP FORT

The Roman name for Housesteads is thought to have been Vercovicium. It stands on the bedrock of the Whin Sill, where the Wall follows the sinuous contours of the ridge. The fort's overall plan is rectangular, with the four corners rounded like those of a playing card.

The site covers 5 acres and, inside, archaeologists have identified the headquarters building, commandant's house, barracks, hospital, granaries and latrines. Excavations – not yet completed – have brought life to the blueprint; the main gate is to the east and careful exploration has exposed deep ruts made by Roman cart and chariot wheels.

The nerve centre of Housesteads was the headquarters building, built according to a standard plan for garrison forts, with a military temple (the Roman equivalent of a regimental chapel), administrative rooms, armouries and the hall where official announcements were made. Near by was the commandant's house, a fairly spacious building with its own private latrine. Excavation in the lavatory revealed a gold ring, lodged in a crack in the sewer, whose loss must have caused much frantic searching and recrimi-

nation in the household at the time.

The Romans, of course, were great plumbers, and one of the most evocative buildings at Housesteads is the main latrine block, to the right of the south gate. The building was open plan, accommodating a dozen men at a time, and no doubt rang to bawdy laughter in its day. The soldiers sat in rows to either side of a central platform and cleaned their sponges in basins after use. The latrines had wooden seats, positioned above deep sewage channels. A tower at the south-east corner held a rainwater tank, and the lavatories were flushed from a connecting stone channel, the waste draining downhill.

The granaries at Housesteads betray the same functional ingenuity. The corn stored here was kept dry by an underfloor ventilation system, clearly visible today. Provisions of dried meat, fish, oil and wine were also kept in the building, and doled out from a serving door.

Outside the fort was an extensive civilian settlement, where excavation has again added a vivid touch of human interest. Under the floor of a shop or tavern, known today as the Murder House, the bones of a man and woman were found; and piercing the man's ribs was the point of a sword. The remains date from the early 4th century and had obviously been buried in secrecy. What drama was enacted here? Retribution for a thief, a pimp or an adulterer? Whatever the motive for the crime, the find amply illustrates the rough side of life in the frontier township.

THE SHIFTING FRONTIER

Hadrian's Wall was a clear-cut barrier, but the human frontier of northern England was more complex. On the home side of the Wall there were unruly tribes such as the Brigantes of the Pennines; north of the line were friendly groups such as the Votadini whose traders must have been welcome guests at Housesteads. And astonishingly, Hadrian's successor Antoninus Pius seems to have felt that the whole Wall was a mistake. In AD 139, he decided that the barrier should have been built further north and erected a new rampart of turf, known as the Antonine Wall, from the Firth of Forth to the Clyde. But campaigns north of the old Wall never brought long-lasting success, and Hadrian's rampart remained the base-line for offensive operations. Three times it was itself breached by wild northern tribesmen: in AD 197, 296 and 367. Though there were long periods of peace, when acute boredom must have been the chief peril facing the garrison at Housesteads, the sentries had to keep watch from the Wall.

In the 3rd and 4th centuries, Housesteads was the garrison of the First Cohort of Tungrians, a unit originally raised in Belgium. But soon recruits were enlisted locally. Some Spaniards, Gauls, Africans and Italians may have manned the rampart and yearned for Mediterranean sunshine, but most of the soldiers were probably Pennine farm-boys already familiar with sombre skies and moorland views. The fort itself housed some 1,000 men, and perhaps twice that number lived in the civil settlement. Though House-

steads can never have been a rich centre of cultural life, it must have seemed strikingly cosmopolitan to recruits drawn from the lonely Northumbrian hills.

WALKING THE WALL

Today, in the summer months, Housesteads attracts visitors from all parts of the world. From every point of view it is best seen off-season, when brooding skies augment the drama of the setting. There is a car park at the bottom of the hill and a small museum near the site. The fort is maintained by the Department of the Environment, but the site is open and movement unrestricted.

The classic viewpoint is at the north-east corner of the fort, looking east towards milecastle 36. In the foreground is the little valley of Knag Burn, where there is a gateway through the Wall. In Roman times it had two sets of doors so that travellers passing through could be locked in while frontier guards examined their baggage.

But the best way to experience the romance of the site is to walk the Wall itself. To the east there is a fine track leading to Sewingshields Crags, but the ancient barrier disappears in places. Westward lie many miles of solid rampart where the track runs along the top of the Wall. This is a lordly walk; the causeway rises and falls with the crest of the Whin Sill, winding past dizzying cliffs where glorious views unfold. Only a few hundred yards from Housesteads is milecastle 37, the most dramatic on the Wall and built by men of the Second Legion who commemorated their achievement with an inscribed stone. A mile further on, the walkway reaches the beautiful waters of Crag Lough, a green jewel set among faces of raw rock.

This whole stretch of the Wall might have been laid out by a landscape artist purely for its scenic appeal – but it was not. Tread this track and you are following the route of the imperial frontier guards. Your views are their views – the moors have not changed in 2,000 years.

HOME OF THE LEGIONS *The North Gate at Housesteads. The fort housed a garrison of some 1,000 legionaries – superbly trained soldiers who signed on for 25 years, and were capable of marching 30 miles a day with 50 lb packs on their backs. The life of those stationed on the Wall was a round of patrols, minor skirmishes and constant drill.*

RANNOCH

Highland

A zone of bog and peat hag tangled with pools and burns, Rannoch embodies all that is most sombre in the Highland landscape. Here, you feel, Macbeth might have met his three witches; the mood is both desolate and malign. The landscape is bare. Though the winds which ruffle its sullen waters also snarl through a few battered trees, nothing else that is upright arrests the ranging eye until it meets the moor's dark, enclosing mountains.

Countless memories and folk tales linger about the grim, remote expanse. Rannoch merges in the north-west into Glen Coe, the spectacular Glen of Weeping where the Macdonalds were massacred one infamous night in 1692. The moor itself is the legendary haunt of supernatural creatures, and a historic refuge of outlaws. Robert Louis Stevenson used the wild setting in his novel *Kidnapped*, while the poet T. S. Eliot evoked its listless menace in verse. His *Rannoch, by Glencoe* captures the doom-laden aura of the land-scape in its opening image: 'Here the crow starves...'

THE LONELIEST STATION IN BRITAIN

Rannoch Moor is Scotland's most famous and most awesome moor. As an expanse of raw Highland wilderness it has few rivals today, and has been much studied by naturalists and geologists.

From its tip at Glen Coe, the moor expands east and south to form a broad wedge bounded by lochs Rannoch and Tulla. Comprising some 60 sq. miles of inhospitable terrain, the waste is both high and secluded. Its plateau averages some 1,000 ft above sea level, but this is enclosed by much higher mountains – those of Glen Coe to the west and the Black Mount to the south-west, the ridges of Beinn Achaladair to the south and A Chruach to the north.

The eerie triangle of Rannoch Moor is geologically quite different from the high walls around. While the mountains are composed chiefly of schist and quartz-ite, the moor is floored with granite whose poor drainage has created a waterlogged habitat.

The terrain was scoured by an ice sheet 10,000 years ago and left pitted with dips and strewn with grey moraine. When the retreating glacial masses spilled out of the basin they shaped the main lines of drainage seen today. Rannoch's main system of water is an eastward-flowing chain of lochs and rivers which practically bisects the moor via Loch Bà, Loch Laidon and Loch Rannoch. You can swim almost the entire breadth of the moor in summer – or skate across it in winter if you prefer.

Apart from the major lochs, there are countless smaller pools and streams. High rainfall has allowed

AWESOME WASTELAND *Looking down from Beinn Achaladair, the road skirting Rannoch Moor snakes between Lochan nah Achlaise and Loch Bà. Beyond, a wasteland pock-marked by an infinity of inky pools, stretches for mile upon desolate mile.*

LONE TREE *Few trees now survive on Rannoch Moor itself, those that do usually grow on islands in the lochs. But baulks of iron-hard black timber that are found in the peat show that in earlier times the moor was densely wooded.*

BLACK WOOD OF RANNOCH

Some of the finest Scots pines in Britain grow along the southern shore of Loch Rannoch. Rising above a carpet of heather, their orange-gold trunks carry magnificent crowns of blue-green needles. This is the Black Wood of Rannoch, a remnant of the ancient forest that once covered much of northern Scotland.

Scots pine
Pinus sylvestris

peat to accumulate in sodden beds up to 20 ft deep – they often quiver and squelch underfoot. No road crosses the heart of the moor, though the road from Crianlarich to Glencoe village traverses its western extremities. The main artery of communication is the old West Highland Railway line to Fort William, whose construction in 1892–3 called for much ingenuity from its Victorian engineers. Huge quantities of brushwood had to be laid as a foundation for the track, and packed out with soil and ash.

MYSTERY AND MASSACRE

Before the railway was built, Rannoch was an emptiness on the map. Dr John Maccullough, an early 19th-century pioneer of Scottish travel writing, wrote of it in 1811: 'It is indeed an inconceivable solitude; a dreary and joyless land of bogs, a land of desolation and grey darkness.' There were no roads at all at this time; travellers had to pick a track for themselves through the waste.

Yet for centuries this watery fastness had been friend to bandits and rebels. William Wallace and Robert Bruce both used it as a base from which to make forays against the English. They kept company with the phantoms and water-horses, or kelpies, alleged in folklore to lurk in its secret waters.

Rising to the east is the strangely immaculate cone of Schiehallion (3,547 ft) whose name means 'fairy hill of the Caledonians'. On its slopes is a well, once believed to be enchanted, where white-clad Highland maidens used to bring garlands on May Day as offerings for the fairies. Schiehallion was also known

as a haunt of the Cailleach Bheur, the witch of Ben Nevis, and thought to contain a cave from which there was no return. Even in recent times, the shadow of a ghost dog has been reported to come from nowhere and follow passers-by in the area.

While Schiehallion dominates the horizon to the east, the western views lead to the bare rock triangle of Buachaille Etive Mór (3,345 ft), the 'Great Herdsman of Etive', who guards the entrance to Glen Coe. In this valley, on February 13, 1692, some 40 members of the Macdonald clan were butchered by a company of troops led by a Campbell.

THE LIVING TWEED

Schiehallion and the peaks of Glen Coe – places of magic and melancholy – mark two of Rannoch's natural extremities. Seen from their heights, the moor itself stretches out as a great torn fabric of moor grass, stained black with peat hag and rumpled with knots of grey rock. Here and there, glimmering, ragged-edged waters shine out through rips in the sombre tweed. The air is often damp and vaporous.

When sunlight illuminates the landscape though, it brings its subtle texture to life. Thread your way over the drier ground and you see that the tweed is flecked with innumerable colours. Sphagnum moss provides much of the blanket cover, a green, water-loving plant which dies and decomposes to form the peat on which new generations of moss will grow. Through it rise the stems of yellow-flowering bog asphodel and white cotton grass, while all about are low shoots of heath, heather and bog myrtle. Growing on the

ABOVE THE MOOR *The mottled tweed-coloured blanket of the moor stretches out below the summit of Buachaille Etive Mór (3,345 ft) which guards the eastern entrance to Glen Coe. The snow-dusted summits to the left mark the northern limit of the moor, while in the far distance a gleam of sunlight strikes blue from the waters of Loch Laidon.*

surface of the sphagnum itself you may find purple liverworts and sundew – a carnivorous plant, whose spoon-shaped leaves both trap and digest any small insects which alight on them.

Once in a while you may come upon mouldering hunks of black wood lying in depressions in the peat bed. These are the remains of ancient Caledonian pines. For thousands of years after the Ice Age, Rannoch Moor seems to have been thickly forested, but when the climate became wetter the peat grew to smother the woodlands beneath its spongy blanket. East of the moor, however, where the ground is steeper and better drained, is the largest surviving expanse of ancient pine forest in Scotland. This is the Black Wood of Rannoch, where magnificent trees of immense age soar to heights of 60 ft.

The moor itself is not entirely treeless; small islands on the lochs are quite thickly wooded with birch and rowan as well as pine. But they rise in pathos in a vast bare wilderness which is the domain of curlew, snipe and lapwing. Nearly 4,000 acres of the moor fall within a National Nature Reserve, and its jig-saw of waters abound with ducks and swans. Black and red-throated divers visit the lochs, and the silences are sometimes broken by the melodious 'tu-tu-tu' of the greenshank. Very occasionally you may catch a glimpse of the noblest bird of all – the golden eagle – which nests in the crags around.

Rannoch teems with wildlife, and the crows do not 'starve' as in Eliot's evocation. The poet goes on to write that 'here the patient stag/Breeds for the rifle', a more exact image, for red deer flourish on the moor and its forest slopes, prey both to landowner and to poacher. The Black Mount to the south-west is especially famed for its huge stags.

THE LOCH-SIDE WALK

Rannoch Moor can be reached by the main road from Crianlarich to Glencoe, or the minor road to Rannoch Station. In poor weather, when mists shroud the landscape, it is a dangerous place for the peat can be treacherous and give way beneath the feet of the unwary walker. Seen under gloomy skies it is at its most malign – and the menace is no poetic fiction.

In summer sunshine, however, there is safe and splendid walking to be had on the wide, drier ground between the pools. The best known route crosses the moor on the south sides of Loch Bà and Loch Laidon. The backdrop of the mountains is especially impressive at the outset, where the immense Coireach à Bà presents a staggering spectacle from the roadside. Gouged out of the Black Mount range between Clach Leathad (3,602 ft) and Stob Ghabhar (3,565 ft), this is the largest corrie in Scotland.

The enclosing mountains are part of Rannoch's unique attraction. If you stripped them from the horizon you would be left with a huge moor remarkable in itself, but utterly bleak in character. As it is, they lend drama to the scene, inviting the imagination to play around the wasteland's eerie desolation. And when sunlight turns their grey silhouettes to blue, the moor gains an unexpected quality. Wild, remote and hostile to man, Rannoch Moor becomes staggeringly beautiful.

TREGARON BOG
Dyfed

The wonder of the scene does not grip you immediately. At Tregaron Bog there are none of the crags, gorges or watery cascades for which the Welsh landscape is chiefly famed. It is, in fact, a spectacular nothingness; even the River Teifi which runs through its heart seems to disappear in places, emerging into full view only at the other side.

Tregaron Bog presents one of Britain's barest canvasses, and absorbs colour according to nature's moods. Seen from the north, under the lowering skies of winter, it is a forbidding waste of beige which stretches almost as far as the eye can see. In late spring it is flecked with the radiance of cotton flowers; in autumn it burns red with the hues of dying sedges. But the dramatic tone changes tell only part of the story. Linger awhile at any time of year and its aura begins to haunt you. The appeal is subtle but enduring – once visited, Tregaron Bog will not be forgotten.

THE RED MIRE

The old name for the bog is *Cors-goch Glan Teifi* (Red Mire on the banks of the Teifi), evoking the vivid tones of autumn. Situated in a valley beneath the Cambrian Mountains, it lies 3 miles north of the town of Tregaron, once an important droving centre.

Technically it is a raised bog, formed over thousands of years by the slow accumulation of peat. The Ice Age set the scene; about 20,000 years ago a melting glacier came down from the mountains to litter the Teifi valley with ridges of rock debris. The town of Tregaron stands on one such ridge which dammed up the course of the river. Upstream, a shallow lake developed, 4 miles long, which gradually filled with sedimentary clay and silt.

At first a fenland of reed and alder emerged, but it did not survive a period of increased rainfall. The waters rinsed nutrients from the soil and the bog-moss, sphagnum, took over; smothering the fen with its green, spongy carpet. Decayed remnants of one generation of mosses formed a humidified foundation for the next. Today, the peat has accumulated in domed beds up to 30 ft above the river level.

The river itself flows slowly through the bog, so choked in places with pondweed and water lilies that it seems to vanish completely. But its course still defines the contours of the peat beds to east and west.

The huge West Bed is a classic, convex plateau – the finest in Europe – which has hardly been affected by mankind. It is at the summit that the peat growth is most active. Here the green bog-mosses thrive around pools of ill-drained rainwater; the ground level rises

SLOW WATERS *It is spring, and fresh young club-rush is sprouting up to hamper the already slow-moving waters of the River Teifi as they flow towards the southern limit of Tregaron Bog. The vast tract of the bog stretches out to the north where the foothills of the Plynlimon Mountains reach down to contain it.*

One of the rarest birds in Britain, the red kite can sometimes be seen soaring over Tregaron Bog scanning the terrain for carrion and prey – small mammals, frogs, lizards and insects. The kite's last stronghold in Britain is in the mountains of mid-Wales where it nests and roosts in remote oak-woods, though ranging far and wide in search of food. When soaring, with its tail spread to give lift, the kite can be mistaken for a buzzard, a similar-sized bird, but in direct flight the kite's distinctive fork in the tail is revealed and is unmistakable.

Red kite
Milvus milvus

until the peat is dry enough to support heather on top and the build-up ceases for a while. Then the hummock may collapse and a new pool form in the depression. Imperceptibly, the summit has swollen; at the margins, where the water drains best, the peat growth is less significant.

On the other side of the river are two domed beds, North East and South East, which evolved in essentially the same way. They, however, have always been more accessible to man, and have been excavated by generations of local peat-diggers. On these eastern beds the curvature is distorted by pools and dry ridges; it is sculpted wilderness which bears witness to human need.

EEL WATERS, CURLEW SKIES

The region of Tregaron is rough farming country, and the dusky expanses of the bog give way to distant vistas of low green hills dotted with oakwoods. The sheep-grazed uplands are sparsely populated; not long ago, country doctors would visit their patients on horseback. Peat was valued as a source of fuel; it was cut in early summer, stacked to dry and carted off in autumn before the rains made the mire impassable. In addition, the bog was a source of rushes for grazing and animal bedding.

Peat cutting had ended by 1960, and the bog-mosses are reconquering their domain. Though there is still some grazing and rush-gathering, the area is carefully protected today as a unique peatland habitat.

It is only in the long views that Tregaron Bog seems a monochrome emptiness. In the near view the plant life is extraordinarily varied, and on the West Bed fascinating for its arrangement in concentric zones of vegetation. The steep margins are clad chiefly with tussocks of purple moor-grass. Above them is a zone of cotton and deer grasses, tangled with heather and birch scrub. At the waterlogged summit the acid soil nurtures a host of flowering wetland delights: white beak-sedge, hare's tail, cross-leaved heath, cranberry, crowberry, bog rosemary and sundew. On the eastern beds the zones have been confused by peat cutting, while on both sides of the river are willow swamps formed in flooded hollows.

The wildlife is superb. More than 3 sq. miles of the bog now form the Cors Caron National Nature Reserve, and it boasts over 40 species of nesting birds. This, above all, is curlew country, its silences broken often by the melancholy 'coorli' call from which the bird derives its name. Buzzards, red kites and sparrowhawks are regular predators of the open terrain, while sedge warblers and reed buntings frequent the damp places.

In summer, the reserve rings to the calls of skylarks and meadow pipits, and the incessant buzzing of grasshoppers. Otters flourish in the Teifi's eel waters and on summer nights, when the last bird call has died, polecats come down from the hills to prey on the frogs and water voles which abound there.

The mood of the bog varies as much through its wildlife as through its seasonal colour changes. With the grey skies of winter, flocks of whooper swans

arrive from Greenland to settle on the open water, while migrant hen harriers fly in from Europe to join the resident predators. And the fastness of the mire offers nature lovers a chance of a really exotic sighting. Among the species recorded at Tregaron have been white stork and purple heron.

THE RAILWAY WALK

The town of Tregaron was once an important intersection of drovers' roads. From medieval times until the middle of the last century the hill tracks around were regularly traversed by clamorous flocks of sheep, and lowing herds of cattle – not to mention pigs and even geese and turkeys – which were driven east over the Cambrians to markets in England. The drovers themselves often went on horseback, with corgis as herding dogs, and Tregaron still sees more than its share of horse riders, as a popular centre for moorland pony-trekking.

The routes, of course, avoided the mire, for its wild acres were no friend to man or beast. The railways brought the end of the droving era, and in 1866 a line was laid over the north-east tip of the bog, connecting

Tregaron with Aberystwyth. The track was closed some 20 years ago, and today the disused railway line provides a delightful mile-long walk into the wilderness. It is open to the public, and safe too, for the Victorian navvies used huge quantities of slag and brushwood to provide a foundation for the track.

The walk begins at a hut beside the road to Pontrhydfendigaid, about 2 miles north-east of Tregaron. This is a raised section of line where pastoral farmlands give way to thick growths of rushes. Saplings of oak, ash and birch thrive on the margins of the track where they have been allowed to establish themselves in the lime-rich soil of the navvies' ballast. You pass through a cutting and over another raised section before the track bends into the bog itself.

As you enter the bog, long views open up, extending to the hills of the north. To the right especially, the landscape is ridged and ditched by peat diggings, and there are green sphagnum-covered pools fringed with horsetails, bogbean and cotton grass. Eventually you arrive at a tributary of the Teifi, where an observation tower commands splendid views over the northern bog. In the immediate foreground are thick willow swamps, hung with lichens, which teem with dragonflies in summer. Below the tower, the Nature Conservancy Council has excavated a pool to attract wildfowl and waders; it is a place for silence – and keen eyes.

Beyond the tower, access is available only to permit holders. Exploring the wetland is, in any case, for those with some knowledge. Gumboots are sensible footwear, for flooding affects sections of all the marked footpaths. Outside the reserve proper are some areas of the bog where you may wander freely, but the willow swamps and old peat diggings are especially dangerous. A basic rule of thumb – known to all lovers of wetland solitudes – is to keep to the tussocks of heather. They indicate dry ground, while the inviting green places where bog-mosses flourish can be treacherous in the extreme.

The bog is a vital organism, its peat beds perpetually regenerating themselves, expanding and contracting with climatic change. The irony of this Welsh nothingness is its very vibrance. The appearance of emptiness is an illusion; Tregaron Bog is one of Britain's most living landscapes.

AUTUMN GOLD *In late summer and autumn the banks of the Teifi glow with gold as the stems of reed canary-grass ripen. A deep-rooted grass that thrives in shallow water, reed canary-grass spreads into dense masses by means of underground roots which send up new plants at frequent intervals. It grows up to 6 ft tall, providing cover and food for buntings and other small birds and insects.*

URRA MOOR

North Yorkshire

U p on the North York Moors the sky is open and the wind blows so free that you can practically lean against it. The upland is one great rolling plateau which covers 553 sq. miles stretching inland from the North Sea coast. The central ridge runs east-west, but is indented by delectable pastoral dales to either side, lightly scattered with farms and villages of stone which glow gold or glower grey according to the season. On the high tops you can walk all day and not meet a soul for company. You hear precious little either, except for the bleating of black-faced sheep and the chuckle of grouse in the heather.

At Urra Moor, to the north-west, the upland reaches its highest point of 1,489 ft, and eastward the heather is everywhere, extending in one vast undulating carpet to the furthest horizons. For two weeks in August, Urra's dome glows with a purple so intense that it might have been lit with neon – an improbable, unforgettable sight. In winter the scene is entirely different. The same heather darkens the whole land-scape with a sombre fleece to which the upland mass owes its old local name; the Blackamoor. Urra then is gaunt and forbidding, seeming to embody the very spirit of the wilderness.

That appearance, however, is an illusion. For the great heather waste is an accident of human toil, and imprinted with relics of man's presence.

AN ACCIDENTAL WASTELAND

The North York Moors provide the largest expanse of heather upland in England; the mass of tiny purple flowers of August have been estimated at 3,000 million to the square mile. But long ago the hills, chiefly of sandstone, supported extensive woodland: alder, birch, hazel and scrub oak. From the Bronze Age to medieval times, people cleared the trees to make farm fields and sheep runs, and to provide charcoal for fuel. Stripped of its cover, the soil was drained of nutrients, becoming lean and acid.

The heather then took over. Tough and wiry, thriving on acid soil and adapted to harsh physical conditions, the plants blanketed the treeless waste. Heather is the archetypal vegetation of moorland, and intimately connected with its landscape. In fact, moor-land is sometimes defined quite simply as 'country abounding in heather'. And when the plants die, their decayed remnants form a constituent of peat – the source from which new generations will draw suste-nance.

Urra Moor lies among the Cleveland Hills, in an area well known to Bronze Age tribesmen in the period when it was still partly wooded. They raised

WALKING COUNTRY *The route of the Lyke Wake Walk follows the heather-clad skyline across Cold Moor to the flat top of Hasty Bank. From there, the route descends before climbing again to Urra Moor, one of the finest stretches of the whole walk.*

MOOR AND VALLEY *From the great medieval earthwork above the tiny hamlet of Urra the view extends south-eastwards along the western flank of Urra Moor. Below are the green fields and hedgerows of the tiny valley carved from the moor by the waters of Bilsdale Beck.*

countless circular burial mounds, known as howes, on its high places. On Urra itself, the summit is capped by a huge tumulus known as Round Hill, or Botton Head. In addition, a 3 mile earthen bank and mound follows the moor's western escarpment. Its dating and purpose are uncertain – was it a fortification or boundary line? Certainly, the mysterious dyke is a major man-made modification of the landscape – like the heather itself, which is managed as a source of livelihood.

Sheep and grouse both thrive on the new green shoots of heather, and moorland economy has grown up around them. Left to themselves, the heather plants have a lifespan of some 15 years, growing thick and woody to over 3 ft in height. To accelerate the generation of new shoots, controlled burning is carried out by farmers and gamekeepers. Known in Yorkshire as 'swiddening' – it is 'muirburn' in Scotland – the burning of old growth takes place between November 1 and March 31, when great clouds of smoke may be seen rising from the old Blackamoor.

It is an alarming phenomenon to the uninitiated visitor, but in fact it is carefully regulated by the use of

firebreaks – paths stripped of heather to prevent flames spreading. The fires are lit, moreover, at a time of year when the peat is still damp and will not heat enough to damage the plants' roots.

In reality, Urra is a wilderness tamed. Blinded by the initial shock of August purple, you may not notice that the heather is growing at different heights in different places; and that its leaf tones vary accordingly from pale green to deep olive and dark brown. A chequer-board field system has been overlaid on the wilderness – though no field crops will grow in its soil.

THE FIREBREAK PATH

Several great moorland walks come together on Urra and follow the same track to its top. Among them, none is more colourful than the celebrated Lyke Wake Walk, a 40 mile endurance test running from Osmotherley in the west to Ravenscar on the coast. Steeped in a bizarre lore of witches and warlocks and funereal coffins, its challenge is so strenuous that few entrants have time to linger over the scenery; they may be seen, wild-eyed and perspiring, taking the moor's gentle gradients at a near gallop.

You do not have to be a walking fanatic to experience Urra's high heatherscapes. The moor may be approached by the road from Stokesley to Helmsley. It is a fine drive which climbs steeply from the lowland plain to the north, reaching the moor's edge at a parking place near the summit of Clay Bank.

At the car park itself there are splendid panoramas, and up to the right on Hasty Bank hill is a magnificent outcrop of bare rocks. Known as the Wainstones, they command huge views north and along the edge of the scarp which forms the boundary of the moor. The rocks are so named because they once resembled haywains in shape – though the likeness has been lost through subsequent erosion. Grouped in a tumbled confusion of slabs and pinnacles, they are well known to climbing enthusiasts.

To get up on to Urra, however, you take a path to the east of the road as it cuts through a natural pass. A narrow rock cleft leads to the moor's edge, where a cluster of stunted larches are grouped – the last trees before a 17 mile stretch of open moorland begins. Lyke Wake walkers have to brace themselves at this point, for this is where their loneliest ordeal starts.

The path first runs roughly parallel to the earthen dyke, rises to a peaty ridge, and cuts straight through the heather by a broad firebreak. Looking back down the track is a grand view of Urra's Cleveland Hill neighbours: Hasty Bank, Cold Moor and Cringle Moor. Their long, rounded tops jutting into empty space. You lose sight of the green plain below and are far – very far – from the bustle of traffic.

The firebreak itself follows an old road across the moors, its gentle undulations known both to Romans and Danes. It is said that on Urra, William the Conqueror saw smoke rising from the fires in York. The track is partially paved in places, and there are old stone crosses and marker stones by the wayside. Near the summit is the delightful Handstone, a crudely carved pillar erected as a signpost in the 18th century. It bears two chiselled hands and the inscriptions 'This way to Stoxla' (Stokesley) and 'This way to Kirkby' (Kirkbymoorside). Further along the firebreak is the much older Face Stone, which once marked the boundary of Cleveland.

This must always have been a lonely road, even in its heyday. With no habitation for miles around, it served smugglers as a 'trod' by which they brought contraband inland from the coast. It is not hard to imagine their nocturnal processions across the moor by moonlight.

THE HEATHER-LOCKED HEIGHTS

The great hump of Round Hill, capped by an Ordnance Survey triangulation pillar, commands no wide-ranging vistas. The broad dome of the moor locks you into the wilderness, so that even the brows of the neighbouring Clevelands have almost disappeared. This is a place of high solitude at the edge of heather and sky. You are not entirely alone though – ramble around the ancient mound and you are almost bound to be startled by the sudden, low whirring flight of red grouse and their distinctive call: 'ge'bak, ge'bak'. It is a familiar cry, known to all moorland walkers. Grouse are found only where heather abounds, favouring its young shoots for food and its older tangled growth for nesting cover.

Though Round Hill's prospects are featureless, you have only to wander a few hundred yards to obtain surprise views from the moor's edge. From a rocky outcrop to the south, for example, is a magnificent view down the long sweep of tranquil Bilsdale. The Cleveland Way long-distance footpath swings northeast here, round Greenhow Bank, while the firebreak itself leads eastwards on to the track of the old Rosedale Railway, once the second highest in England, which used to haul ironstone over the moors for processing at Durham and Teesside. The track offers 6 miles of fine, easy walking which never drops below 1,000 ft. The way rounds the head of lovely Farndale, famed for the wild daffodils which grow in profusion in spring, and you only come within striking distance of human habitation at the lonely Lion Inn at Blakey. Dating from 1553, this marvellously bleak building stands on the road to Hutton-le-Hole; the first artery of modern life which you encounter.

AN ISOLATED CONE

To turn the excursion on to Urra into a circular 6 mile walk, however, it is best to head west from Round Hill and descend from the moor's top by a bridlepath to the ancient earthen dyke. As you follow it back round the edge of the moor, a startling prospect opens up. Framed by the gap between Urra and Hasty Bank, Roseberry Topping comes into view to the north, a splendid and isolated cone of a hill which is constantly cropping up in surprise views from the moors. Just in front of it and slightly to the east is Captain Cook's Monument on Easby Moor, a 60 ft obelisk erected in 1827 to commemorate the great navigator who spent his boyhood at Great Ayton below.

For some there is only one time to visit Urra – during the magical two weeks in late August when the heather blooms most intensely. The purple is there for a much longer period though, persisting through September in more muted tones. And patches of bell heather and the lighter pink cross-leaved heath anticipate the display by flowering during July.

Throughout the summer months the empurpled vision is matched by pervasive scents and sounds. Heather exudes a heady aroma, redolent of the magic of wild places, and yields a rich nectar which causes the moor to hum with the flight of innumerable bees.

But Urra is a marvel for all seasons: green and exhilarating with the breezes of spring, when the flanking dales are garlanded with primroses or bluebells; mellow in late autumn when the heather tones die into indigo and the dale heads burn red with bracken; austere in winter when its tangled carpet protrudes in blackened knots through stark sheets of snow. Throughout the year, the months conspire with the landscape to calendar the moor with wonder.

A PERFECT MATCH

Heather moorland and the red grouse are inseparable – until August 12, the Glorious Twelfth, when the shooting season starts. Heather provides the cover beneath which the birds nest and shelter from predators. It also provides them with most of their food. Walkers know the red grouse as well as the hunters. A bulky bird, with stubby, rounded wings, it flies low and fast, taking off with a barking cackle when disturbed.

Red grouse
Lagopus lagopus

THE MALVERNS FROM HANGMAN'S HILL, HEREFORD AND WORCESTER

THE HAUNTED UPLANDS

Britain's hills have been kind to humanity – from the earliest cave-dwellers who sought refuge in the holes lining the tremendous water-worn gorge at Cheddar, to the Iron Age men who built thriving tribal capitals on the high places. It is now some 2,000 years since the hill sites were abandoned. Yet Britain's uplands remain imprinted with ditch and rampart and burial mound. Earthwork fortifications may be seen ringing the summits of mighty Mam Tor, or the faery Eildons, or White Horse Hill and, supremely, of Maiden Castle. Today, the hills of Britain fascinate through their lore, enchant through their beauty and inspire as viewpoints commanding sweeping vistas over the lowlands below.

BROADWAY BEACON

Hereford & Worcester

You do not expect high drama from the Cotswolds. Explore the broad upland by footpath or car and you may scarcely be aware of the hilltops at all. You travel instead through a gently enfolding landscape of honey-coloured villages and old manor houses, glimpsed by rippling brook or among lightly wooded slopes. Even the place names have a rustic tranquillity in them: Adlestrop, Minster Lovell and Chipping Campden, for example. The rivers partake of the same mellow aura – who could imagine a more delectably named stream than the Windrush or the Evenlode?

Approach Broadway Beacon by the main road from the east and you climb at a fair gradient through the golden stonework of Bourton-on-the-Hill. You are aware then that the ground is rising, but it soon levels again, although with mild undulations. A signposted side road leads left to Broadway Tower Country Park, to which you drive by some tumbledown drystone walling. The splendid folly comes quickly into view, its grey turrets looming on the brow of the hill to the right. Pay the admission charge, walk back towards the tower; and suddenly an astonishing vision opens up.

At your feet, the whole Cotswold escarpment tumbles away into a vastness of unbounded space. Down below is the great sweep of the Vale of Evesham with Bredon Hill rising like an empurpled island from the flat green farmlands. Beyond, the eye travels to the long blue crest of the Malverns, and further still, in the hazed distance, you may glimpse the Black Mountains of Wales 100 miles away.

At 1,024 ft above sea level, Broadway Beacon is the second highest point on the Cotswolds and is much more than a local attraction. Situated at the upland's edge, on the threshold of immense vistas, it is one of the finest viewpoints in the British Isles.

A DARK TOWER – BY REQUEST

The Cotswolds are old sheep-farming hills, owing their wonderful stone-built churches, villages and manors to the wealth of the medieval wool trade. In Tudor times, the sheepmasters used to maintain vast flocks on the hillsides, and Broadway Beacon was common grazing land. Bonfires were lit at the top to signal news across country and to celebrate great events. Strictly speaking, the term Broadway Beacon refers only to the summit knoll – the hill itself goes by the name of Fish Hill, or Broadway Hill.

In 1771 the land became part of the Earl of Coventry's estate, which covered parts of both Gloucestershire and Worcestershire. The crowning tower was added in 1797, perhaps to mark the centenary of the Coventry earldom. It is said, however, that the chief inspiration for the folly came from the countess who wanted to see whether the high point could be seen from Croome Court, the family seat 16 miles away to the north-west near Pershore. She asked that a bonfire be lit on the summit, and when she saw its flames twinkling in the far distance caused the earl to build a tower on the site.

Rising to 65 ft above the hilltop, and so topping Cleeve Cloud (1,083 ft) the highest point in the Cotswolds, the folly presents a romantic silhouette from a distance; close up it is a glorious absurdity. Built in a mish-mash of styles combining Norman with Saxon influences, it is plonked on the summit like a piece from a giant's chess game. The architect James Wyatt (1747–1813) was responsible for the design, and deliberately chose a more sombre stone than the local yellow Cotswold for its construction. His aim was to create a 'dark tower' effect, which he completed with scowling gargoyles near the top.

ARTISTS AND ECCENTRICS

The approach road to the site is Buckle Street, part of an ancient hill track extending between Bidford-on-Avon and Bourton-on-the-Water. And the tower has a fascinating history in itself. In 1827 it was bought by Sir Thomas Philipps, a famous collector of manuscripts and something of an eccentric besides. It was his declared wish to possess a copy of every book in the world, and he so crowded his home at Middle Hill near by with volumes that, it is said, his wife could barely reach her dressing table. In the folly, then very dilapidated, Philipps set up a printing press from which transcribed manuscripts were published.

Later in the 19th century, the tower came into the hands of an Oxford lecturer, Cornell Price, who had it repaired and redecorated. Price was a friend of William Morris, the artist-craftsman and socialist, who used to spend holidays in the folly in the company of the Pre-Raphaelite artists Dante Gabriel Rossetti and Edward Burne-Jones. Between them the group did much to promote the unspoiled charm of the Cotswolds, which had been little admired before. They must have gloried in the tower's tremendous views, though Rossetti is said to have grumbled about having to carry food all the way up from the village of Broadway below.

Later occupants included William Sherratt, who used the folly as a farmhouse. He was a renowned local storyteller, one of his yarns concerning a milk-maid blown off Fish Hill by a strong gust of wind and carried sailing away by her breeze-filled petticoats. No such fate befell a certain Mrs Hollingsworth. The last person to use the tower as a home, she lived in it for 40 years, as caretaker, without mains water, electricity or sewerage, managing to bring up a family in the turreted fantasy – and leaving as recently as 1972.

ON COTSWOLD STONE

Broadway Tower stands today in a delightful country park where a small flock of the now rare Cotswold sheep are maintained. The heavily fleeced breed descends directly from the old Roman longwool breed, but had practically disappeared from the Cotswolds by the mid-20th century; it is now expanding again. On the first floor of the tower is a room illustrating the history of sheep-farming in the Cotswolds, while the second floor is maintained as a

William Morris room. The third floor contains a relief model of the surrounding countryside, and six viewing porthole windows with 'keys' illustrating what may be seen through them.

The views are, of course, Broadway Beacon's great glory, and it is not necessary to climb to the rooftop platform to enjoy them. It is the great open arc stretching from south-west to north-east which most enthrals, and it may be experienced in all its splendour from the hillside.

Down below the stonework of Broadway, the Cotswolds' most famous village, speckles the green plain, and you can make out the towers of Tewkesbury Abbey, Worcester Cathedral and Warwick Castle as well as a dozen parish church steeples. The surrounding hills are exquisitely beautiful, and many famed through the poetry of A. E. Housman. Bredon, for example, where the poet went to 'see the coloured counties' with his love, is superbly delineated, a whalebacked Cotswold outlier rising abruptly from the plain. You can see, too, the 'high reared head of Clee' and even the celebrated cone of the Wrekin far to the north, whose 'forest fleece' heaved in the winds which troubled Wenlock Edge in *A Shropshire Lad*.

NATURE'S MOODS

No viewpoint in Britain can guarantee its panoramas in all weathers, and Broadway Beacon is as subject to nature's moods as any other. Sometimes, for example, a heat haze rising from the Vale of Evesham can veil both the plain and its hills, leaving the lovely spurs of the Cotswold escarpment curving into a void of white mist, with the bleating of sheep and the call of the skylarks dropping from nowhere.

Then is the time to explore the hill for its own sake. Three nature trails have been laid out in the country park, each with its own attraction. One winds through shaded woodlands of ash, beech and sycamore which in springtime are flooded with bluebells and aromatic with the scent of white-flowering wild garlic. The second descends steeply downhill by steep slopes tangled with hawthorn scrub to views of Broadway's spires through the haze.

The third walk leads gently along the edge of the escarpment to the pleasing little Fish Inn, erected as a gentleman's summer house in about 1775. Like so many buildings in the neighbourhood it is built of the golden limestone for which the Cotswolds are famous. Technically it is an oolitic limestone, consisting of tiny compacted spheres of calcium carbonate. It weathers in a variety of shades, from dove-grey to an extraordinarily rich yellow – the yellow of egg yolks or of sunshine itself. Just by the inn is a small private quarry where the stone can be seen in its raw state.

And if rainfall has not rinsed the air by the time that the walk is over, there is Broadway itself to explore. The village is easily reached by marked paths down the escarpment – a fitting destination for the walker.

FOLLY VIEW *Clouds break over Broadway Beacon and a breathtaking prospect of woodland, field and hedgerow stretches to distant hills on a misted horizon. The artist Dante Gabriel Rossetti stayed in the splendid tower folly – and carped at carrying groceries from Broadway below. Now the way up the 1,024 ft hill is marked for walkers to enjoy.*

CHEDDAR GORGE

Somerset

It has been called the English Grand Canyon. Cheddar Gorge cuts for over a mile through the Mendip Hills of Somerset, flanked by stupendous limestone cliffs which soar to 450 ft above a winding road. Cragged and fissured, the pale immensities of rock are strewn with ivy and clustered with ash and yew. Overall, the effect is extraordinary; as if the upland mass had been sundered and the chasm embroidered with foliage.

The gorge is dry; follow the tarmac strip of the road through it and you meander where, you feel, a river ought to run. Yet within the ramparts to either side is a hidden life of water, trickling and gurgling in a million streams which are eating the heart out of the hills. Come down the pass from the north and you arrive at the village of Cheddar, where water-worn caves give access to a prehistoric underworld in which the relics of Stone Age man have been found. Fantastically ornamented with stalagmites and stalactites, the caves lead through time as well as the landscape.

IN PRAISE OF LIMESTONE

Limestone underlies much of southern England's uplands, and has shaped a rolling landscape of downland and wold. The rock is sedimentary in origin, and formed out of primeval sea-beds where the debris of innumerable marine animals accumulated. Their skeletal remnants, compacted under great pressure, yield the carbonate of lime to which the rock owes its name.

Heaved to the surface by ancient earth movements, the bedded rock has tended not to form bold crags or tors; limestone weathers too easily, is softened by rainfall and readily clothed with grass. The poet W. H. Auden evoked the maternal gentleness of the scenery in his *In Praise of Limestone*, rightly attributing its character to the simple geological fact that the rock dissolves in water:

Mark these rounded slopes
With their surface fragrance of thyme and, beneath,
A secret system of caves and conduits; hear the springs
That spurt out everywhere with a chuckle,
Each filling a private pool for its fish and carving
Its own little ravine whose cliffs entertain
The butterfly and the lizard.

The lines well express the spirit of the Mendips, which extend across Somerset from the Bristol Channel to the Wiltshire border. Turf-topped and thyme-scented, the whalebacked plateau of carboniferous limestone is dipped and hollowed by watercourses both wet and dry. The hills are low, barely exceeding 1,000 ft at their highest point, and given over chiefly to peaceful farming and grazing. To come upon the spectacular cliffs of the Cheddar Gorge in this tranquil landscape is an unforgettable experience. What unimaginable upheaval or other natural cataclysm, you may wonder, could have fashioned it?

The fearsome cliffs have been known for centuries past. The 10th-century monarch King Edmund, for example, nearly had a fatal accident at the 'immense precipice and horrid gulf' as a medieval chronicler called the gorge. In 941, it seems, the king was out hunting in the Mendips, and pursued a stag which plunged to its death in the gorge; the hounds followed over the edge and the king halted only just in time. A 12th-century traveller, Henry of Huntington, described the cliffs as ranking among the 'four wonders of England'.

Many theories were advanced to explain the gorge's origins. It was once believed, for example, that an ancient earthquake had ripped the hills apart. It was also suggested that the cleft was eroded by the sea at a time when its level was higher; and that the gorge is the remnant of a cavern whose roof has collapsed.

THE VANISHED RIVER

Today it is widely accepted that the gorge was in fact cut by a river whose course has since disappeared underground. Probably the erosion occurred in two stages. First, a stream from the Mendip plateau carved out the lines of the gorge, boring out the cave system in its flanks before sinking below ground. Then, during the Ice Age, the caverns became choked with frozen mud and the gorge flooded with torrents of meltwater which deepened and sharpened its contours.

The water rises today near the end of the gorge, in an area which is honeycombed with caves. There are two principal systems open to the public. The first was

BRIGHT UNDERWORLD *Concealed lighting turns Cox's Caves into a glowing fairyland of tall stalagmite pillars roofed by a hanging forest of stalactites.*

discovered accidentally in 1837 by a mill-owner named George Cox, who broke into a hole while quarrying the hills for limestone. Cox's Caves, as they are known, form a complex of grottoes glistening with stalagmite pillars and hanging curtains of stalactites. The second system, known as Gough's Caves, is grander in scale, reaching for a quarter of a mile into the hills. It was discovered in 1890 by Mr Richard Gough who was consciously seeking out a new complex of caverns. He blasted 12 ft through solid rock to reach what is known today as the Grand Passage – then went on digging through a blocked

tunnel to discover the great chambers of St Paul's and King Solomon's Temple.

In 1903, during excavations near the entrance to Gough's Caves, a 10,000-year-old skeleton was unearthed. Now reconstructed and exhibited at Gough's Museum, the so-called Cheddar Man belonged to one of the Stone Age tribes which abounded in the Mendips, hunting wild horses and reindeer with flint-tipped arrows. Thousands of flint implements have been found just inside the entrance to Gough's Caves, which may have been an implement factory for a whole community. Much mystery, of course, still lingers about this era, as it does about the caves themselves. They have only been partially explored even today; only in 1976, a new tunnel 270 ft long was discovered at Gough's Caves.

BY JACOB'S LADDER

The village of Cheddar is something of a tourist trap, famed for its cheese as well as its gorge and caves. Cheese-making is an ancient Somerset art, and Cheddar's speciality has been celebrated for centuries. In 1170, for example, Henry II bought 80 hundredweight of it, describing it as the 'best in England'. Daniel Defoe, who visited Cheddar in 1772, echoed the medieval king's sentiments, declaring: 'Without all dispute, it is the best cheese that England affords, if not, that the whole world affords.'

The whole world today, of course, knows pallid imitations of true Cheddar cheese. Farmhouse cheeses are still made in the Mendips according to traditional recipes, but much of the land today is given over to strawberry farming. Tourism, too, is an important local concern. The caves have become an electric fairyland, lit by artificial means and thronging with visitors in high season. There is even a Caveman Restaurant, complete with Grotto Bar and a neon skeleton beckoning at the roadside.

The road through the gorge becomes very congested in summer. But, in any case, it is best experienced on foot, for no view from a car window can do justice to the scale of the cliffs around. The walk also allows you to look closely at a series of small caves where Jack Plumley, a highwayman, used to hide out with his horse. To escape the crowds you have only to climb up on to the high ground where huge and exhilarating views open up. The simplest ascent is by Jacob's Ladder, a steep flight of steps at the side of the gorge. It was constructed by Roland Pavey, a 19th-century caving enthusiast who failed in attempts to discover a cavern like Gough's or Cox's and so made his own – by blasting out an old river passage to create artificial galleries. Man-made waterfalls have been introduced, illuminated with coloured lights.

From the Waterfall Cave, Jacob's Ladder climbs directly up the side of the gorge, and with 300 steps cannot be taken at a run. At the top is an observation tower with magnificent views, which extend in fine weather as far as Exmoor and the Bristol Channel. From the top of the ladder there is also one of the West Country's finest walks, leading along the clifftop to Black Rock Gate at the head of the gorge.

The views down into the abyss are giants' views, in which the cars and sightseers so recently left behind have shrunk to miniscule proportions. And the formations are superbly delineated from above: the Pinnacles, for example, biting like fangs into the chasm, and the Horseshoe Bend where the road almost encircles a limestone outcrop.

The core of the rock is bared to the eye in tiered beds up to 10 ft thick. The horizontal or tilted bedding planes are most marked, but you can also see the innumerable vertical joints which make the cliffs appear as if they have been constructed of massive rectangular blocks. The colour varies according to the time of day. In full sunlight the naked rock seems stark white; when shadows fall it turns grey-brown, finally

turning in twilight to a rich, glowing purple.

These are jackdaw heights, colonised by squabbling communities of the birds and ringing to their 'tchak-tchak' cries. And the plant life is extraordinarily varied. Trees sprout in the most improbable places, whitebeam flourishing among the clustering ash and dark, evergreen yews.

Cheddar Gorge is especially famed for the delightful Cheddar pink, but there are other rarities. There are several unusual species of hawkweed, for example, including *Hieracium stenolepiform* which grows nowhere else in the world. Here, too, you may find mossy saxifrage, rock stonecrop and lesser meadow-rue, while growing in profusion are ox-eye daisies and yellow Welsh poppies. Red valerian is also widespread and flowers from June to August.

All are lime-lovers, but that does not quite explain the distinctive character of the gorge's plant community. It is likely that the very steepness of the cliffs and the multitude of ledges have contributed to the variety of species. The wind-blown seeds of frail or rare plants may settle in isolated pockets of soil and grow without being crowded by close neighbours competing for nourishment.

With the drama of the cliffs and the mystery of their weird, glittering underworld, the flowers of Cheddar Gorge have conspired to make the Mendips' ravine unique. Widely famed and much visited, it remains a marvellous phenomenon with no parallel in the whole of the British Isles.

LIME LOVERS *Whitebeam, ash and yew flourish on precarious footholds in the gorge. So does a type of hawkweed which grows nowhere else in the world. Saxifrage, poppy and valerian bloom, and ivy spreads . . . all thriving in a lime-rich environment.*

THE EILDONS

Borders

They surge as one three-crested wave from a tranquil sea of farmland. Mysteriously isolated and distinctively contoured, these are fairy hills of ancient enchantment. Once, it is said, the Eildons formed a single upthrust which was split into three on a wizard's orders; and within the bosom of the hills, a medieval poet is said to have been entertained by the Queen of Elfland. An 18th-century poet, Andrew Scott, wrote:

> *O Eildon Hills, huge sisters three,*
> *As fair you rise as ony,*
> *Scotia has higher hills than thee,*
> *But few gleam half as bonny.*

Yet through the tapestry of Eildon legends is woven a harsher reality. Smoke from the peat fires of Iron Age encampments once curled from the Eildons' summits. The Romans knew these fortified heights and later, when bandit mosstroopers ravaged the Scottish-English Borders, the Eildons looked down on centuries of bloodshed and villainy. Sir Walter Scott, Border poet supreme, wrote: 'I can stand on Eildon Hill and point out forty-three places famous in war and verse.'

The Eildons are much more than a feature of the countryside. Steeped in folklore and the tumults of time, they embody the romance of the Borders.

BALLADEER LANDSCAPE

Tour around the middle reaches of the Tweed and you drive through a balladeer's landscape. Among the sheep hills and the cattle-grazed farmlands are a number of ruined abbeys – Melrose, Jedburgh, Kelso and Dryburgh – gutted by the English during centuries of invasion which lasted from the 13th to the 17th centuries. For much of that time, this 'Debatable Land' was despoiled too by Border brigands, known as mosstroopers or reivers, from whose feuds, murders and moonlit rides an epic tradition of balladry emerged.

Sir Walter Scott (1771–1832), who lived for much of his life at Abbotsford House near Melrose, drew inspiration for many of his novels from the songs and sorrows of the region. And the three Eildon Hills, rising sudden and lovely above Melrose, lie at the very heart of Scott country.

They are the most conspicuous landmarks in all the old county of Roxburghshire, visible, for example, from Carter Bar, high in the Cheviots to the south. Running from north to south, the Eildons attain heights of 1,327 ft (North Hill), 1,385 ft (Middle Hill), and 1,216 ft (Wester Hill) respectively. The three hills

LEGENDARY HILLS *The Eildons rise spectacularly from tree-girt fields and pastures – formed, says legend, from a single mound split into three by order of an ancient wizard. Iron Age encampments once crowned all three hills.*

owe their abrupt elevation to ancient volcanic action – here molten rock broke through the older sedimentary beds of the Tweed basin. And though beautifully delineated from a wide area around, the Eildons have one classic viewpoint. Two miles to the east of the triple peaks is a prospect so intimately connected with Sir Walter Scott that it has become known quite simply as Scott's View.

The viewpoint is on Bemersyde Hill, overlooking an exquisite loop in the Tweed. Bemersyde House near by is the ancestral home of the Haigs, and Scott was a frequent visitor at the house. He took an intense delight in the dramatic vista from the hill, with the Tweed curving amid a foreground of woods, and the broad, undulating farmlands beyond pierced by the three peaks on the skyline. So often did the novelist linger by the roadside that at his funeral, when the cortège was rounding the hill on its way to Dryburgh Abbey, Scott's horses, pulling one of the carriages, halted of their own accord – as if their master still required them to pause. Scott's View remains as hauntingly beautiful today, and is clearly indicated by signposts and lay-bys.

THE FORT OF THREE HILLS

Sir Walter Scott was not the first to discern a special quality in the Eildons. From the earliest times, warriors must have coveted the commanding heights, purely for strategic reasons. Apart from their elevation, the triple hills overlook the confluence of the Tweed with its tributary the Leader Water, so covering important river routes.

On North Hill, the second highest of the Eildons, is a huge circular earthen rampart in which some 500 hut circles have been identified. Dating from the Iron Age, the encampment must have held a population of 2,000 to 3,000 people within its 40 acres, making it the largest hill-fort in Scotland. It was, perhaps, the tribal capital of the Selgovae, a people who occupied much of this part of the Borders.

The Romans in their turn saw the site's advantages. At Newstead, just to the east of Melrose, they built their largest fort in all the Borders, calling it *Trimontium* (the three hills) in tribute to the backdrop of the hills. Using Hadrian's Wall as a base line, the legionaries made many expeditions deep into Scotland and built a great road known as Dere Street as their chief thoroughfare. It stretched from Corbridge on the Tyne as far as Inveresk on the Forth, and Trimontium lay on its path. Up on North Hill, the site of the old Iron Age encampment, the Romans placed a signal station to cover the route.

The Newstead fort is practically invisible today, and marked only by a roadside sign. But excavations at the site, now overgrown, have filled a whole room at Edinburgh's National Museum of Antiquities with

SCOTT'S VIEW *The Eildons from Bemersyde Hill – a view that compelled Sir Walter Scott to linger long and often on the road here. So often that during his funeral, horses drawing one carriage halted of their own accord at the spot. They were Scott's own horses.*

RAIDING COUNTRY *Look south-east from the Eildons' heights (facing page) and a peaceful panorama of sheep-dotted meadows and snug stone farms recedes to a blue haze of hills – the Cheviots. But for centuries this quiet landscape echoed to the war-cries of Border reivers.*

STATELY SHELL *The English made a habit of despoiling stately Melrose Abbey – most notably in 1322 and 1385. The Earl of Hertford finally gutted it in 1545, but it remains a magnificent shell, with flying buttresses and fine tracery decorating its sadly empty windows. By tradition the heart of Scotland's hero Robert Bruce lies buried in the chancel under one of those windows.*

tools, weapons and household utensils both Roman and native in origin.

THE RHYMER'S HILLS

An established walk from the small town of Melrose takes you up to the summits of the Eildons. It begins at a car park near the old market cross, and you start climbing by fields and stiles. Then, as you ascend, making for the saddle between the two northern peaks, the fields give way to steep slopes of gorse, bracken and heather. A broad path takes you steeply up to the top of North Hill, where a huge panorama opens up.

Look north and Melrose is at your feet, with its ruined abbey founded by the Cistercians. The little burgh itself boasts fewer than 2,000 people – a smaller community than that of the tribesmen who once thronged these breezy heights. On the northern horizon you can make out the silhouettes of the lonely Lammermuirs, one of the loveliest Border ranges. Turning south-east, where the Tweed glides round by Dryburgh, the eye travels to the long wall of the Cheviots. And from the central summit, where there is a view indicator, you look south-west to the faraway hills of Galloway.

Did the Romans, knowing the use of these heights, also have a sense of their beauty and mystery? Certainly one medieval laird did: he was Thomas Learmonth (1220–97) of Ercildoune, a few miles up

the Leader Water. A nobleman, born at what is now Earlston Castle, he is better remembered as Thomas the Rhymer. In his own time he was known as a seer, and among his innumerable predictions he is said to have foretold the death of the Scottish king, Alexander III, and the Battle of Bannockburn.

The Rhymer was also the author of a wonderful ballad recounting a long sojourn in Elfhame – the Scottish fairyland – to which he was introduced by the Queen of the Fairies on the Eildons' slopes:

> *True Thomas lay on Huntlie Bank;*
> *A ferlie he spied wi' his e'e;*
> *And there he saw a ladye bright*
> *Come riding down by the Eildon Tree.*

The Rhymer was taken into an enchanted country within the Eildons by his 'ladye bright' and spent seven years there with the queen. It was a pleasant time, marred only when she gave him an apple to eat which was supposed to make him speak only the truth. 'A gudely gift ye wad gie to me!' protested the outraged Rhymer, who was noted for his honest tongue.

If you come down from North Hill by its eastern slope, you can see the Eildon Tree Stone, situated in Eildontree plantation, marking the site of the supposed meeting between poet and fairy.

BY WIZARD'S COMMAND

The magic of the Eildons is inextricably linked with the saga of the Rhymer, but the hills' supernatural lore does not end there. These mystic heights, like certain others scattered throughout the British Isles, are said to contain a cave where King Arthur and his knights lie sleeping. And the hills are also associated with Michael Scott, a 13th-century contemporary of the Rhymer, who is remembered as the Border Wizard.

Possibly born in Fifeshire, Scott was a noted astrologer, physician and mathematician who did service in the courts of Europe and was knighted by Edward I of England. He died in 1292 and was buried in Melrose Abbey.

In Scotland, 'Auld Michael' is remembered as a black magician, the source of innumerable folk tales. One such, told by Sir Walter Scott, attributes the very shapes of the Eildons to the wizard. It was said that the three hills once formed a single cone, but the wizard had to find futile tasks to exhaust the energy of a very active demon. He first told him to build a weir across the Tweed at the town of Kelso downstream; the demon obliged overnight. Then the wizard told him to cleave the Eildon Hill into three; by next morning the task was accomplished. Finally, the wizard set him a truly interminable task of spinning ropes from the sands of the sea. The demon was mastered at last.

Today, the geological origins of the Eildons are well known. But the three hills have lost none of their enchantment. Come upon those dreamy silhouettes by the purple light of the gloaming and you can fancy that the Queen of Elfhame still holds sway within peaks contoured at a wizard's behest.

MAIDEN CASTLE

Dorset

It is a grand testament to man's ambition. Situated among the chalk downs of Dorset, Maiden Castle is the mightiest prehistoric fort in Europe, a saddle-backed earthwork monster nearly half a mile long. Engineered with horn picks, bronze axes and crude wicker baskets, the huge ramparts swirl in tiers around the contours of the hill, banked, ditched and mazed with access corridors to east and west.

The sinuous elegance of the whole is best revealed by aerial photography, which shows the broad grassy summit swelling like an upsurge of green sea and the ramparts as seismic ripples from the dome. From the ground, Maiden Castle is a more brooding presence. Thomas Hardy, whose novels celebrated Wessex heaths and downs, wrote of an animal character in the hills' ribbed immensity, likening it to 'an enormous many limbed organism of antediluvian time'.

Beauty or Beast, Maiden Castle is a quite extraordinary creation, one spectacular lump of nature as organised by man.

OUT OF THE STONE AGE

Scattered upon the face of Britain are some 3,000 earthwork enclosures whose grass-covered banks and ditches once sheltered Iron Age tribes. The settlements were flourishing for centuries before the Romans came – and long before the tiered defences were built on the hill where Maiden Castle stands. With 30 centuries of history behind it, the site was already imprinted by man when the rampart-builders took up their picks.

Maiden Castle lies some 2 miles south-west of present-day Dorchester in Dorset, and its hill is by no means high. It stands only 600 ft above sea level, but rises abruptly from the undulating countryside at some distance from the main downland ridge. The first known settlement was a village of the New Stone Age, situated on the eastern knoll and dating back to about 3000 BC. Pottery and implements of flint, bone and horn have been recovered from the site, with a crudely fashioned chalk idol, perhaps representing a mother goddess.

Little is known of the shadowy people who occupied the hill at that time. But around 2000 BC the camp was abandoned and an immensely long burial mound built at the summit, extending for a third of a mile along the top. At the eastern extremity, a macabre discovery was made by archaeologists. Interred there was the body of a man – about 30 years old – who had been brutally hacked to death. His mutilated remains were buried with care, suggesting a ritual killing.

Did the hill at this time become a place associated

PREHISTORIC POWER *Primitive horn picks, bronze axes and massed muscles built Maiden Castle – mightiest prehistoric fort in Europe. Its true immensity and the complex engineering of its sinuous ramparts and maze of access points are best seen from the air.*

with death and to be avoided? Did folk memories of the burials linger about the summit? Or did the climate simply worsen, discouraging upland settlement in the region? Whatever the reason, from 1500 BC no significant use was made of the hill as a place of habitation. The Bronze Age passed it by, and it was centuries before the rampart-builders arrived.

Around 300 BC, nameless tribes of Celtic farmers came to the Wessex downs in numbers. They were an Iron Age people, in the sense that they were familiar with the metal and some of their families might possess a few iron-tipped tools and weapons. In reality, though, they still relied chiefly on bronze for their domestic hardware, and their most marked characteristic was their habit of stockading their settlements with earthen ramparts. Typically, the earth walls were about 7 ft high, faced on each side with sharpened timbers, and surrounded by a V-shaped ditch.

REVOLUTIONARY WEAPON

At Maiden Castle, the new settlers enclosed about 16 acres of the eastern knoll, setting up timber huts within and digging large storage pits to hold their corn and water. Groups of dwellings were separated by streets, and in time the settlement expanded along the ridge. Within 50 years it had trebled in size to cover the entire summit of the castle – an area of 45 acres. The whole was enclosed by a circuit wall with elaborate double gateways to the east and west.

What caused the sudden multiplication of ramparts was a dramatic development in warfare. Around the 1st century BC the sling-shot was introduced to Britain. It was a weapon as revolutionary in effect as the breech-loading rifle or Maxim gun of later times. Primitive arrows had a range of only some 30 yds; a slung pebble could kill at 100 yds. To counter it, higher and more extensive defences were needed.

A seafaring tribe from Brittany, the Veneti, probably brought the sling to south-western England. With the new weapon came its remedy. At Maiden Castle, limestone slabs were hauled to the site to reinforce the gateways. Stone platforms were set up as vantage points, and the apron slopes of the hill itself became flounced with fantastic tiers of banks and ditches.

Maiden Castle today is usually reached by a side road leading to a car park off the main road from Dorchester to Weymouth. Thomas Hardy, whose *A Tryst in an Ancient Earthwork* satirised an early excavation at the site, well evoked the impression made by coming upon it: 'At one's every step forward it rises higher against the south sky, with an obtrusive personality that compels the senses to regard it and consider. The eyes may bend in another direction, but never without the consciousness of its heavy, high shouldered presence ... The profile of the whole stupendous ruin, as seen at a distance of a mile eastwards, is as clearly cut as that of a marble inlay.'

As you climb up the turfed banks, you know that if this hill is an animal it is a gigantic creature. Three or more tiers of ramparts soar almost sheer in places to heights of 60 or 90 ft. The whole area enclosed by the outer banks amounts to some 120 acres, and even today the best way to enter the summit compound is by way of the ancient gateways. They are more elaborately ridged, and at the great West Gate you have to zigzag through a labyrinth where no fewer than seven ramparts come together. Once at the top, it takes 45 minutes to walk the 1½ mile footpath round the summit bank.

Up to 5,000 people crowded the summit of the castle during its heyday, a sturdy hill folk who went clad in roughly woven garments with dogs at their heels. They tilled the land around in small square plots, maintaining sheep, goats and oxen in addition. And for much of the time that they lived there they must have felt secure enough in their mighty bastion.

Tribes from north-eastern Gaul had begun to arrive on the south coast of England in the 1st century BC and had established themselves as far west as Gloucestershire. But there is no reason to suppose that they came to Maiden Castle as anything other than Celtic cousins, traders and immigrants rather than as warriors. The real test of the ramparts followed the Roman invasion of Britain in AD 43 when, in one dramatic encounter, the sling-shot defenders met the greatest war machine on earth.

THE MAIDEN'S FALL

The inhabitants of Maiden Castle must have been expecting trouble. Vast quantities of sling-stones were laid in, and deposited especially near the gateways. One hoard excavated comprised no fewer than 20,000 pebbles, many garnered from Chesil Beach to the south.

The trouble came in the form of the Second Augustan Legion, headed by the future emperor Vespasian, and bent on the conquest of southern England. Approaching the great hill-fort from the Isle of Wight, the Romans skirted the mighty West Gate and drew up their siege engines at the slightly less daunting entrance to the east.

A devastating barrage of ballista arrows, fired from giant crossbows, was swiftly followed by an infantry assault. Vespasian's troops streamed up the banks and ditches, gained access to the enclosure and fired the huts around. Amid the tumult of smoke and flames, the gates were taken – and the massacre of the defenders ensued.

Archaeologists who excavated the site in 1934–7 discovered grim evidence of the scale of the disaster. There were skeletons buried sometimes in pairs in hastily dug chalk and earth graves, their skulls cleft by sword blades. There was a mass grave in which some 40 bodies were found, including that of a defender in whose backbone a ballista arrowhead remained embedded. It is clear that resistance was fierce, for among the skeletons were many with skulls shattered by axe-blades – Celtic, not Roman weapons.

After the cataclysm, a few families seem to have lingered on the ruined hill. But by AD 70 the site had been entirely abandoned, the population resettling in and around the new Roman town of Durnovaria, present-day Dorchester.

MALHAMDALE

North Yorkshire

A two-tone colour scheme pervades Yorkshire's limestone dales, of pale rock and emerald turf. Here and there the valleys are shaded with woodlands, and often they are topped by dark-hued moorland. But the dales themselves offer acres of open pastureland where the grass grows in vast green carpets on the soluble rock.

Barely 6 miles long and threaded by the babbling headwaters of the River Aire, Malhamdale embodies the attraction of the limestone country. Its hill slopes are criss-crossed with light-coloured drystone walling and nibbled by shaggy Dalesbred sheep. Dippers and wagtails haunt the banks of the shallow river whose course is forded by low, stone bridges.

This is a shepherd's landscape, and long ago drovers used to converge on the village of Malham in their thousands, bringing herds and flocks to a great local fair. Today, in high season, crowds still throng the dale – but not to trade or barter. They come instead to admire the fantastic rock scenery which is grouped around the valley's head. For though Malham's is a miniature dale, its landforms are gigantic, comprising two of Britain's grand limestone spectaculars: Malham Cove, a stupendous horseshoe wall of rock; and Gordale Scar, an awesome cliff.

A minor road, branching north off the main road from Skipton to Settle, winds up the dale to Malham. The area has known settlement since prehistoric times, and the village owes its name to Dark Age homesteaders. It derives from a 6th-century Anglian settler called Malcas; *Malham* means 'Malcas's Place'. The early farmers left their mark on the landscape by creating arable strips on the hillside to ease ploughing, and to conserve the rainwater which drains so easily from the soil of the limestone slopes. Known as lynchets, the strips survive as green terraces curving around the hillsides.

MAJESTIC AMPHITHEATRE

But the true marvels of Malham are entirely natural formations, which date back far beyond the dawn of mankind. Some 300 million years ago, a system of landslips split the earth's crust across this region of Yorkshire. Known as the Craven Faults, the fractures extend from Kirkby Lonsdale to Nidderdale and have cloven the strata of bedded rock to leave cliffs or scars. Malham lies at the heart of the fault zone.

A short walk of barely a mile from the village takes you up to Malham Cove, which bares its grandeur to the eye long before you arrive at its foot. It is a majestic amphitheatre of rock, contoured with a startling symmetry. The sheer walls rise to some 300 ft, and extend in breadth for twice that distance. Dazzling white in full sunshine, the cliffs have a vertical drop

CATACLYSMIC CLIFFS *Easy to imagine an immense waterfall plunging 300 ft over the great crescent lip of Malham Cove. And so it did, when the cliff was old beyond imagining, formed by an earth upheaval 300 million years ago. The lip was straight then – a torrent released by the cataclysm wore it to its present shape. During exceptional rainfall the torrent returns as nearby Malham Tarn bursts its banks.*

ABOVE MALHAM *The limestone plateau above Malham Cove (preceding pages) with its stunning vista of dale country and Malham village snug in a hollow below. Weathering has dissolved and rounded the edges of cracks and fissures in the plateau to leave an extraordinary impression of gigantic blocks of paving stone.*

which is frankly astonishing. They were long considered unscaleable by rock climbers, and have only been conquered in postwar years by Himalayan challengers using them as a testing ground.

The cove was first formed when immensities of limestone dropped clean away along a straight edge. Water shaped the splendid crescent, cascading over the edge at the time of the cataclysm in torrents which gradually cut back the scarp.

The flood must have resembled a Niagara in its time, but has disappeared since the end of the Ice Age. During the era of the glaciers, frozen water sealed up the fissures in the limestone plateau above, so that the torrent streamed over a hard bed. With the melting of the ice, the fissures opened up, and today soak in rainwater like a sponge.

Only after truly exceptional rains has the missing Niagara been re-created. It has occurred when the glacier-formed lake of Malham Tarn, about 1½ miles further north, burst its banks and sent floods down the ancient watercourse. No such grand cascades have occurred in this century, but Thomas Howson's *Illustrated Guide to the District of Craven* (1861) noted: 'Twice in the last forty years the swollen waters of the Tarn have made their way over the Cove, but the torrent has dispersed in one vast cloud of spray before it reached the bottom; its density and the magnificence of the sight may be imagined by the fact that the spectators could not approach within a hundred yards of the foot of the rock without being drenched through.'

Malham Cove is not entirely dry; a little crystal stream, the Malham Beck, issues mysteriously from the foot of the cliffs to wind away among oaks and alders. The water last saw daylight by an old smelt-mill some three-quarters of a mile west of Malham Tarn, before trickling into the limestone underworld and following a subterranean joint to the cliff.

The Pennine Way mounts up the western edge of the cliffs to reach the plateau above. The views back down the dale are magnificent, and if you look ahead you can see the depression of the dry valley which once conducted the waters to the edge. What most engages the eye, is the plateau underfoot. It is paved with a vast expanse of bare limestone blocks.

THE LIMESTONE PAVEMENT

The gleaming limestone pavement is not unique to Malham, though it is one of the most remarkable in the country. Rainwater, acidified by carbon dioxide from the atmosphere, has entered the innumerable vertical joints in the rocks. Its acidic content has dissolved their edges, deepening and widening fissures (if the process continues further, cave systems and potholes will be created).

The limestone pavement extends between the top of the cove and Malham Tarn. Covering 150 acres, this peat-edged water is the second largest lake in Yorkshire, and, situated at 1,229 ft above sea level, the highest lake in the Pennines. It has been famed for centuries for its trout, and is much studied today for its wildlife. The lake bed holds water because the North Craven Fault here thrust up an outcrop of Silurian slate – an impervious rock. A small stream,

BURBLING BECK *Gordale Beck burbles its way past winding wooded banks at Janet's Foss. At Gordale Scar – the Lewthwaite Crag of Charles Kingsley's enchanting novel,* The Water Babies *– the beck presents a different mood, streaming over the rock face in two wild leaps. Kingsley was a guest at nearby Malham Tarn House, which became Hartover Place in the famous story.*

TRANQUILLY WILD *The limpid tranquillity of peat-edged Malham Tarn is a 150 acre paradise for students of wildlife, and its plump trout have been famed for centuries. Formed by glaciers, its high waters are held safely by a bed of slate – an alien outcrop of impervious rock in a region of porous limestone.*

FLOWERING IN CLIFF AND CREVICE

Malhamdale, like Cheddar Gorge, nurtures many lime-loving plants. The botanist John Ray (1627–1705) identified the rare and exquisite blue flower of Jacob's ladder, *Polemonium caeruleum*, growing in a wood 'on the left hand of the water as you enter the Cove from Malham'. It still thrives there summer-long in the deep screes. Among the delights of the hill slopes is mountain pansy, sometimes bearing four pale yellow flowers on a single stem.

Mountain pansy
Viola lutea

however, flows south of Malham Tarn, disappearing into swallow holes in the limestone to reappear at Aire Head Springs – the source of the Aire.

Charles Kingsley, the Victorian novelist, stayed as a guest of the Morrison family at Malham Tarn House (now a field studies centre) near by. And like Wordsworth and Ruskin, who also visited the area, he was deeply impressed by the landforms.

WHERE YOUNG LIONS CROUCH

Kingsley called the cove an 'awful cliff filling up the valley with a sheer rock wall', and found inspiration at the site for his most famous novel. He was asked, as a man of knowledge, what might have caused certain dark markings to streak the face of the cove. In fact, they result from moss growth in moist patches, but Kingsley improvised with a joke. He suggested that perhaps a chimney sweep had fallen over the edge. The quip must have lingered in the writer's mind, for out of it *The Water Babies* was born. Tom, the chimney sweep, meets the babes in the waters of the Upper Aire; Malham Tarn House becomes 'Hartover Place' in the story; and the great Gordale Scar appears as 'Lewthwaite Crag'.

The 'Lewthwaite Crag' of Kingsley's novel lies to the east of the cove, about 1¾ miles from Malham village. It was formed during the same fault period as its neighbour, but in character is entirely different.

You reach Gordale Scar by damp pasturelands and a narrowing valley which earned the wonder its name. *Gore* is an ancient term meaning 'an angular plot of land', while 'dale' probably derives from the Scandinavian *dalr* (little valley).

Gordale Scar comes into view quite suddenly – a mighty gorge overhung by 400 ft cliffs, where the rushing Gordale Beck streams over the rock face in two wild leaps. Its perspectives are extraordinary, of giant rock masses which cast black shadows across to the facing cliffs. The 20th-century artist John Piper is among many who have tried to capture the mood of Gordale Scar in paint. And, like the cove, it has had its fair share of literary admirers. The poet Thomas Gray wrote: 'I stayed there not without shuddering a quarter of an hour, and thought my trouble richly repaid for the impression which will last with life.' William Wordsworth was moved to write of a:

'chasm, terrific as the lair where the young lions crouch'

As at the cove, the original cliffs were created by vertical faulting, and here, too, waters chiselled back their edge. But at Gordale the river went underground to tunnel out a colossal cave. The cave itself eventually collapsed, leaving a roofless abyss.

While the cove is dry, the river continues to run at Gordale because surface clays, brought down in the Ice Age, have plugged many fissures in the rock bed. But water still plays its tricks with the limestone, as you discover if you climb to the summit.

The lower falls at Gordale Scar are easily attained, but it takes some rough rock scrambling to reach the top. Here you arrive at a strange upper valley sculpted by the winding beck. If you walk up the valley you notice something very bizarre; the volume of water *increases* the further upstream you go. This is because the descending waters are being soaked up all the time by joints in the limestone – they only rejoin the beck at springs below the scar itself.

MAM TOR

Derbyshire

The name means 'Mother Hill' and perhaps the sturdy Celts who applied the label saw in Mam Tor the comfort and safety of a maternal bosom. Certainly they built on its high summit the largest hill-fort in Derbyshire. And when seen from the north-west there is a generous amplitude about Mam Tor well fitting its ancient title.

From the south-east, however, the hill presents a different aspect. The whaleback curve of its ridge gives way to a 300 ft precipice, one shattered mass of sandstone and shale which glimmers as if in perpetual motion. Contemplating the strange mirage of a cliff you can well see how the hill earned its colloquial name of Shivering Mountain.

LANDSCAPES OF LIGHT AND DARKNESS

The Peak District of Derbyshire provides the green playground of central England. Hemmed in on all sides by the industrial cities of the North and the Midlands, the area was the first in Britain to be protected as a National Park. And the intervention was timely, for today its 542 sq. miles have managed to survive as an area of remarkably unspoiled natural beauty.

Geologically, the Peak District National Park divides into two distinct regions. To the south is the so-called White Peak, a pale limestone upland dipped with wooded valleys which include the little miracle of Dovedale, scarcely changed in the 300 years since Izaac Walton learned fly-fishing there. To the north is the sterner Dark Peak, where a swathe of sombre gritstone has created shaggy moorland terrain, capped by the wild plateau of Kinder Scout (2,088 ft).

Mam Tor itself lies between the landscapes of light and darkness. Rising to 1,696 ft, its summit crowns a magnificent upland ridge which walls off two renowned Derbyshire valleys. Rural Edale lies to the north, a delightful valley from which the 250 mile Pennine Way begins by rising to the dark wilderness of Kinder. South of Mam Tor is Hope Valley, whose limestone caves and potholes offer some of the most exciting underworld scenes in Britain.

Mam Tor's ridge is one layered mass of dark grey sandstone and shales, laid down in alternating strata some 300 million years ago, at a time when the region lay under the sea. Examine the precipitous south-eastern face of Mam Tor and the parallel beds can be seen very clearly. This should only be done from a safe distance, however, for Mam Tor's 'shivering' is not just an optical illusion. The rock is highly unstable and prone to the landslides which formed the original scar.

Winter frosts disintegrate the fabric of the hill, and at any time of year rainwater, seeping through joints in the sandstone, may erode the softer shale below. Often masses of rock crumble and fall, slithering in miniature avalanches down the hillface to scatter their debris across the Castleton road below.

Situated at the head of Hope Valley, the village of Castleton offers the best long views of Mam Tor's shivering face. The village owes its name to the formidable ruins of Peveril Castle, which brood on a mound above the rooftops. The castle was built by Sir William Peveril, the illegitimate son of William the Conqueror, and was immortalised in Sir Walter Scott's novel *Peveril of the Peak*.

But Castleton is equally famed for the labyrinth of caves which pit the limestone hills around. Only a stone's throw from the castle, for example, is the awesome Peak Cavern, a pothole whose mouth yawns wider than any other in Britain; it is 60 ft high and twice as broad. A mile of passageways connects its stupendous subterranean chambers, and a community of ropemakers used to live in the cavern in cottages overhung by stalactites. The settlement flourished from the 16th century well into this century, and though the dwellings have gone now, the soot from their chimneys still stains the roof.

A CLUTCH OF WONDERS

From Castleton, a superb circular walk of some 4½ miles takes you up to the summit of Mam Tor by way of a whole clutch of wonders. Near the outset, the walk passes the famous Speedwell Cavern, where a 500 yd underground canal tunnelled by 18th-century lead-miners opens into a chamber known as the Bottomless Pit. The route then leads up through the Winnats Pass, an amazing pinnacled ravine which is one of the Peak's great natural show places.

Above Winnats Pass, somewhat to the left, is Windy Knoll Cave where in 1875 thousands of bones of

BATTLEFIELD *Lose Hill, left, looks across the valley of the River Noe, beyond which the tip of Win Hill peers above the rim of Hope Brink. The hills were named after a battle that took place more than 1,200 years ago between opposing Saxon armies.*

STRONGHOLD *Clearly visible from a mile off are the great ditch and rampart which encircle the summit of Mam Tor (far left). Standing 30 ft high in places and enclosing an area of 16 acres, the massive earthwork was thrown up by Iron Age Celts nearly 2,000 years ago. It remains largely intact except at the point where the shivering cliff cuts into the perimeter.*

SHIVERING MOUNTAIN *The constantly crumbling south-east face of Mam Tor has given the hill its local name of Shivering Mountain. Here, the alternating layers of shale and sandstone which slip against one another and cause the crumbling are exposed to view.*

prehistoric animals were discovered. It seems that they were washed into the cave by a watercourse long since vanished. The remains included bison and reindeer, grizzly bear and sabre-toothed tiger – all creatures which once stalked the Derbyshire hills.

The walk is so rich in interest that brisk climbing does it scant justice; visitors with time to spare will want to give each wonder the attention it deserves. But for those in a hurry, the summit of Mam Tor can be quickly reached by the main road from Castleton. About 2 miles from the village a side road leads to Edale, and from it a footpath climbs to the hilltop. You may feel the raw wind as soon as you leave the car, presaging that exhilaration known to all upland walkers. But the gradient is easy, and you quickly reach the ramparts which girdle the summit of the Shivering Mountain.

The panorama which unfolds at the summit of Mam Tor is extraordinary; a great airy compass which unites the two landscapes of the Peak. South and south-east lies the limestone country of Hope Valley, where quarries bare the pale rock to the eye. Look north across the green, quilted trough of Edale and the eye meets dark country in the swarthy heights of Kinder, its shapeless moorland brow ever frowning against the horizon.

Mam Tor itself was evidently known to the Bronze Age tribes of the Pennines, for two burial mounds dating from their era lie within the circuit of the later Iron Age ramparts. It is hard to imagine what drove the earthwork builders to fortify such a high and remote position. Hill-forts of any size are rare in this part of the Pennines, and at Mam Tor the ramparts stand some 30 ft high in places, enclosing 16 acres.

It is clear that the Iron Age defenders had a primitive understanding of the hill's geological structure. They heaped up their earthen walls on layers of hard sandstone, digging into the softer shale to make their ditches. It is not known whether the shivering abyss of the south-eastern cliff was incorporated in the ring of defences. The circuit is broken by the hideous drop, and some at least of the ramparts have clearly been lost to erosion.

Recent research into the hill-fort suggests that the earthworks were raised in about AD 50–70. A coarse type of pottery excavated at the site indicates that the people were probably Brigantes, the dominant tribe of the Pennines in the 1st century AD. In all, the most plausible explanation for the fort's existence is that it was set up in some haste by the Brigantes as a stronghold when the Romans advanced into northern England.

Was it taken by force? One thing is clear: when the Romans came, they came to stay. Down in Hope Valley, barely 2 miles from the tor, they built their own fort of Navio at the confluence of the river Noe and the Peakshole Water. And soon they were mining the slopes under Mam Tor for a rare mineral known as Blue John – found nowhere else in the world. A banded rock of many colours, it was sculpted to make vases and other ornaments which found their way from the remote land of the Brigantes to grace homes in Pompeii and elsewhere.

Mam Tor's ridge is about 4 miles long. Look west from the windblown summit and the eye travels down the long mass of Rushup Edge; look east and a splendid walk along the humped spine of the upland beckons. This is in fact the finest ridge walk in the Peak District, dramatic, but never hazardous.

A tumbledown stone wall runs the whole length of the ridge, and its sinuous course along the crest dips and rises to new viewpoints overlooking the valleys on either side. At the col of Hollins Cross (1,349 ft), for example, you have intimate views of the village of Edale on one hand and the gaunt nobility of Peveril Castle on the other. Ahead are the crumbling cliffs of Back Tor (1,332 ft), capped by woods and adding a dimension of savagery to the views. From Back Tor the walk climbs to shapely Lose Hill (1,562 ft), crowning the eastern end of the ridge.

SISTER PEAKS

Lose Hill commands sweeping views down into the valley of the Noe, and across to the cone of Win Hill (1,516 ft). Win and Lose hills are sister peaks which earned their names from a battle fought in AD 626. Edwin, King of Northumbria, camped on Win Hill, and his adversaries on the facing peak. The king won the day and gave his high point its name, while the other hill was labelled after the losers.

Looking back from Lose Hill you can see the path winding like a ribbon along the massive barrier of the ridge. It is a tremendous prospect, showing the whole upland in relief as it curves back to the great bulks which flank the horizon – Rushup Edge and mighty Mam Tor itself.

PATH TO THE TOP *The windswept crest of Rushup Edge forms a 2 mile long causeway, 1,600 ft high, leading to the summit of Mam Tor. Walkers can follow the ridge, while car drivers can follow a parallel road about 300 ft below the crest.*

WHITE HORSE HILL

Oxfordshire

THE OLDEST ROAD *The vast rectangular ramparts of Uffington Castle (facing page) command the Ridge Way as they have done for centuries. But long as the castle has stood there, it is modern when compared with the Ridge Way, which men have walked for 10,000 years or more. This is the oldest road in Britain, if not the whole of Europe, and is still in use today.*

THE HORSE *The oldest, largest and most dramatic of Britain's white horses strides across the hill which bears his name. Viewed, like this from the air, he can be seen in full perspective. From any other viewpoint he is always foreshortened, and in close-up the bold chalk strokes that delineate him are a jumble – and a source of wonder at the skill of the artists who created him.*

The ancient White Horse rides like the wind above his downland scarp. The whole fluid sweep of his body, from head to tail, is expressed in two bold curves. Two of the legs are detached in stylised fashion, while the head is curiously birdlike, suggesting a creature of mythology. This is a primitive tribal image; and yet there is immense artistry in its graceful execution. Measuring 374 ft in length, the White Horse of Uffington is not only the emblem of the Berkshire Downs – he is woven into the folklore of a nation.

Who placed him there, and for what purpose? Scattered around the chalk uplands of southern England are a number of animals, crosses and giants scoured from the turf. Very few date back earlier than the 18th century. Among the host of white horses, Uffington's is unquestionably the oldest. Streaking above the vale which bears his name, he is the grandsire of them all – the ancestral stud.

For centuries the galloping steed has haunted people's imagination. He is first mentioned in the 12th century; in the 14th century he is named as one of the Wonders of Britain, second only to Stonehenge. By popular tradition, the great White Horse was the emblem of King Alfred who was born at Wantage, 6 miles to the west. Allegedly, the hillside was branded with his insignia to commemorate the king's victory over the Danes at the Battle of Ashdown (871).

Others have associated the creature with Hengist, an earlier Saxon leader who also bore a white horse on his banner. But, somehow, the White Horse seems a feature of the hillside from time immemorial. The writer G. K. Chesterton evoked this impression in his *Ballad of the White Horse*:

> *Before the gods that made the gods*
> *Had seen their sunrise pass,*
> *The White Horse of the White Horse Vale*
> *Was cut out of the grass.*

Whatever the creature's origins, his enchantment is undisputed. A great enigma, a weaver of dreams, the White Horse strides out of England's past caparisoned in mystery.

Modern archaeologists tend, like Chesterton, to identify the White Horse with a period much earlier than King Alfred's, and the hill itself offers some clues to the emblem's origins.

Rising to 856 ft, White Horse Hill is a magnificent downland viewpoint. Its summit is crowned by a roughly rectangular earthwork fort known as Uffington Castle, a hilltop arena measuring some 250 yds long by 200 yds wide with a single entrance to the north-west. It was probably built by Iron Age Celts in about 350 BC. They may have been members of the Dobunni tribe, for one of their silver coins has been found at the site.

The wind-blown ramparts offer sweeping panoramas over five counties. Today the scene below is one of rich farmland patchworked with green fields, copses and hedgerows. But in ancient times the clay valleys were thick with inhospitable forest and marsh. Travellers followed the Ridge Way, an upland track on which the stronghold is situated.

It is now thought that the White Horse was the emblem of the tribe who built Uffington, a cult figure set up to bond the local people through their shared mythology and blood relationships. A Celtic goddess, Epona, was known as the protectress of horses, and it is possible that the Uffington emblem was dedicated to her.

Horses played a vital role in Celtic life. Sturdy ponies drew their two-wheeled war chariots and carried their reckless cavalrymen into battle, while immense craftsmanship was lavished on riding accoutrements. Stylised horses, resembling the chalk-cut Uffington figure, are depicted on certain Celtic coins, buckets and other items. Though the White Horse cannot be dated with any certainty, the 1st century BC is generally thought to be his period of origin.

THE MISSING VIEWPOINT

For present-day pilgrims, White Horse Hill's fascination often begins with a sense of perplexity – even of irritation. Where is the emblem supposed to be viewed from?

The church of Uffington offers one classic viewpoint, but the angle is oblique. The village of Woolstone is closer, lying right under the hill; but the height of the horse foreshortens the view. Approach-

NIGHT RUNNER *Mystery and power radiate from the White Horse as the rising moon strikes light from his galloping form. Motionless for more than 2,000 years, yet he seems to move through the darkness where everything else bar the moon is still.*

ing the emblem, the mystery deepens. From the flanks of the hill itself, the creature can only be seen at a drastic slant. In close-up the whole picture disintegrates in a maze of white tracks and tussocks.

The best frontal views of the horse on his hill are obtained from some 4 miles back, on a minor road which leads from Uffington to Compton Beauchamp. (Railway passengers on the Reading–Swindon line cross this road and are granted the same splendid vision.) But although the galloping steed is marvellously delineated at this distance, he remains tilted skywards. The full picture – as it appears on postcards – has only been achieved by aerial photography.

DRAGON HILL

How did the ancient designer plan his creation? Flying was not a Celtic accomplishment, so the question remains deeply puzzling. However, a curious flat-topped knoll on the hill's lower slopes provides some clues.

Known as Dragon Hill, this weird truncated hummock is a miniature wonder in its own right. Legend asserts that St George, patron saint of England, slew the famous dragon on the green table-top. There is a bare patch where the grass never grows; by tradition,

the monster's blood poisoned the soil. Enthusiasts for the legend see the revered White Horse as in fact representing the dragon.

Dragon Hill looks like an artificial podium sculptured into the landscape. In fact, it seems not to have been man-made, but soil tests have indicated an unusually high level of potash. Perhaps beacon fires once flared upon it, or Druidic sacrifices were offered there. It is also possible that the podium was used as a vantage point from which to direct the cutting of the horse.

The view of the White Horse is foreshortened from the top of Dragon Hill. But if a wooden platform or tower were erected upon it, it might offer the missing vantage point. It is conceivable that such a structure was built up for the ceremonial cutting, and subsequently destroyed. The horse would then remain a noble landmark for the eyes of men; but the one immaculate vision would be reserved for the heavens.

Pure speculation – but the site invites the imagination to roam. Scramble down the tufted slopes of Dragon Hill and you find yourself in a deep downland combe, or hollow, at the very foot of the horse. The flanks of the natural amphitheatre are curiously ribbed and terraced, and the air is still after the gusty hillside. The place is known, appropriately enough, as the Horse's Manger.

Standing here, the ceremonial altar of Dragon Hill looms to your left, and the great steed streaks in white slashes across the ridge above. The Horse's Manger must surely have been a place of assembly for the tribe, a hallowed downland womb where members gathered to observe the now forgotten rites enacted on the hill.

THE FESTIVE SCOURINGS

An aura of reverence seems to have lingered about the hill from the time when the horse was first cut. One impressive tribute to the place's sanctity survives in the memory of the great scourings.

For generation after generation, local people kept their landmark radiant and intact in a ceremony of cleansing. It was the custom to go up on the hill at periodic intervals and collectively scrape away any encroaching turf. The practice is first mentioned in the 16th century, and in 1677 a writer described it as a formal trust: 'Some that dwell hereabouts have an obligation upon their hands to repair and cleanse this Land marke, or else in time it may turne green like the rest of the hill and be forgotten.'

Forgotten it never was. Incredibly, the scourings seem to have persisted from the time of Boudicca and Caractacus until the early 20th century. How else could the image have survived the green trespass of the turf?

By the 18th century, the scourings had become a rustic celebration which took place in an atmosphere of carnival gaiety. Thomas Hughes, Victorian author of *Tom Brown's Schooldays*, was born in Uffington and commemorated the ancient custom in *The Scouring of the White Horse* (1858). Although written in the form of a novel, the book set much fascinating factual material before the public.

It seems that booths and stalls were set up in the high arena of Uffington Castle, and it was here that many of the revels took place. Events for the scouring of 1776, for example, included horse races and sack races ('every man to bring his own sack', according to a handbill). In one contest, asses ran for a 'flitch of Bacon'. In another, participants had to remove a bullet from a tub of flour by mouth; the winner would receive 'a Waistcoat, 10s. 6d. value'. Ladies ran for smocks, while lusty youths wrestled and battled with cudgels for buckskin breeches and silver buckles. There were races for cheeses which were rolled down the steep slopes of the Horse's Manger.

Gipsies, pickpockets, hustlers and mountebanks thronged to the revels. No doubt much ale was consumed, and lads and lasses frolicked profanely on the sacred hill. And yet, like so many ancient rural festivities, the scourings had a solemn, underlying purpose. The great emblem of the vale had to be maintained according to ancestral tradition. A nameless generation had inaugurated the rite; and for 2,000 years their descendants kept the trust.

DRAGON HILL *Since modern scholarship throws doubt not only on the existence of dragons, but of St George himself, it seems unlikely that he slew his dragon on this hill. However, it may once have carried a scaffold from which some prehistoric genius masterminded the cutting of the White Horse – a wonder as awesome as any dragon.*

GAZETTEER

An A–Z guide to more than 200 of the most beautiful and
awe-inspiring features of the British landscape.

ABERFELDY BRIDGE *Tayside*

The River Tay, conceived in the waters of Loch Tay, collects water from eight tributaries on its 120 mile journey to Dundee on the Firth of Tay. The river is famous for its salmon, castles and craggy hills. Beauty spots abound and one of the most delightful is Aberfeldy, where in 1733 General Wade built the handsome bridge as part of his military road programme. It is still in use today, not least by visitors admiring the view of the river.
LOCATION *The bridge carries the B846 over the Tay to Weem.*

AILSA CRAIG *Strathclyde*

Now a bird-watcher's paradise, Ailsa Craig, plugging the mouth of the Firth of Clyde, is the remnant of an extinct volcano. This produced bluish-grey granite of a unique structure and boulders from it have been used to trace the movements of glaciers during the ice ages. Pieces of rock from the Craig have been found as far south as the Lake District. A modern-day use for bluish-grey granite has been in the production of curling stones. The cone-shaped island rises to 1,100 ft, with a fringe of sheer cliffs 500 ft high. Around these cliffs gannets breed in thousands, and razorbills, guillemots and puffins line even the narrowest of ledges.
LOCATION *Ten miles off the Strathclyde coast. Regular boats run from Girvan during the season.*

ALDERLEY EDGE *Cheshire*

The magic cave of the 'Wizard of the Edge', glorious woodlands and the Bronze Age lead mines of Alderley Edge are only 20 miles from Manchester. At the highest point of the Edge – a sandstone escarpment – is a stone mound marking the site of a beacon, one of hundreds which formed Britain's early warning system in time of war before radar was invented. To the south is the saucer-like disc of the radio telescope at Jodrell Bank.
LOCATION *On the B5087 south of the town of Alderley Edge.*

ALLEN GORGE *Northumberland*

For 5 miles the River Allen rumbles and rushes through a wooded gorge which at times is 250 ft deep. A path runs for 2 miles beside the river.
LOCATION *On the A686 Alston to Hexham road, 12 miles W of Hexham.*

ALMOND AQUEDUCT *Lothian*

Scotland can boast three remarkable aqueducts on the Union Canal between Edinburgh and Falkirk which was opened in 1822. These cross the River Almond, River Avon and the Water of Leith. Almond Aqueduct is 76 ft high and 420 ft long and has five stone arches supporting a sunken iron trough which carries the water. It is set in a beautiful and secluded river valley.
LOCATION *Off the A706, 2 miles SW of Linlithgow.*

ARBOR LOW *Derbyshire*

Stand among the recumbent stones of Bronze Age Arbor Low on a misty morning and in the mind's eye erect the 47 massive limestone slabs, each weighing more than 8 tons. Watch the mist lift and the pink light of dawn reflect from the stone and you have a genuine rival to Stonehenge. A rock-cut ditch and an outer bank surrounds the circle of stones which had two opposed entrances in its 200 yd circumference. On the edge of the bank is a later Bronze Age barrow and a linear earthwork which was probably a territorial boundary. Gib Hill, less than a quarter of a mile west, is an early Bronze Age barrow built over even earlier graves.
LOCATION *Beside a minor road off the A515, 9 miles S of Buxton.*

ARBROATH CLIFFS *Tayside*

A nature trail, the Arbroath cliff walk, leads up from the main promenade in the town. It follows a line of old red-sandstone cliffs carved into arches, blowholes and stacks. House martins and white-rumped rock doves breed in their natural habitat, and the rusty cliffs form the perfect backdrop for tufts of pale yarrow, blue harebells and yellow trefoil.
LOCATION *The A933 from Brechin and the A92 from Montrose converge in the centre of Arbroath, where the cliffs are clearly signposted.*

ASHDOWN FOREST *East Sussex*

King's Standing was once a place in the forest where the king stood to watch deer being hunted. Many trees have gone, but the 14,000 acres between Forest Row in the north and Maresfield in the south are still wooded, although interspersed with patches of heathland.
LOCATION *King's Standing is 4 miles S of Hartfield on the B2188.*

LOCH ASSYNT *Highland*

The scenery at Loch Assynt differs from much of the surrounding area because extensive limestone outcropping has brought lusher shades of green and a greater variety of plant life. This is best seen around Inchnadamph where bladder fern, mountain avens, stone bramble, the rare grass *Agropyron donianum*, a sedge, *Carex rupestris*, and the splendid dark red helleborine bloom in some profusion.
LOCATION *The A837 runs along the north shore of Loch Assynt.*

AVEBURY *Wiltshire*

Avebury, dating from about 1800 BC, is among the most important early Bronze Age monuments in Europe. The stones are smaller than those of Stonehenge, 18 miles to the south, but the Avebury complex is larger. It has been sadly depleted and only 30 of the original 100 stones remain. The circle is 360 yds in diameter, and within it are smaller circles, not to mention the old village of Avebury. A huge earth bank punctuated by four entrances surrounds the circle.
LOCATION *Avebury is on the A361, 12 miles S of Swindon.*

LOCH AWE *Strathclyde*

The 3,695 ft hulk of rock called Ben Cruachan glowers down at the northern end of Loch Awe over the Falls of Cruachan and the Pass of Brander. Loch Awe is 22 miles long, but seldom exceeds 1 mile across. Several fortified castles show how important it was to the Clan Campbell who used Loch Awe as a defensive moat.

Forestry Commission trails through Inver-liever Forest on the western shore are good places to see buzzards, hen harriers and a host of other birds.

LOCATION *From Lochgilphead follow the A816 Oban road as far as the B840. This follows the eastern shore of the loch. A minor road follows the western shore. From Oban the A85 reaches Loch Awe via the Pass of Brander.*

AXE EDGE *Derbyshire*

The high limestone, grit and shale ridges of central Derbyshire are sliced by the three magnificent valleys of the Wye, Derwent and Dove. The most famous, the Dove, runs through the rich scenery of the Peak National Park and forms the barrier with Staffordshire. The River Dove rises, with the smaller River Manifold, in the moorlands below Axe Edge, the highest point between Leek and Buxton. Near by is Flash, at 1,518 ft the highest village in England. It was from here that counterfeit coiners operated, and the word 'flash' has been used for such money ever since.

LOCATION *Off the A53, 3 miles SW of Buxton.*

AYSGARTH FALLS *North Yorkshire*

Aysgarth Falls are set in beautiful woodlands in Wensleydale. The River Ure is spanned by a single-arched bridge from which the first of three great falls can be viewed. The second fall follows quickly after the first, and the third is reached by a woodland footpath of about 1 mile. Beyond the falls, the river meanders through the grounds of Bolton Hall, under the bridge at Wensley and on to Masham.

LOCATION *On a minor road off the A684, 1 mile E of Aysgarth.*

BADBURY RINGS *Dorset*

Three huge ramparts rising one above the other to a plateau are the remains of one of the most important Iron Age forts in Britain. The Romans eventually overran Badbury, but realising its strategic importance they strengthened it and ran four roads into the complex. One of these, Ackling Dyke, is still visible at the north-west corner and a very substantial road it was, 13 yds wide and elevated to a height of 4 to 6 ft. From the top rampart the views extend over Dorset into Hampshire and Wiltshire beyond.

LOCATION *Off the B3082, 3 miles NW of Wimborne Minster.*

BALA *Gwynedd*

Llyn Tegid (in English, Lake Bala) is the largest lake in Wales. It is 4 miles long, almost a mile wide and shelves suddenly to a depth of 150 ft. In its depths lurks the gwyniad, a fish of the salmon family which lives more than 80 ft down and is caught only by net. There is a small promenade and a narrow-gauge railway runs lakeside trips with views across the water to the wild hill country beyond.

LOCATION *Bala village at the head of the lake is at the junction of the A494 and the A4212.*

BASS ROCK *Lothian*

A long chain of reefs and islands punctuates the often stormy seas off North Berwick. The largest of these is the Bass Rock, a plug of volcanic basalt rising to a height of 420 ft with a comparatively flat and grassy top. Up to 20,000 pairs of gannets – Britain's largest sea-bird – breed there. Visitors crossing from North Berwick are treated to exciting diving displays by the gannets, whose scientific name *Sula bassana* is derived from the island. Overlooking the landing stage on the south side are a ruined castle and the modern lighthouse, now the only inhabited building on the island. A path leads up to the gannets, passing the ruined chapel of St Baldred. The views across to Tantallon Castle on the mainland and the Isle of May out to sea are breathtaking, and the roar of the sea driving into the caves at the foot of the cliffs is a never to be forgotten sound.

LOCATION *Reached by boat from North Berwick during the season. Crossing takes 25 minutes.*

BEACON FELL *Lancashire*

Standing 873 ft above the Forest of Bowland, Beacon Fell offers attractive all round views to Lakeland, the Dales and, on a crisp clear day, to the mountains of Snowdonia in Wales. It was once a link in the chain of signal fires which were used to proclaim victories or to warn of impending danger in the days before electric signalling – though with an annual rainfall of more than 60 in., getting the fire going could have been a problem.

LOCATION *On a minor road which leaves the A6 at Bilsborrow, 7 miles N of Preston. A one-way ring road winds clockwise around the hill and offers wonderfully varied views.*

BEALACH NA BÀ *Highland*

Translated from the Gaelic, Bealach na Bà means 'Pass of the Cattle'. It is the nearest thing to an alpine pass in Britain and is often sealed by snow. It reaches a height of 2,054 ft, has gradients of 1 in 4 and some frightening hairpin bends. In past winters the people of Applecross could get provisions only by boat, but now an easier coastal road runs from Shieldaig. But it is still worth travelling the old road and stopping to view the magnificent scenery. On a clear day the Cuillins on Skye, 30 miles west, stand out like a saw-edge.

LOCATION *The pass is signposted, 'Applecross Scenic Route', along a minor road off the A896, 2 miles N of Kishorn.*

BEN NEVIS *Highland*

See page 36. (Map, page 174.)

THE BLACK MOUNTAIN *Dyfed*

See page 40.

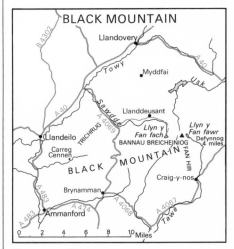

BOLTON PRIORY *North Yorkshire*

The priory ruins are set in green rolling fields bounded by woodland on a site overlooking the River Wharfe. It was built in the 12th century by Augustinian monks, and the nave is still a functional part of the parish church. A visitors' centre leads to extensive riverside walks illuminated by flowers and serenaded by bird song. All paths lead to The Strid (Old English for 'turmoil'), a fissure in the Wharfe's channel where the river narrows to about 6 ft. Rain certainly brings turmoil, when the peat-brown waters crash over the limestone ledges of the river bed.

LOCATION *Beside the B6160 close to its junction with the A59, 7 miles E of Skipton.*

BOSCASTLE *Cornwall*

The village of Boscastle is perched on a cliff-top 400 ft above its harbour, which was rebuilt in 1584 at the expense of Sir Richard Grenville. Access can never have been easy, but despite this the harbour thrived during the 18th and 19th centuries, importing coal and fertiliser and exporting slate, china clay and corn. A short scramble over rocks from the jetty leads to startling views and the sounds of a blowhole, blasted into voice by the insistent sea.

LOCATION *On the B3263, 3 miles NE of Tintagel.*

BOWDER STONE *Cumbria*

East of the road from Seatoller as it sweeps into Borrowdale is a huge boulder balanced precariously on its edge. But it is quite stable – and there is a ladder to climb to the top. The stone is estimated to weigh 2,000 tons. It may have fallen from the slopes above, but it is more likely to have been left by the retreating ice. From the top can be seen the 'jaws of Borrowdale' and Derwent Water.

LOCATION *Beside the B5289, 5 miles S of Keswick.*

BRECON BEACONS
Powys/West Glamorgan

The Beacons are a compact 10 mile long range of sandstone hills and mountains once used as positions for signal fires. The area is rich in spectacular waterfalls and it shares 519 square miles of National Park with the Black Mountains. Pen y Fan (2,906 ft) is the highest peak, but the easiest to climb is the 1,995 ft Sugar Loaf. Just north of Coelbren are the Henrhyd Falls which have a 90 ft drop. One mile from Penderyn are the Scwd yr Eira Falls, on the River Hepste, behind which visitors can walk. The area is rich in wildlife including alpine flowers, red kites and buzzards.

LOCATION *The town of Brecon stands close to the northern boundary of the Brecon Beacons National Park.*

BRENT TOR *Devon*

Brent Tor towers 1,100 ft over the western edge of Dartmoor. Its conical peak is not only a landmark for miles around but also contrasts sharply with the other tors on the moor. These are granite crags exposed by erosion, but Brent Tor is an actual volcanic cone. There is a church on top, built for the monks of Tavistock Abbey and dedicated in 1319. A previous church there was called St Michael on the Rock and it dated from the middle of the 12th century.

LOCATION *Off a minor road 4 miles N of Tavistock.*

BRIDESTONES *North Yorkshire*

It was once thought that the Bridestones were carved by prehistoric man and were used in Neolithic marriage ceremonies. But it is now known that wind, rain and hard frost wrought their dramatic shapes, not the hand of man. The rocks are composed of 150-million-year-old layers of hard and soft sandstone which erode at different rates. The upper set of Bridestones are in a rough horseshoe shape, and the lower set are in a fairly straight line. From the upper stones a path leads to Bridestones Griff (a ravine cut by a stream) sheltering rowan trees, their berries adding a dash of scarlet in autumn.

LOCATION *Off the Dalby Forest Drive, a toll road reached by a minor road running N from Thornton Dale on the A170 Scarborough to Pickering road.*

BRIMHAM ROCKS *North Yorkshire*

See page 102. (Map, page 173.)

BROADWAY BEACON
Hereford and Worcester

See page 132.

LOCH BROOM *Highland*

From Ullapool a passenger ferry crosses Loch Broom to Allt no L'Airbhe and gives splendid views over the sea to the outer loch, with the Summer Isles, looking every bit as attractive as their name, and Stac Polly rising 2,009 ft behind them. Only one island is occupied, but until the herring stocks ran out many had their own fishing communities.

LOCATION *Ullapool is reached on the A835 from Braemore which runs for some distance alongside Loch Broom.*

BROWN WILLY *Cornwall*

Cornwall's highest granite tor is affectionately known as Brown Willy, and he surveys Bodmin Moor from his 1,377 ft summit. The name comes from the Celtic *Bryn Huel*, which means 'the tin mine

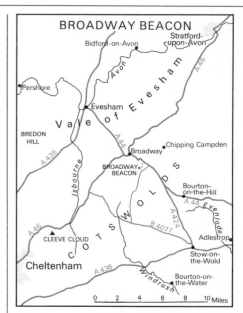

ridge'. There is an Iron Age fort on the summit. On a fine day the views to the coast are as dramatic as any in the land, but with an annual rainfall of 80 in., days of mist when the views are obscured are more common.

LOCATION *About 2 miles NW of Jamaica Inn on the A30.*

BUCKLAND BEACON *Devon*

The climb up to Buckland Beacon on Dartmoor is often a blaze of colour as gorse shines out from the heather where stonechats perch to chatter. The top is rocky and exposed, as are most of the tors, and was a perfect place to light a signal fire. The views to the South Devon coast are inspiring, presumably explaining why a former lord of the manor had the Ten Commandments carved on the rocks at the summit.

LOCATION *Off the A38, 3 miles NW of Ashburton.*

BULLERS OF BUCHAN *Grampian*

The 200 ft deep cauldron known as the Bullers of Buchan is in fact the chamber of a sea cave of which the roof has collapsed. A surviving part of the roof forms a dramatic arch under which the sea roars into the cauldron. The sea, especially when driven by high winds, belches forth to justify the name the 'Boilers of Buchan', made famous by the writings of many authors, including Boswell, Dr Johnson and Sir Walter Scott.

LOCATION *Signposted off the A975, 6 miles S of Peterhead.*

BUTSER HILL *Hampshire*

Butser Hill is the highest point of the South Downs. It peers down into a ravine studded with yew trees. Many ancient tracks led there, and some are still used. One leads to Ramsdean Down where outlines of Celtic fields can be seen near three Bronze Age round barrows. To the east are views over the Weald, while to the south, Portsmouth, the Solent and the Isle of Wight can be seen.

LOCATION *Off the A3, 3 miles S of Petersfield.*

BUTTERTUBS PASS *North Yorkshire*

Buttertubs Pass links Muker in Swaledale with Hawes in Wensleydale, carving its way between Great Shunner Fell (2,340 ft) and Lovely Seat (2,213 ft). The pass reaches a height of 1,726 ft close to the Buttertubs, remarkable shafts up to 100 ft deep eroded from the limestone and named after their resemblance to butter tubs. Cliff Beck, which rises in the tubs, flows down to Muker. There are merlins and peregrines on the surrounding moors, and the Kearton Brothers, pioneers in bird photography who lived in Muker, were never short of subjects.

LOCATION *Hawes is on the A684. Muker is on the B6270. Buttertubs Pass links the two.*

CADBURY CASTLE *Somerset*

South Somerset has few high hills, but it does have the sloping mound on which stands the supposed site of King Arthur's Camelot. It is now accepted that at the beginning of the 6th century a powerful British king was waging war against the Anglo-Saxons. He must have had a fortified site, possibly constructed on an old Iron Age camp and providing essential panoramic views. Excavations at Cadbury have shown just such a layered history from Stone Age camp to Bronze Age fort, Iron Age settlement, Roman armoury and burial ground, and the expected 6th-century settlement as well as a Saxon mint of later date.

LOCATION *On a minor road off the A303 east of the junction with the A359, 7 miles NE of Yeovil.*

CADER IDRIS *Gwynedd*

The highest point of Cader Idris is the 2,927 ft Pen y Gadair, and its volcanic rocks stretch for 10 miles across north-west Wales, forming an ancient barrier between Gwynedd and Powys. Cader Idris means 'the seat of Idris', who was possibly a Celtic chieftain active around AD 630. Cader Idris is second only to Snowdon as a tourist attraction and viewpoint in Wales. To the west, on a good day, the Mountains of Wicklow can be seen across the Irish Sea, and to the east the view extends right across Wales to the Shropshire hills.

LOCATION *Cader Idris can be seen at its best from Machynlleth or from the A493 Machynlleth to Dolgellau road. Several paths lead to the summit from Dolgellau.*

CALLANISH *Lewis, Western Isles*

A soggy peat moor overlooking a grey heaving sea and swept by rain driven by a howling Hebridean wind is hardly the place to expect human settlements. Callanish, however, a stone circle dating from the early Bronze Age is substantial enough to rank among Europe's most spectacular henges. At the centre of the circle of greyish-pink gneiss stones is a Neolithic burial cairn, and from this standing stones radiate outwards with a 270 ft long avenue running northwards. The Hebrides appear to have been settled 4,000 years ago and Callanish was at the centre of the settlers' religious life.

LOCATION *Car ferry to Stornoway from Ullapool. Flights from Inverness to Stornoway. Callanish is 16 miles W of Stornoway off the narrow A858.*

CAPE WRATH *Highland*

All but the most determined travellers fail to reach Cape Wrath, the remotest spot on mainland Britain, because they run out of road at Durness. In summer, however, a passenger ferry across the Kyle of Durness connects with a minibus which runs 10 miles over a narrow winding road to the lighthouse on the cape. The 70 ft tall lighthouse stands on a headland 360 ft high, but still, in winter, is washed by salt spray driven by 100 mph winds. At Clo Mór, 3 miles south-east of the lighthouse, are the highest cliffs on the mainland, towering 921 ft above the Atlantic. Inland lies the Parph, a trackless, uninhabited wilderness of peat bog and heather across which the occasional walker treks north from Sandwood Bay to the lighthouse. The reward is breathtaking views of towering cliffs, sandy beaches and rocky coves haunted by seabirds, while over the peat hags there is more than a chance of seeing golden eagles patrolling in search of prey.

LOCATION *The ferry is signposted 4 miles S of Durness on the A838.*

CARN GOCH *Dyfed*

Perched 700 ft above the Vale of Tywi is Carn Goch (the Red Cairn), site of the largest Iron Age fort in Wales. The iron-wise Celts of 200–300 BC built their fort over 2,000 ft long and 500 ft wide, and there are traces of one, perhaps two, smaller structures. The main fort is known as *y Gaer fawr*, 'the big fort', and in the event of attack the whole population plus the livestock would retreat within. It is thought that *y Gaer fach*, 'the little fort', was an outer defence work designed to hold off an enemy until the defence of the larger fort was organised. The view from the top is uplifting, especially on a cool spring day, but the view from Bethlehem Church where a flower-lined footpath starts its climb to the fort is awe inspiring. It must have been terrifying to the troops of an invading army, especially those chosen to lead the attack.

LOCATION *On a minor road off the A4069, 3 miles SW of Llangadog.*

CASTLERIGG *Cumbria*

Evening sunshine highlights this majestic circle of 38 stones of which all but five are still standing. Castlerigg, 706 ft above sea level between Keswick and Thirlmere and flanked by Skiddaw and Helvellyn, probably dates back about 4,000 years to the Beaker People of the late Neolithic or early Bronze Age. This circle has a diameter of 102 ft, and within this a further ten stones are arranged in a rectangle. The purpose of this, and indeed the whole complex, is still the subject of debate. The setting suggests a temple, but the arrangement of the stones indicates the possibility of a solar calendar used to measure the agricultural year.

LOCATION *On a minor road off the A66, 2 miles E of Keswick.*

CATERTHUNS *Tayside*

Surprisingly little is known about the Picts, and they are often represented as prehistoric barbarians, but the strangely beautiful pair of Caterthuns do something to dispel the belief that they were totally uncivilised. The Caterthuns are hill-forts dating from about 200 BC, one being brown the other white. Each stands proudly on its own

1,000 ft peak and faces its partner across a steep but narrow gorge. Five concentric earth-covered ramparts explain the name of the Brown Caterthun; pale stone outer defences are the mark of the white fort.

LOCATION *The Caterthuns overlook the minor road to Bridgend which runs NW off the A94, 1 mile N of Brechin.*

CERNE ABBAS GIANT *Dorset*

A 180 ft tall, masculine figure, brandishing a huge club in his right hand, is inscribed on the chalk hillside above the village of Cerne Abbas. One belief is that he is about 1,700 years old and depicts the Roman god Hercules. A more likely suggestion is that he is some 300 years older and was a Celtic fertility god.

LOCATION *The giant is seen at his best from a lay-by on the A352 just N of Cerne Abbas.*

CHEDDAR GORGE *Somerset*

See page 134.

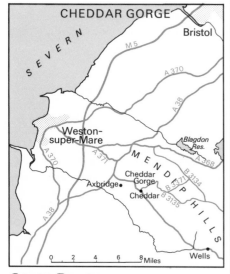

CHESIL BEACH *Dorset*

A great sweeping bank of shingle extends 18 miles from Burton Bradstock in the west to the Isle of Portland in the east. This is Chesil Beach, a natural breakwater formed of pebbles which have been graded by the sea. At the Portland end they average 3½ in. in diameter, decreasing gradually along the length of the beach to under 1 in. at the western end. The still expanding shingle has already impounded a stretch of water called the Fleet. Close by is Abbotsbury, settled by Benedictine monks in 1044. The area is famous today because of the Swannery where 500 pairs of mute swans nest in the shallows.

LOCATION *Best seen by walking from the large car park at Fortuneswell reached via the A354, Weymouth to Portland road.*

THE CHEVIOTS *Northumberland*

A perfect blend of history and natural history, the Cheviot Hills are grass-covered but imposing uplands with heather and bracken towards their summits. The highest point is the Cheviot (2,676 ft), and cutting into it are the two deep ravines of Henhole and Bizzle in which may be found wild goats, ravens and many wild flowers, including dwarf cornel and star saxifrage. The College Burn rises in the Henhole and meets the River Glen at Kirknewton, a settlement associated with the Roman missionary Paulinus. Visible from the Cheviot is Chillingham where since 1220 a herd of fierce wild white cattle has roamed free in 300 acres of parkland.

LOCATION *Wooler, on the A697, 16 miles S of Berwick-upon-Tweed, is a good base from which to explore the Cheviots.*

CHISLEHURST CAVES *Greater London*

Some of the extensive labyrinth of caves and tunnels at Chislehurst are without doubt prehistoric, and it has been suggested they were the site of a Druid's College. Others were possibly dug by the Romans and by the Saxons, but the proof is difficult to establish. What is sure is that the caves, which extend for many miles through the chalk, were efficient air-raid shelters during the Second World War.

LOCATION *The entrance to the caves, which is signposted, is close to Chislehurst station just off the A222, three-quarters of a mile W of the junction with the A208.*

CHOLLERFORD BRIDGE *Northumberland*

Few rivers are so maligned as the 35 mile long Tyne, one of Britain's shortest rivers. Although the industrialised 19 miles of navigable river are heavily polluted, the upper reaches are as clean as they were when Hadrian was building his wall. There are majestic views from the 17th-century Chollerford Bridge which is only half a mile from Chesters, once a vital part of the Roman defence network. Many ruins remain and a museum bulges with artefacts including a bronze tablet, a Roman soldier's equivalent of his discharge papers.

LOCATION *The B6318, which runs parallel to*

Hadrian's Wall, is carried over the Tyne on Chollerford Bridge, 4 miles N of Hexham.*

CHUN CASTLE *Cornwall*

A whitewashed boulder on the crest of a hill marks the site of Chun Castle, an Iron Age fort overlooking the rocky Cornish coast. The fort consists of two concentric stone walls with staggered entrances, all surrounded by a broad ditch. Chun Quoit is close by and is a burial chamber in use from 2500 BC to 500 BC. The views of the coast are spectacular.

LOCATION *Off a minor road, signposted to Penzance, which leaves the B3306 1 mile NE of Morvah. From Trehyllis Farm a steep footpath, which is signposted, leads to the castle.*

CLO MÓR CLIFFS *Highland*

Mainland Britain's highest cliffs, at Clo Mór on Scotland's north coast, are composed of sandstone. They look terrifying when they loom out of the fog, but stunningly beautiful when caressed by the filtered light of a summer sunset.

See Cape Wrath.

CRICCIETH *Gwynedd*

Snowdonia, Cardigan Bay and Harlech Castle can be seen from the headland at Criccieth. The rock, which is black and pitted with grottoes and small caves, is topped by a 13th-century castle. Lloyd George, who was Prime Minister from 1916 to 1922, married a girl from Criccieth and lived near by.

LOCATION *On the A497 from Porthmadog to Pwllheli.*

BEN CRUACHAN *Strathclyde*

In 1965, deep in the bowels of the twin-capped 3,695 ft Ben Cruachan, a huge cavern, the size of Coventry Cathedral, was blasted out of solid rock to house a hydroelectric power station. Water to power the turbines comes from a reservoir, created by a dam 1,300 ft up on the mountain. A minibus takes visitors almost a mile through tunnels to the station deep inside the mountain. From Cruachan's slopes can be seen Loch Awe to the south and the twisting Pass of Brander to the west.

LOCATION *Cruachan Power Station is beside Loch Awe on the A85 between Dalmally and Taynuilt.*

THE CUILLINS *Highland*

See page 46.

DAN YR OGOF CAVES *Powys*

Where is it possible to meet The Nuns, The Elephant Head and The Flitch of Bacon? They are all near to the Trojan Waterfall and are the names of stalactites and stalagmites in the Dan Yr Ogof caves, first investigated in 1912 by two brave Welsh brothers in a coracle. The mile-long cavern is illuminated, revealing the grotesque shapes with such colourful names. *Ogof* is Welsh for 'cave', and there is another cave system to the east called Ogof-Fynnon-Ddu, the longest and deepest cave complex in Wales. This has even more spectacular shapes and an underground lake, but is accessible only to experienced cavers.
LOCATION *Off the A4067, 16 miles NE of Swansea, just beyond Craig-y-nos.*

DERWENT WATER *Cumbria*

A stroll from Keswick leads to Derwent Water and Friar's Crag where the Borrowdale Fells form the perfect backcloth to the water and the green foothills beyond, clothed in hardwood trees. It was on Friar's Crag that pilgrims waited to be ferried to St Herbert's Island. This Celtic saint was friendly with St Cuthbert, and according to legend they died on the same day. There are three other islands on the lake which are all owned by the National Trust, who also care for most of the lake shore. A 2 mile nature trail runs along the shore.
LOCATION *The B5289 from Keswick runs along the eastern shore of Derwent Water to Borrowdale.*

DEVIL'S BRIDGE *Dyfed*

In a 25 mile journey from Plynlimon Hill to the sea at Aberystwyth the River Afon Rheidol falls 1,750 ft and is one of the most impressive rivers in Wales. The River Mynach rises even higher and near Devil's Bridge the two join in a gorge where their hissing torrents pour over falls, the highest of which is 300 ft. The bridge is really three bridges built over one another. The top bridge is 19th century, the middle 18th, but the well-preserved lower structure was probably built in the 12th century.
LOCATION *On the A4120, 12 miles E of Aberystwyth.*

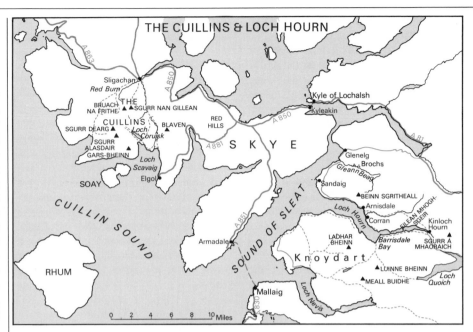

THE CUILLINS & LOCH HOURN

THE DODMAN AND VERYAN BAY *Cornwall*

In 1919 the National Trust purchased Dodman Point, 1 mile from Gorran Haven, and have been adding to the estate ever since. Paths have been cut from Hemmick to previously isolated beaches rich in multi-coloured pebbles. On the summit are traces of an Iron Age fort and a granite cross erected in 1896 as a reference point for fishermen at sea. A 19th-century coastguard tower is a reminder of the days of sail when officers toured the cliffs keeping a weather-eye open for wrecks and smugglers.
LOCATION *Gorran Haven is on a minor road, 3 miles S of Mevagissey. Dodman is 2 miles further S by footpath.*

DOLGOCH *Gwynedd*

At Dolgoch, waterfall-watching is made easy. In 1865 the Talyllyn railroad was built to carry slate from Abergynolwyn to Tywyn, a coastal town in the foothills of the Cader Idris range. The railway runs past the falls and from the halt at Dolgoch its waters can be seen crashing down for 125 ft.
LOCATION *Dolgoch halt is beside the B4405, 4 miles NE of Tywyn.*

DOVE DALE *Derbyshire*

Dove Dale is a lovely limestone valley richly clothed with woodland. It is about 2 miles long, a wonderland of fantastic scenery and rock formations, among them the

Dove Holes, caverns formed by river and rainwater slowly dissolving the rock, and Reynard's Cave, an arch left when a cave roof collapsed. Outcrops of limestone abound and have been christened Jacob's Ladder, the Twelve Apostles, Tissington Spires and Lovers' Leap.
LOCATION *A footpath through the dale runs N off the minor road from Thorpe to Ilam. Thorpe is 4 miles N of Ashbourne on a minor road off the A515.*

DOVER CLIFFS *Kent*

The first written record of the White Cliffs was provided by Julius Caesar, and around AD 43 the Romans were building the Pharos lighthouse. This is the most complete Roman structure in Britain and is contained within the walls of Dover Castle, built mainly in the 12th and 13th centuries, and still the strongest fortification in the land. The views from the castle and elsewhere along the flower-strewn chalk cliffs are truly magnificent.
LOCATION *Dover Castle stands above the town and is well signposted.*

DOZMARY POOL *Cornwall*

Bodmin Moor suggests mist, rain, howling wind, Jamaica Inn and blood-thirsty smugglers. But below the tors are gentler tracts of countryside and the shallow, tranquil lake, Dozmary Pool. This, Tennyson tells us, was where Sir Bedivere threw Excalibur, King Arthur's sword, as the king lay dying. A strange pile of rocks known as the Cheesewring is close by on the western slopes of Stowe's Hill. Below is Sibylbank, a county reservoir.

LOCATION *Dozmary Pool is 2 miles S of Bolventor on a minor road off the A30.*

LOCH DUICH *Highland*

The Kyle of Lochalsh leads into Loch Alsh and beyond it Loch Long and Loch Duich. These three important waters are dominated at Dornie by Eilean Donan Castle, built by Alexander II of Scotland in 1220.

LOCATION *Eilean Donan Castle is beside the A87, 9 miles E of Kyle of Lochalsh.*

DUNCANSBY HEAD *Highland*

Duncansby Head is memorable for the mathematical precision of the layering of the sandstone rock and the 200 ft high sandstone pillars, including the magnificent Muckle Stack. Access to the area is not easy, there being no recognised path, but it is worth the struggle to see Long Geo, an inlet some 100 yds long with 200 ft vertical walls and situated just west of the lighthouse. Birds are everywhere, gliding across a backdrop formed by the Pentland Firth and beyond this the outline of Orkney.

LOCATION *About 2 miles up a minor road which runs E off the A9, just S of John o'Groats.*

DUNGEON GILL *Cumbria*

Dungeon Gill, in the shadow of the Langdale Pikes and Harrison Stickle, has been a major attraction for a century. A great cascade of water plunges over steep rocks for almost 100 ft, 60 ft of it an unbroken torrent, on the way to a fairly tranquil basin. A path from the Dungeon Gill New Inn car park leads to Stickle Gill, a smaller but still impressive waterfall, which must have been a mighty torrent before the stream was dammed to provide power for a mill.

LOCATION *On the B5343, NW of Skelwith Bridge.*

DUNKERY HILL *Somerset*

Dunkery Hill glowers down over the wooded bird-rich valleys of Exmoor to Blue Anchor Bay. It is a haunt of red deer and in autumn the stags stamp, pace and roar to keep their hinds together. Dunkery Hill, 1,705 ft, is the highest point of Exmoor and Somerset.

LOCATION *About 1 mile W of Weddon Cross* on the B3224. A minor road runs off NW to skirt Dunkery Hill.

DUNNET HEAD *Highland*

Dunnet Head is 2 miles closer to the Arctic circle than nearby John o'Groats, which, with its signpost indicating Land's End 876 miles, normally gets the credit for being Britain's northernmost point. The old red-sandstone cliffs have a unique beauty, and birds soar and call from the ledges. It was here in 1905 that fulmars were first recorded as nesting on mainland Britain, and kittiwakes breed below the lighthouse which beams out towards the Pentland Firth and across to Hoy.

LOCATION *On the B855, 12 miles NE of Thurso.*

DUNNOTTAR CASTLE *Grampian*

This substantial and well-preserved fortress was built mainly in the 14th and 15th centuries on a rock towering over the sea, 1 mile south of Stonehaven. It was the last castle in Scotland to surrender to Cromwell, in 1652, after an 8 month siege. The Parliamentarians were desperate to capture the castle, which housed the Scottish crown jewels. Earlier, the cliff was, in turn, the site of an Iron Age fort, an early Christian chapel dedicated to St Ninian, and finally a parish church which was incorporated into the castle.

LOCATION *Off the A92, 2 miles S of Stonehaven.*

EAS COUL AULIN *Highland*

From Loch Beag a stream runs steeply towards a cliff edge at Eas Coul Aulin, then tumbles 658 ft to rocks below. Britain's highest waterfall roars and smokes with spray, and is reached only after a 3 mile hike over rough country. But it is set in savage scenery and so impressive that the effort is fully rewarded.

LOCATION *By footpath off the A894, 10 miles N of Inchnadamph.*

EDGEHILL *Warwickshire*

Few vantage points command views of Shakespeare's native countryside, but a splendid exception is Edgehill, the site in 1642 of the first battle of the Civil War. A tower, built in 1750, makes a good vantage point over the rolling landscape. At the southern boundary is the King's Stone, a Bronze Age monument.

LOCATION *Off the A422, 12 miles SE of Stratford-upon-Avon.*

EGGARDON HILL *Dorset*

Situated among and dominating the rolling chalk plains of Hardy's Wessex, Eggardon Hill affords exhilarating if often breezy views over Dorset and beyond. Milkwort, bird's-foot trefoil, bedstraw, eyebright and gorse provide colour and perfume to lighten the step of the weary traveller. From prehistoric times Dorset's chalk ridgeways have provided dry routes for travellers. What better spot to keep a watch on these routes than from the 827 ft peak of Eggardon, which still has the remains of a substantial Iron Age fort.

LOCATION *Off a minor road leading from the A35, 5 miles NE of Bridport.*

THE EILDONS *Borders*

See page 138.

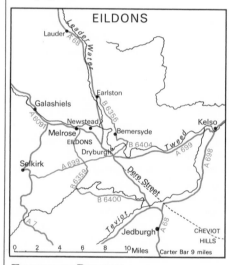

FINCHALE PRIORY *Durham*

Finchale (pronounced 'finkle') Priory is dominated by woods which slope steeply down to the River Wear. It must have been a healthy as well as a secluded beauty spot, because St Godric had his chapel there after a startling life as pedlar, pirate and priest. He left his retreat only three times from 1115 to his death at the age of 105 in 1170. From the 14th century until the Dissolution the priory was used as a rest home by monks from Durham.

LOCATION *Off the A690, 3 miles NE of Durham.*

FINGAL'S CAVE *Strathclyde*

See page 10.

FLAMBOROUGH HEAD *Humberside*

Despite an ever increasing number of trippers, Flamborough Head remains a paradise for birds and is riddled with fascinating caves. There are two light-houses, but only one in use – a huge structure constructed as long ago as 1806. It replaced an old chalk lighthouse of 1674. The name Flamborough derives from the Saxon *flaen*, which means 'arrow-head' and perfectly describes the shape of the promontory. Some 3,000 years ago the headland was fortified, and a rampart called Dane's Dyke still remains. To the west is Bempton Cliffs, a bird reserve, which has the only colony of gannets breeding on mainland Britain. There is an enormous variety of flowers, and observation points along the cliffs make bird-watching safe.
LOCATION *On the B1259, 5 miles NE of Bridlington.*

FLATFORD *Suffolk*

Many rivers are famous for their turbulent upper reaches, others for sweeping estuaries, but the real magnificence of English rivers is in the middle reaches. Mills nestle snugly into the banks, ancient bridges span the streams and more than a dash of colour is added by yellow water-lilies and kingcups, pink marshmallows and blue water forget-me-nots. Such settings are perfect for artists, and Constable has ensured that Flatford on the Suffolk bank of the Stour is known throughout the world. Many buildings which he painted still stand, including Flatford Mill and Willy Lott's Cottage, but only the thatched cottage by the small wooden bridge is open to the public – it is now a riverside cafe.
LOCATION *On the B1070, 1 mile W of the A12.*

FOUNTAINS ABBEY *North Yorkshire*

Set in the peaceful and fertile valley of the River Skell, Fountains Abbey, built by the Cistercians in 1132, is one of Britain's most beautiful ruins. When Henry VIII dissolved the monasteries in the 1530s, abbeys like Fountains suffered badly, but the magnificent cloisters and a great part of the church, infirmary, cellars and workshops remain. Fountains Hall near by, made from stones removed from the abbey, is also a beautiful building. It is perched on a knoll, commanding sweeping views of the abbey and the valley.
LOCATION *On a minor road off the B6265, 3 miles SW of Ripon.*

FOYERS *Highland*

Foyers, a village on the eastern shore of Loch Ness, has two claims to fame. Britain's first hydroelectric scheme was pioneered there in 1896, and it has a waterfall, a magnificent cataract of white foaming water, which is renowned throughout Scotland. A path runs down from the post office to the two-tier force, with the main drop tumbling 90 ft. After a brief respite in a deep pool the River Foyers picks up speed through a wooded gorge and then slows gradually before entering Loch Ness.
LOCATION *On the B852, 18 miles SW of Inverness.*

FURNESS ABBEY *Cumbria*

A wooded valley and a peaceful stream close to a sandy coast rich in fish made the Vale of the Deadly Nightshade an obvious choice for a monastery. The Cistercians did not miss chances like this, and they built a magnificent red-sandstone abbey after taking over Furness from the Savigny Order. Furness Abbey, with its vast income from sheep and iron ore, became so powerful that of all the northern abbeys only Fountains could rival it. Although close to the shipbuilding town of Barrow-in-Furness, the abbey still retains the tranquillity which attracted the monks over 800 years ago.
LOCATION *Off the A590, 1 mile S of Dalton-in-Furness.*

LOCH FYNE *Strathclyde*

The head of Loch Fyne is Campbell country and dominated by their splendid castle at Inveraray. The family have provided beauty as well as grandeur in Sir George Campbell's gardens at Crarae, which are now open to the public. The rhododendrons can be seen from road and loch. At the seaward end the inlet of Loch Gilp leads to Lochgilphead and the Crinan Canal, which is only 9 miles long yet took eight years, from 1793 to 1801, to build. This small cut saved many a sailing ship from the treacherous 130 mile long journey round the Mull of Kintyre.
LOCATION *Lochgilphead is 25 miles SW of Inverarary on the A83, with Crarae between the two. Crinan is 6 miles NW of Lochgilphead on the B841.*

FALLS OF GLOMACH *Highland*

It takes a couple of hours of tough going through the grand scenery below Glen Elchaig to reach the Falls of Glomach, which plunge 370 ft into a deep pool. They are hidden within the folds of the hills, and the weather can change suddenly. Walkers should bear this in mind. Boots and protective clothing are essential.
LOCATION *Footpath from minor road leading from Ardelve on the A57, 8 miles E of Kyle of Lochalsh.*

LOCH GOIL *Strathclyde*

The 6 mile long Loch Goil is often looked upon as a minor water because it is an arm of Loch Long. Lochgoilhead is mainly Victorian, but its church, restored in 1955, has a chantry altar dating back to 1512. To the south-east is a range of 2,000 ft peaks called Argyll's Bowling Green. The ruins of

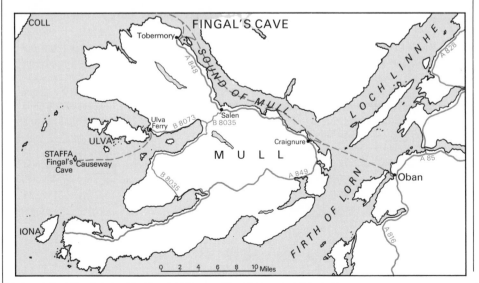

Carrick Castle, the home of the Argylls before it burned down in 1685, look down the loch. The road from Lochgoilhead north-west to Loch Fyne climbs through Hell's Glen, a steep pass reaching a height of 719 ft.

LOCATION *Lochgoilhead is 12 miles W of Arrochar, on the B839.*

GOLDEN CAP *Dorset*

The 626 ft Golden Cap, overlooking Lyme Bay, is the highest cliff on the south coast. It is best seen from the sea, from which angle the band of bright orange sandstone stands out, running above the grey rocky base. The National Trust owns the hill and the surrounding estate which includes farms, woodland, common, undercliff and a 7 mile stretch of coast running from the Spittles rocks just east of Lyme Regis to Eype Mouth near Bridport. The views seawards from the Cap are often breathtaking, especially towards the white cliffs of Portland when they are being lapped by the gentle swell of a blue sea.

LOCATION *Several lanes off the A35 Lyme Regis to Bridport road lead to Golden Cap Estate.*

THE GREAT GABLE *Cumbria*

See page 52.

GREAT ORMES HEAD *Gwynedd*

Llandudno is a town built recently (since 1840) on a strip of land linking the mainland with a former offshore island, the Great Orme, the summit of which can be reached by cable tramway. The cliff paths offer magnificent views, but it is the wonderful variety of plant and animal life which is the real joy, the speciality being a unique sub-species of butterfly. The typical grayling is *Hipparchia semele anglorum*, but the Great Orme variety is much duller and smaller and has been named *Hipparchia semele thyone*.

LOCATION *Llandudno is on the A546, and Great Ormes Head is reached from the promenade.*

GREY MARE'S TAIL
Dumfries and Galloway

High up on the grassy fells and scree slopes above Moffat is a stunning waterfall, formed where the 200 ft Tail Burn from Loch Skene shoots over a cliff. The loch cannot be seen from the falls because of a fringe of high crags. The description Grey Mare's Tail has also been given to two other Scottish falls, but the Tail Burn fall is by far the most impressive.

LOCATION *On the A708, 10 miles NE of Moffat.*

GRIMSPOUND *Devon*

Grimspound is an excellent example of a Bronze Age shepherd settlement huddled into the folds of Dartmoor, and has the well preserved remains of 244 huts within a stone compound. The positions of door lintels and stone sleeping shelves can still be detected. Grim was an alternative name for Woden, a god of the Anglo-Saxons. The atmosphere of Grimspound was well known to Sir Arthur Conan Doyle, who used it as Sherlock Holmes's hiding place during the unravelling of the case of *The Hound of the Baskervilles*.

LOCATION *On a minor road off the B3212, 5 miles SW of Moretonhampstead.*

HARDROW FORCE *North Yorkshire*

There cannot be many waterfalls which can be approached by paying a small fee and passing through an inn door. The footpath outside the back door of The Green Dragon leads to the fall, which at 98 ft is one of Britain's highest waterfalls. Near the falls are the remains of a bandstand, and at one time folk came from miles around to make music in company with the tumbling water. Hardrow Force is at its best in winter when, after a hard frost, icicles gleam like diamonds when struck by shafts of low sunlight. Its most exciting feature, however, is the footpath which actually passes between the rock face and the waterfall.

LOCATION *On a minor road off the A684, 1 mile N of Hawes.*

HARESFIELD BEACON *Gloucestershire*

Haresfield Beacon stands some 700 ft on top of a wooded slope, and is the perfect watch tower. It is hardly surprising to find the remains of an Iron Age fort and a Roman military site. What was surprising was the discovery during the last century of a cache of 3,000 Roman coins. The views from the beacon are spectacular. Gloucester, marked by the limestone Robin's Wood Hill; the Severn, wide and brown; the Forest of Dean; and, beyond, the Welsh mountains.

LOCATION *On a minor road from Edge on the A4173, 6 miles S of Gloucester.*

HARTLAND POINT *Devon*

Hartland Point thrusts out bravely into the Bristol Channel, and despite the lighthouse perched on the 325 ft sandstone summit the savage rocks below are still a potential graveyard for ships. A stream empties over

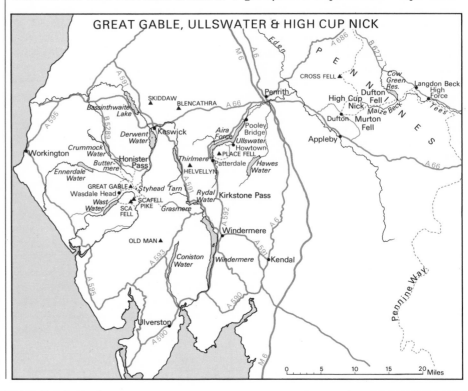

GREAT GABLE, ULLSWATER & HIGH CUP NICK

the eroded cliffs, just one of the many coastal waterfalls which are part of the magnificently varied scenery.

LOCATION *On a minor road from Hartland on the B3248, 12 miles W of Bideford.*

HELVELLYN *Cumbria*

The quickest but not the easiest way to the 3,118 ft summit of Helvellyn is a 3 mile path from the car park of the Forestry Commission's Swirls Forest Trail. It climbs above Thirlmere, which is now 3 miles long but before 1879 was two smaller lakes. The upper lake was dammed to provide water for Manchester, and the rise in level created the one lake. Striding Edge and Swirrel Edge can be seen, and on a clear day Thirlmere and Ullswater. The path up from Glenridding via Red Tarn, the easiest route, can also be seen.

LOCATION *Glenridding is on the A592 at the south end of Ullswater. The Swirls car park is on the A591, 4 miles N of Grasmere.*

HEREFORDSHIRE BEACON *Hereford*

Looking down on harebells nodding in the breeze and at wild mignonette and milkwort, or up to admire linnets or larks, nature lovers will delight in the richness of the Herefordshire Beacon. Taking time to rest during the climb towards the 1,115 ft summit makes the magnificent views even more memorable. In the 3rd century BC the clatter of weapons and marching feet would have echoed across the valleys as Ancient Britons prepared for war. The British Camp on the summit of the Beacon was a 32 acre enclosed fort of immense proportions. It is said that Caractacus, the most famous of British chiefs, made his last defiant stab at the Romans somewhere close to the Beacon, before his capture.

LOCATION *Off the A449, 1 mile W of Little Malvern.*

BEN HIANT *Highland*

The name Ben Hiant means the 'Holy Mountain'. At its feet is a gentle bay called Camas nan Geall, and close to the shore is a cross dedicated to St Ciaran. After Ciaran's death in 548, St Columba called him 'the light of this isle'. Ben Hiant, 1,729 ft, is an extinct volcano and stands out clearly from the rounded tops of the nearby hills. The upper slopes have views east across Loch Sunart, and south across the Sound of Mull. The area is, however, out of bounds during the deer-stalking

season, which starts on August 15.

LOCATION *On the B8007, 10 miles W of Salen.*

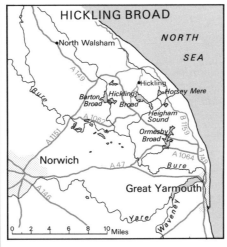

HICKLING BROAD *Norfolk*

See page 78.

HIGH CUP NICK *Cumbria*

See page 106. (Map, facing page.)

HIGH WILLHAYS *Devon*

Dartmoor National Park is 110 square miles of high, wet moorland known as Dartmoor Forest. It has been a hunting ground since 1307, and still belongs to the Duchy of Cornwall. It has regal views from granite tors over sweeping moorland, tree-studded valleys, stone circles, bogs and peaty streams. The highest tor – and the highest point in southern England – is High Willhays (2,038 ft). Those visiting high spots like Willhays or nearby Yes Tor (2,030 ft) should do so preferably with a guide, and always with extreme caution. Both hills are in a military firing area and should not be approached when red flags are flying.

LOCATION *Both High Willhays and Yes Tor can be seen from the A30 close to its junction with the A386, 4 miles SW of Okehampton.*

HONISTER PASS *Cumbria*

Honister Pass, reaching a height of 1,176 ft, connects Seatoller at the end of Borrowdale with Buttermere. The area is rich in good-quality slate, but the industry has done little to disturb the scenery. From Seatoller, the Johnny Wood Walk has been laid out by the Lake District Naturalist Trust

and leads through a natural old oak wood which also contains some introduced exotic conifers.

LOCATION *The B5289 passes from Seatoller through Honister Pass, and alongside Buttermere and Crummock Water.*

HOUND TOR *Devon*

See page 109.

LOCH HOURN *Highland*

See page 22. (Map, page 165.)

HOUSESTEADS *Northumberland*

See page 114. (Map, page 170.)

HUNTER'S TOR *Devon*

The 5 mile stretch of Dartmoor's River Teign above Fingle Bridge has scenery as dramatic as any in Scotland's Highlands. At Hunter's Tor the river drops into a steep tree-lined gorge and crashes its way towards Fingle Bridge, a magnificent arched structure of granite dating back to Elizabethan times. The views from the bridge and the paths leading from it are spectacular. Within strolling distance of the bridge is the Iron Age fort known as Prestonbury Castle.

LOCATION *6 miles from Drewsteignton, reached by minor roads from Dunsford on the B3212.*

INCHNADAMPH *Highland*

Ring ouzels, ravens and soaring eagles can be spotted at the 3,200 acre nature reserve at Inchnadamph, but it is dominated by the past. In a remarkable cave system have been found the fossilised remains of lemmings, brown bears, Arctic foxes and reindeer, and human skeletons some 8,000 years old. The route to the caves passes areas rich in alpine plants, among them rare club mosses, mountain saxifrage and mountain avens.

LOCATION *On the A837 close to the head of Loch Assynt.*

IONA *Strathclyde*

Sands of dazzling white speckled with dark green pebbles, blue sea and the sound of soaring larks ensure that Iona's tranquillity makes a lasting impression. Although the highest point, Dun Hill, is only 330 ft, there are wonderful views from its summit, both seawards across to the Small Isles and also towards Mull, less than a mile away and to the mainland beyond. St Columba is remembered by a cairn on Dun Hill and by the remains of the 6th-century chapel from which the Gospel was spread to Scotland and beyond. A lovely abbey maintains the holy traditions of an island also famous as a burial place for kings: 59 lie there, 48 Scots, 4 Irish and 7 Norwegians.

LOCATION *Passenger ferry from Fionnphort, Mull via Oban–Craignure ferry.*

JEDBURGH ABBEY *Borders*

Jedburgh, once a popular residence for the kings of Scotland, was always in the thick of fierce battles against the invading English. Things got so bad at one point that the Scots parliament ordered the castle to be demolished in 1409 because the English seemed to gain more advantage from it than the natives. The abbey was also knocked about a bit. From its foundation by Prince David (later David I) in 1118 it was sacked several times and in 1523 totally wrecked. The Earl of Surrey then tried to burn it down and yet it stands today as defiant as ever. Its Norman tower, tiered arches and tracery of a rose window have been restored and the abbey is now one of Scotland's finest.

LOCATION *On the A68, 11 miles N of Carter Bar on the border with England.*

KILBURN WHITE HORSE
North Yorkshire

Unlike many carvings on chalk hillsides in southern England, the Kilburn White Horse is neither chalk nor of prehistoric origin. In 1857 John Hodgson, the local schoolmaster, assisted by his pupils, carved

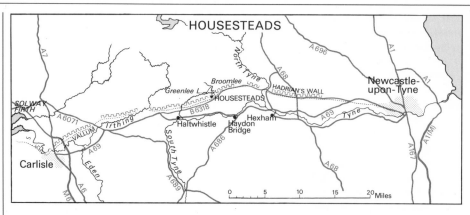

the 314 ft long, 228 ft high horse in the gritty limestone. They then used 6 tons of lime to whiten the figure, which is still freshened up from time to time. Steps lead from a car park up to the horse, from where there are fine views over the Vale of York.

LOCATION *About 1 mile along a minor road south off the A170, 5 miles E of Thirsk.*

KILLIECRANKIE PASS *Tayside*

The pass of Killiecrankie, owned by the National Trust for Scotland, lies north of Pitlochry. 'Bonnie Dundee' (Graham of Claverhouse, Viscount Dundee) was killed winning a battle there for James II of England (James VII of Scotland) in 1689. From the well-appointed visitors' centre, a wooded gorge alive with the sound of the tumbling waters of the River Garry leads down to the 'soldier's leap'. There, at the narrowest point of the gorge, a terrified soldier leaped across to escape the royalist Highlanders.

LOCATION *On the A9, 3 miles N of Pitlochry.*

KINDER SCOUT *Derbyshire*

The flat moorland plateau of Kinder Scout reaches 2,088 ft, and many an over-confident walker has fallen or become lost there through treating it too lightly after visiting the Highlands, the Lake District or Wales. The summit is spongy with peat which makes walking difficult, but the views over the Peak District are worth the effort. Kinder can be reached from the Snake Inn via Fairbrook Naze.

LOCATION *The Pennine Way footpath runs up Kinder Scout from Edale where there is a National Park Information Centre.*

KINNOULL HILL *Tayside*

Kinnoull Hill on the River Tay is only 728 ft high, but from its summit on a clear day

can be seen Cairn Toul, 4,241 ft, 50 miles north, and Ben More, 3,843 ft.

LOCATION *Follow the A85 Dundee road out of Perth. After crossing the Tay, Kinnoull Hill is signposted left via Manse Road.*

KISDON FORCE *North Yorkshire*

It is hard to imagine that a century ago the charming dales village of Keld was the centre of the lead-mining industry. It was originally called Appletreekeld, meaning the spring of the apple tree. Evidence of the industry is everywhere, and the delightful lead-loving plant, spring sandwort, grows over the spoil heaps. Waterfalls abound. Kisdon Force is reached after a walk up the Swale which empties its leaping waters over one limestone edge after another. Half a mile upstream by a riverside path is Catrake Force, and the more turbulent Main Wath is 1 mile above that.

LOCATION *Keld is on the B6270, 10 miles SE of Kirkby Stephen. A half mile signposted walk leads to Kisdon Force.*

KYNANCE COVE *Cornwall*

See page 14.

THE LAIRIG GHRU *Grampian*

See page 60.

LAND'S END *Cornwall*

The soaring majesty of the cliffs at Land's End is in complete contrast to the commercialism surrounding England's westernmost point. The view south-east to Gwennap Head is incredible, the Scillies are visible on a clear fine day, the Armed Knight rock looks like a gigantic crusader rising from the sea, and Enys Dodman is a huge archway of granite. Caves are found everywhere, flowers cover the cliffs and the sound of wind, waves and birds make a visit to Land's End still memorable for those who love wild places.

LOCATION *At the western end of the A30.*

BEN LAWERS *Tayside*

Ben Lawers is the highest mountain on Tayside and towers 3,984 ft above Loch Tay. It is renowned for its alpine flowers including purple saxifrage, moss campion, yellow mountain saxifrage, alpine lady's mantle and alpine club moss which, together with the splendid views, make the climb worth while. Butterflies such as the small pearl-bordered fritillary and small mountain ringlet may be seen in summer.

LOCATION *Above the A827, 14 miles SW of Aberfeldy.*

LEIGHTON MOSS, SILVERDALE *Lancashire*

This 321 acre marshland nature reserve is administered by the Royal Society for the Protection of Birds, and has an Information Centre and bookshop at Myers Farm. There are hides for which a permit is required, but a public causeway with two hides crosses the reserve and public access here is free. Good views of otters are a regular feature of the reserve but it is also famous for its bitterns, bearded reedlings, water rails and reed warblers. The marsh is fed from the surrounding limestone hills which overlook Morecambe Bay. The hills are clothed in yew, juniper and ash which shelter rare orchids, while the Moss harbours cowslips, hemp agrimony, iris and great water dock. Close by is Leighton Hall, which during the summer organises displays by birds of prey.

LOCATION *On a minor road about 3 miles N of Carnforth.*

LEITH HILL *Surrey*

Leith Hill, 965 ft, is the highest hill in south-east England. In 1766, Richard Hull who lived there built a 64 ft folly tower on its summit. Hull's tower is worth climbing for a view said to embrace 13 counties. In spring, surrounding woodlands are a sea of bluebells.

LOCATION *On a minor road off the A25, 4 miles S of Dorking.*

LINDISFARNE *Northumberland*

See page 18.

LLANDDWYN *Anglesey*

Although connected to the mainland by a land bridge, Llanddwyn has the remoteness and mystery which attract holy men and women. A holy well and a ruined 15th-century church are both connected with St Dwynwen, who is said to have sought the solitude of the island after an unhappy love affair in the 5th century. Near the church is a rock said to have been split to form a chair in which the dying St Dwynwen could sit and admire the scenery. She must have died happy, since the views of Anglesey, the Lleyn Peninsula and to the east Snowdonia are truly spectacular.

LOCATION *Reached by a 3 mile walk from Newborough on the A4040.*

LOCH LOMOND *Central, Strathclyde*

Loch Lomond, 23 miles long and up to 5 miles wide, is Britain's largest lake. It is 630 ft deep and full of fish, including trout, pike and powan, a white fish of the salmon family, found only in the deep lochs of Scotland and Wales. Wildlife is protected in a nature reserve at the south-east corner. The 30 islands which enhance the attraction of the loch have been sanctuaries for religious men since the 5th century AD. On the largest, Inchmurrin, 1 mile long, St Mirren founded his monastery in the 6th century. There are lay-bys on the road following the west bank, but the best way to see the loch is from a boat.

LOCATION *Alongside the A82, 15 miles NW of Glasgow.*

THE LONG MYND *Shropshire*

The 10 miles of ridge called The Long Mynd (*mynd* is Welsh for mountain) is one of Shropshire's most remarkable features. The highest point is 1,695 ft and 4,530 acres of it are owned by the National Trust. Where once the Welsh and the English battled, only birds now claim territories – curlews, merlins, larks and short-eared owls. Bog mosses, bog pimpernel, tormentil and butterwort twinkle around the stream edges. The Long Mynd is best explored from Church Stretton.

LOCATION *Off the B4370 near Church Stretton. Several minor roads lead to footpaths up to The Long Mynd.*

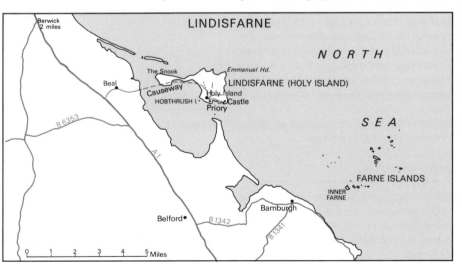

LULWORTH COVE *Dorset*

Lulworth Cove is a round bay on the Dorset coast, almost land-locked by limestone and chalk cliffs. To the east are fossilised tree stumps and to the west are twisted rocks eroded by the sea. Through a spectacular offshore limestone arch, called the Durdle Door, can be seen the Man o' War beach. The arch will eventually collapse, leaving two pillars.

LOCATION *On the B3071, 8 miles SW of Wareham.*

LUNEDALE *Cumbria*

The writer John Ruskin described the view of the Lune valley from Kirkby Lonsdale as 'one of the loveliest in England – therefore in the world'. The 53 mile long Lune is certainly magnificent, from its rising in the Cumbrian hills to its meeting with the sea beyond Lancaster. Spanning the Lune close to the A65 is the 13th-century Devil's Bridge, no longer used for traffic but linking two car parks on each side of the river. Below the bridge, dippers dip, wagtails wag their tails to keep their balance on rocks and skin-divers dive into the clear deep waters full of salmon and trout. A footpath follows the river from the splendid old town of Kirkby Lonsdale to Devil's Bridge.

LOCATION *Kirkby Lonsdale is on the A65, 15 miles SE of Kendal.*

LYDFORD GORGE *Devon*

Foaming water, giant trees and abundant wildlife fill this mile-long chasm cut by the River Lyd. Paths run along both sides of the river, canopied by huge oaks and bordered by ferns, mosses and a profusion of wild flowers, including, in season, herb robert and wild garlic. Herons and dippers are among the birds which fish the river. But the highlight of the walk is the river itself, cascading over smooth dark rock and climaxing in the White Lady Falls, which plunge 100 ft into the gorge at the southern end.

LOCATION *On a minor road off the A386, 8 miles SW of Okehampton.*

LYNTON *Devon*

The Victorians built Lynton on a dome-like cliff overlooking Lee Bay and on the fringes of Exmoor. They built it for the view and because Lynmouth, crushed between the cliff and the sea, could not meet the

demands for accommodation. A cliff railway, built in 1890, connects them. A walk of 1 mile from the top leads to the Valley of the Rocks.

LOCATION *On the A39, 16 miles west of Minehead.*

BEN MACDUI *Grampian*

The Cairngorms have four peaks over 4,000 ft – Cairn Gorm (4,084), Cairn Toul (4,241), Braeriach (4,248) and Ben Macdui (4,296), the second highest peak in Britain after Ben Nevis (4,408). Indeed, until accurate means of measurement were developed in the 19th century, Ben Macdui was usually considered to be the highest mountain in Britain. Ben Macdui derives from *Ben Mhic Dhuibh*, which means 'Macduff's Hill'. The Cairngorms attract ornithologists and botanists as well as mountaineers and skiers. There are ptarmigans, snow buntings, dotterels and golden plovers. Alpine rarities include brook saxifrage, pearlwort and several club mosses.

LOCATION *Ben Macdui can be approached from the Linn of Dee, 6 miles from Braemar, along a minor road off the A93.*

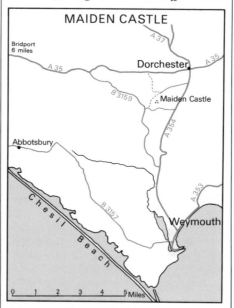

MAIDEN CASTLE *Dorset*

See page 144.

MALHAMDALE *North Yorkshire*

See page 147.

MAM RATTACHAN *Highland*

From the hamlet of Glenelg a twisting turning road, the Mam Rattachan Pass,

reaches a height of 1,116 ft with views of the mountain range known as the Five Sisters of Kintail, the eldest sister, Sgurr Fhuarar, soaring to some 3,505 ft. Dr Johnson, who took the summer ferry from Glenelg to Skye with Boswell on their 'Journey to the Western Isles', described the pass as 'a terrible steep'. The best view of it is from an observation point built by the Forestry Commission to soften the objections to their growing trees obstructing one of the most dramatic views in the Highlands.

LOCATION *At the western end of a minor road off the A87 at Shiel Bridge.*

MAM TOR *Derbyshire*

See page 152.

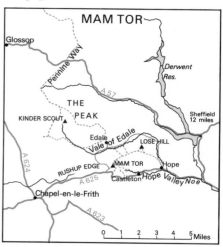

LOCH MAREE *Highland*

Loch Maree is cradled between sweeping hills and dominated to the east by Slioch, 3,260 ft of Torridon sandstone. The tree-lined Loch Maree is 12 miles long and dotted with islands. One of the smallest, Isle Maree, is also the most famous. St Maelrubha had his hermitage there in the 7th century, and a corruption of that spelling gives both loch and island their name. Pine marten, wild cat and golden eagle are all found in the area which is controlled by the Nature Conservancy, and there are several nature trails.

LOCATION *The A832 from Gairloch to Kinlochewe follows the south-western shore of the loch.*

MARLOES SANDS *Dyfed*

A very pleasant walk of less than half an hour from the National Trust car park at Marloes leads to the sands, watched over by sandstone cliffs. At the western edge of

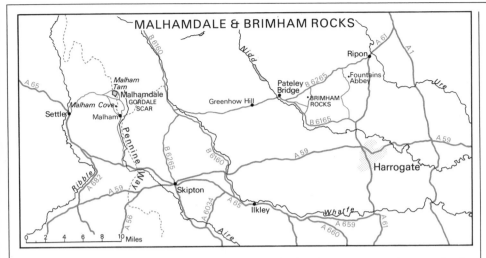

MALHAMDALE & BRIMHAM ROCKS

the beach is the island of Gateholm, meaning goat island. This is cut off at high tide, and although uninhabited today there are the remains of a substantial Iron Age settlement. At the eastern end are the Three Chimneys, which are vertical columns of sandstone. The Pembrokeshire Coastal Path follows the Marloes Sands and leads to the Dale Peninsula.
LOCATION *On a minor road off the B4327, 9 miles SW of Haverfordwest.*

FALLS OF MEASACH *Highland*

Towering menacingly over the Ullapool road, the barren peaks of An Teallach, 3,483 ft, and Beinn Dearg, 3,536 ft, make one think of almost anything except lush woodlands and tumbling waterfalls. But from the car park at Corrieshalloch a steep path descends through dense trees and rare ferns to an observation platform overlooking the River Droma, pouring through a gorge a mile long and 100 yds wide. Sir John Fowler, one of the designers of the Forth Bridge, designed and paid for a small suspension bridge giving a view from above the falls. Ravens nest there and buzzards and occasionally peregrines sweep along the ledges.
LOCATION *Corrieshalloch Gorge, 12 miles SE of Ullapool on the A835.*

THE MENDIP HILLS *Somerset*

The 27 mile long Mendips, composed of limestone over old red sandstone, are botanically spectacular and peppered with caves and potholes. They lie across Somerset from Weston-super-Mare to Frome like a tired dog, but Wells is really the capital of the Mendips. The highest point is Black Down, 1,067 ft, but it looks higher, especially when a storm is brewing. The hills overlook the water-meadows of the Somerset levels. There are Old Stone Age long barrows dating from 3000 BC, and stone circles of the Bronze Age built about 1,000 years later.
LOCATION *The Mendips are best seen via the A371 from Wells and from the B3371.*

MENTEITH LAKE *Central*

Menteith is 1 mile long, and is the only stretch of inland water the Scots will call a lake rather than a loch. On the small island of Inchmahome, reached by ferry, is a priory built in 1238. Monks fished for pike which breed in the lake. Mary, Queen of Scots was sent to the priory when she was only five, after the Scottish defeat by Henry VIII's army at the Battle of Pinkie in 1547.
LOCATION *The A81 runs along the north shore of the lake, 3 miles E of Aberfoyle.*

MERRICK *Dumfries and Galloway*

A forest walk through wooded glens from Loch Trool leads to the granite block known as the Bruce Stone, which stands on top of a scenic hill. Below are the Buchan Oakwoods, splashed by spray from the burn which blasts through a granite ravine. In 1307, Robert Bruce could see something else – the English. His men rolled rocks on to the enemy and began the struggle that ended in his victory at Bannockburn in 1314. From the stone can be seen the Fell of Eschorian. Beyond it a path leads towards the peak of Merrick, 2,765 ft, the highest point in southern Scotland.
LOCATION *On a minor road off the A714, 7 miles N of Newton Stewart.*

MERRY MAIDENS *Cornwall*

The 'maidens' are standing stones dating from the Bronze Age. There are 19 stones averaging 4 ft in height, with a further pair called the Pipers about a mile to the north-east and measuring almost 15 ft. Another, a single upright called the Fiddler, is situated to the east. These stones provided the music for the merry maidens, who according to legend were turned into stone as a punishment for dancing on a Sunday.
LOCATION *Off the B3315, 4 miles SW of Penzance.*

LOCH MOIDART *Highland*

If Loch Moidart is approached from the sea the 13th-century Castle Tioran can be seen perched like a cormorant on an isolated rock. At full tide the sea forms an impregnable moat, but at low water the castle can be reached on foot. It was built by the MacDonalds of Clanranald to keep off their arch-enemies, the Campbells. The MacDonalds burned it down themselves after the 1715 rebellion failed, rather than let the Campbells take it. At the head of the loch are crofters' cottages near Kinlochmoidart, with seven birch trees planted in memory of seven followers who came with Bonnie Prince Charlie from France. The trees face one of Scotland's most impressive seascapes.
LOCATION *On a minor road off the A861, 2 miles N of Salen.*

MONTROSE BASIN *Tayside*

The 2 mile wide basin formed by the River South Esk looks like an inland sea, filled in winter by wildfowl and ringed in summer by garlands of flowers and blossom. About 10 miles north is the National Nature Reserve at St Cyrus, which has a 2 mile coastal walk strewn with flowers including vetch, viper's-bugloss, clustered bellflower and the hairy violet. Nets are staked out into the sea to catch salmon by one of the most ancient methods, called haaf-netting. Rock doves and house martins breed on the sandstone cliffs.
LOCATION *On the A92, 12 miles N of Arbroath.*

MOORFOOT HILLS
Lothian and Borders

Prehistoric hill-forts indicate pagan settlements at Eddleston. It has a 17th-century hotel, the Black Barony, once the clan home of the Murrays, and a miniature railway. From the valley of its stream, Eddleston Water, rise the Moorfoot Hills,

famous for their grouse shoots. Highest point is Blackhope Scar, 2,136 ft.
LOCATION *Eddleston is 4 miles N of Peebles on the A703.*

LOCH MORAR *Highland*

The most difficult way to reach Loch Morar – by boat to Tarbet on Loch Nevis then a half-mile climb – is also the most beautiful. Although only 30 ft above sea level and less than a mile wide, Morar, at 1,017 ft, is Scotland's deepest freshwater loch. It is said to be the home of a monster called Morag, a beast every bit as elusive as its cousin Nessie.
LOCATION *2 miles S of Mallaig on the A830.*

MOUNTAIN ROAD *Dyfed*

The Forestry Commission plantations at Cwm Berwyn have added some deep greenery to the mountain road which spans the 15 miles between Tregaron and the tiny settlement at Abergeswyn. The route reaches a windswept height of 1,600 ft, and the description the 'desert of Wales' seems well-earned. But it was an important drovers' road and cattle, pigs, sheep, geese and turkeys set off on the trip to markets as far south and east as Kent and Essex. The drovers and their corgi dogs must have been stretched to the limit to keep their stock together, and the birds' feet were often coated with tar for protection on the rough roads. It is worth following their steps for the sheer majesty of the panoramic views.
LOCATION *Off the B4343, 10 miles N of Lampeter. The mountain road to Abergeswyn is signposted from Tregaron.*

MULL *Strathclyde*

The island of Mull was formed by volcanoes spewing out lava. Even the huge Ben More (3,170 ft) consists of layer upon layer of lava flows. On the Ross of Mull, the longest peninsula of the island, are the huge Carsaig Arches, tunnels formed by the sea continually battering the basalt cliffs. Geologically, the tiny island of Staffa, 8 miles to the west of Mull, is very similar to this area, and originally the two islands must have been part of the same land mass.
LOCATION *By car ferry from Oban.*

MULL OF GALLOWAY
Dumfries and Galloway

The Mull of Galloway, at the southernmost

point of the Rinns of Galloway, forms the south-western tip of Scotland, and the turbulent water beneath its towering cliff, topped by a lonely lighthouse, is caused by the meeting of seven tides. There is much for the naturalist to enjoy including rock sea lavender, rock sea spurrey and golden samphire, which reach the northern limit of their distribution on the Mull. Seabirds, among them auks, kittiwakes, fulmars and cormorants, seem to occupy every tiny ledge on the sandstone cliffs.
LOCATION *On a minor road off the B7041, 20 miles S of Stranraer.*

MULL OF KINTYRE *Strathclyde*

The Mull of Kintyre is for walkers rather than motorists, but beyond Campbeltown cars can go as far south as the Gap, a vantage point overlooking the sheer cliffs rising 300 ft above the sea. A lighthouse built in 1788 can be reached by a steep, descending path. Along a tough mile track is Sron Uamha, a late Iron Age fort, with views typical of the wild untamed area.
LOCATION *Half a mile beyond the end of a minor road off the B842, 10 miles S of Campbeltown.*

THE NEEDLES *Isle of Wight*

The three huge chalk stacks of The Needles poke up from the sea off the westernmost tip of the Isle of Wight close to Alum Bay. They are all that remain of a chalk ridge that once linked the Isle of Wight to Studland in Dorset. North of The Needles is Alum Bay, bounded by cliffs which are partly composed of bands of sand coloured white, black, brown, yellow, red and green. From the Downs above the bay there are views across the Solent to the mainland, with Portland Bill, 35 miles west, often in view.
LOCATION *Leave Yarmouth on the A3054 signposted to Totland, where the B3322 leads to Alum Bay.*

LOCH NESS *Highland*

See page 80.

NEW FOREST *Hampshire*

The 90,000 acres of prime English woodland largely untouched for 900 years have matured into a wildlife refuge with deer, ponies, squirrels, otters, badgers and rare birds. There are also planted sections. The Tall Trees walk, just west of Lyndhurst, is

among them but, nevertheless, is one of the forest's most striking areas. It consists of huge redwoods, firs and cypresses which were planted in 1859.
LOCATION *Lyndhurst, 'capital of the New Forest', stands at the intersection of the A35 and the A337, 10 miles W of Southampton. From Lyndhurst, roads radiate to all parts of the forest.*

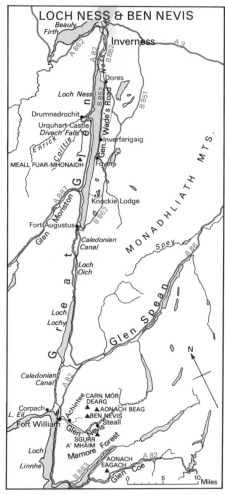

LOCH NESS & BEN NEVIS

NORBER BOULDERS
North Yorkshire

A glacier moved the massive Norber Boulders, some of them weighing 20 tons, from Crummock Dale and Ribblesdale to the southern slopes of Ingleborough. The boulders resist much erosion and protect the ground beneath them from wind and rain, while surrounding areas are worn away. The result is that the boulders stand perched on limestone pedestals like golf balls on tees.
LOCATION *About 6 miles NW of Settle near the village of Clapham on the B6480. From Clapham the boulders are signposted via a bridlepath called Thwaite Lane.*

OFFA'S DYKE
English–Welsh Borders

Offa was King of Mercia from 757 to 796, with joint capitals at Tamworth and Lichfield. The dyke was constructed around 784–96, from Prestatyn on the north Welsh coast to Chepstow on the Severn, to mark the border between Mercia and Wales. It ran a total of 168 miles, of which 81 miles can still be traced. Even today, it is still 30 ft high in places and 60 ft broad. From the National Trust property at Bradnor Hill, a 1,284 ft ridge near Kington, the dyke is seen to have two ditches, suggesting that two separate gangs of builders must have been working there. The Offa's Dyke Path, opened in 1971, follows the course of the dyke over its full length.

LOCATION *Kington is 14 miles W of Leominster on the A44.*

OLD HARRY ROCK *Dorset*

The chalklands of Dorset end where the impressive hills of the Isle of Purbeck meet the sea in dramatic 500 ft high cliffs at Handfast Point. The clifftop here, at the edge of Bullard Down, is known as Old Nick's Ground. There are imposing views but with an element of danger because of constant erosion. Below are wave-punched arches and two eroding chalk stacks standing out to sea – Old Harry and his Wife. Despite associations with the Devil, this lovely spot is more like heaven, especially on a blue day in high summer. Looking out beyond Old Harry and his Wife, the view extends to their cousins, The Needles, 15 miles away off the Isle of Wight.

LOCATION *Handfast Point is reached along the waymarked Dorset Coast Path, 1 mile east of Studlands.*

THE OLD MAN OF HOY *Orkney*

See page 26.

ORFORD NESS *Suffolk*

Orford was once such a busy port that in the 12th century Henry II built a huge castle with an 18-sided keep to protect it. Gradually, however, the long shingle spit of the Ness grew out and strangled the port. Amber and the pink semi-precious stone cornelian can be found on the beaches.

LOCATION *Orford is on the B1084, 10 miles E of Woodbridge.*

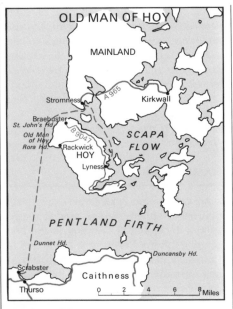

PENDLE HILL *Lancashire*

Sandwiched between Burnley, Nelson and Clitheroe, Pendle has been described as a large ridge tent with one pole shorter than the other, as a sleeping whale and as a cowering lion. Although it fails to reach the status of a mountain (2,000 ft) by a mere 169 ft it dominates the rolling green countryside below it and broods a clutch of picturesque villages. On the Burnley side are Roughlee, Blacko, Barley and Newchurch, where lived the Pendle Witches who were tried and put to death at Lancaster in 1612.

LOCATION *Barley is on minor roads 5 miles N of Burnley.*

PENTRE IFAN *Dyfed*

Pentre Ifan is one of the most impressive Stone Age burial chambers in Wales. From

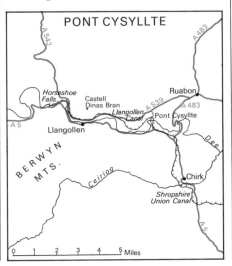

it the views across the Nevern valley are magnificent, especially at dawn and dusk when the stones cast shadows as they have done since about 2000 BC when tribesmen dragged them into place. How they lifted and balanced the 20 ton capstone so precariously on four high pointed uprights is a mystery.

LOCATION *On minor roads off the A487, 10 miles E of Fishguard.*

PEN-Y-GHENT *Yorkshire*

The three great peaks of the Yorkshire Dales are Whernside (2,419 ft), Ingleborough (2,373 ft) and Pen-y-ghent (2,273 ft), all noted for their lime-loving plants, breathtaking views from the summits and the charming villages which surround them. Here also are some renowned potholes – Alum Pot, Long Churn, Calf Holes and Hull and Hunt Pot.

LOCATION *Ribblesdale is on the B6479, 6 miles N of Settle.*

PILLAR *Cumbria*

Pillar Mountain, often called a fell locally, rises to 2,927 ft at the head of Ennerdale. It is worth climbing for its views from the summit, but it is a pillar of rock nearly 600 ft high which gives it the name and attracts the serious climbers. Since it was first scaled by a local man, John Atkinson, in 1826, many a famous mountaineer has learned his trade on its sheer rock face.

LOCATION *Footpaths from Ennerdale.*

PISTYLL RHAEADR
Border of Clwyd and Powys

The spout of the waterfall river is one of the most spectacular falls in the principality. Its waters crash some 300 ft from rock to rock into a lovely valley. Dippers and wagtails are among the many birds which haunt the wooded valley below the fall.

LOCATION *On a minor road signposted from Llanrhaeadr-ym-Mochnant, which is on the B4580, 2 miles W of Oswestry.*

PONT CYSYLLTE *Clwyd*

See page 84.

PORTLAND BILL *Dorset*

The Isle of Portland is a huge block of limestone 4 miles long by 1 mile wide. The stone was used for St Paul's Cathedral, London Bridge and the United Nations

Building in New York, but quarrying has now almost ceased and wild flowers are returning quickly. The old lighthouse at Portland Bill is now a bird observatory and from it the land takes a steep plunge towards Pulpit Rock, a massive offshore pillar with commanding views of the Devon coastline. The isle has long been a naval base and was so important that it had two castles to defend it. From its highest point, 496 ft, Chesil Beach can be seen to the west.

LOCATION *On a minor road leading from the A354, 4 miles S of Weymouth.*

PUFFIN ISLAND *Anglesey*

Off the north-eastern tip of Anglesey lies the blue-grey limestone rock of Puffin Island which is also known as Ynys Seirio, or Priestholm, after a 6th-century Celtic cleric St Seiriol. The puffins have an even greater claim to the island and have proved valuable in commerce from the time of the Danes who sacked the monastery in 853. The Danes filled their larders with sea-birds, and pickled puffins were so much of a delicacy in the high society of the 18th and 19th centuries that the colonies declined, a demise completed by the arrival of brown rats from a nearby sinking ship. A bell on an unmanned lighthouse can often be heard tolling through the swirling mist and could well be regarded as a lament for the priests of old and the puffin colonies, now only a memory on the island which bears their name.

LOCATION *A minor road off the B5109, 2 miles NE of Beaumaris, leads to the headland of Black Point opposite Puffin Island.*

THE QUANTOCK HILLS *Somerset*

The Quantocks, a granite and limestone ridge, overlook the hills of Wales and the Bristol Channel to the north and the Vale of Taunton Deane to the south. Stately manor houses are surrounded by sheep, steep-wooded valleys and flowing streams. The highest point, 1,260 ft, is Wills Neck, Old English for The Ridge of the Welsh Men. The Brendon Hills and Exmoor lie to the west.

LOCATION *The top of Wills Neck is reached from Triscombe Stone on the A39.*

QUINAG *Highland*

Quinag is a fascinating mountain of many peaks, the highest reaching 2,653 ft. There

are so many tiny springs that the hillsides seem to leak, especially in spring as the meltwater pours down the glens to the surrounding lochs. In summer the streams flow more gently, illuminated by patches of yellow mountain saxifrage and clumps of butterwort, bog asphodel and lousewort.

LOCATION *Off the A894 about 2 miles N of Loch Assynt.*

RAMSEY *Dyfed*

Many Celtic saints enjoyed lives of meditation on lonely islands and several visited Ramsey including St Devynog in the 2nd century, followed later by St David and St Patrick. It has no permanent inhabitants save the seabirds, but the once huge puffin colonies have been decimated over the years by the descendants of rats which apparently swam ashore from a wrecked ship. Seals breed in many of the caves which are a feature of Ramsey.

LOCATION *About 1 mile SW of Whitesand Bay. Reached by boat from St Justinian's, 2 miles W of St David's.*

RANNOCH *Highland*

See page 118.

REST AND BE THANKFUL *Strathclyde*

The pass which carries the main road west from Arochar to Inveraray climbs steeply through Glen Croe at the foot of the Cobbler (2,891 ft). The high point of the road, below Beinn Ime (3,319 ft), is 860 ft above sea level. From the summit on the modern motor road there are views towards Inveraray on Loch Fyne and down to

the old military road which twists its way through the glen below. Before the motor car, the journey through Glen Croe was a punishing experience for man and beast, and the summit became known, aptly, as the Rest And Be Thankful.

LOCATION *Off the A83 at the junction of the B828.*

RHOSSILI BAY *West Glamorgan*

A walk northwards from Rhossili, Gower's most westerly village, climbs the 632 ft of the peninsula's highest point, Rhossili Downs. Its top is grassy and botanically rich, the plants thriving on the soil above the parent rock of old red sandstone. The downs overlook the 3 mile sweep of white sand which makes Rhossili Bay one of the finest beaches in Britain. On the downs there are Neolithic burial chambers overlooking the coast of Devon in the south and St Govan's Head in the west. It is said that Sweyne the Viking, who gave his name to Swansea, is buried there. He could not have picked a more beautiful spot.

LOCATION *About 4 miles west of Knelston at the western end of the B4247.*

RIEVAULX *North Yorkshire*

See page 86.

ROSEBERRY TOPPING *Cleveland*

The sacred hill, Roseberry Topping, abode of the mighty Viking war god, Odin, is 1,051 ft of sandstone with seams of coal, alum, iron and jet, the black fossil remains of swamp vegetation. It scans Teesside's fields and industrial landscape on one side, with views of the North Yorkshire Moors

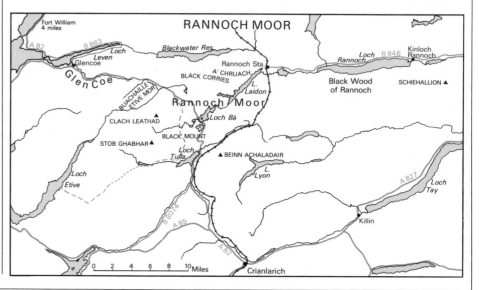

and the Cleveland Hills on the other.
LOCATION *Off the A173, about 1 mile N of Great Ayton.*

ROUGH TOR *Cornwall*

A large part of Cornwall can be seen from the summit of the 1,311 ft Rough Tor on Bodmin Moor. To the north, the views extend to Tintagel Head and the sea, to the south and west they take in not only the moor but the county beyond.
LOCATION *About 2 miles SE of Camelford by a minor road off the A39.*

ST ABB'S HEAD *Borders*

The National Trust for Scotland own St Abb's Head wildlife reserve, a seabird-thronged stretch of coastline soaring more than 300 ft above the sea, the highest cliffs on the east coast of Scotland. A lighthouse built in 1862 stands on the headland and beneath it roseroot, lovage and sea campion bloom amongst the wheeling fulmars, kittiwakes, razorbills and guillemots.
LOCATION *St Abb's village is at the north end of the B6438, 1 mile NE of Coldingham. St Abb's Head is 1 mile from the village by a coastal footpath.*

ST GOVAN'S HEAD *Dyfed*

See page 28.

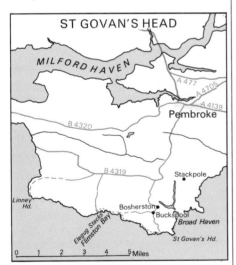

SANDWOOD BAY *Highland*

Sandwood, the reputed haunt of a mermaid, is one of the most remote beaches in Britain, reached after a strenuous 4 mile walk over peat moors and alongside small lochs. The path descends on to a 4 mile stretch of enchanting pale pink sands

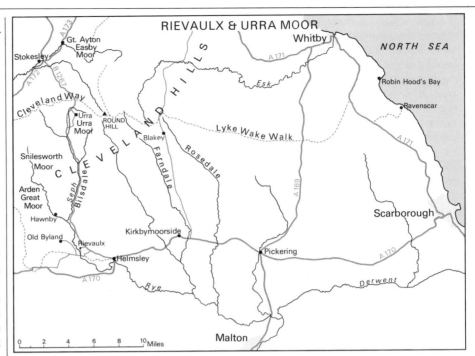

backed by massive grass-covered dunes flanked by contrasting cliffs of dark Lewisian gneiss and red Torridonian sandstone. A huge sandstone stack called the Herdsman (*Am Bhuachaille*) stands on the west of the bay, but two former stacks are now reduced to rock covered by, and bearing witness to, the strength of the sea.
LOCATION *Off a minor road from Kinlochbervie on the B801.*

THE SEVEN SISTERS *East Sussex*

See page 30.

SHEEPS TOR *Devon*

From the rock-strewn summit of Sheeps Tor the expanse of Dartmoor is spread out like a relief map – the deep green of wooded combes slicing into the bare up-

lands. Dartmoor ponies pick their way around the bogs which are rich in summer flowers including bell heather, bog bean, whortleberry and occasionally bee orchids. At the foot of the tor, looking surprisingly natural, is Burrator Reservoir which supplies water to Plymouth.
LOCATION *Off the B3212 about 3 miles SE of Yelverton.*

THE FALLS OF SHIN *Highland*

The stepped rocks whipping the fast-running River Shin into a turmoil of foam make the falls one of the most impressive in Britain. The fish lash and struggle in their efforts to pass from the Kyle of Sutherland to the breeding areas below Loch Shin. Visitors can watch these spectacular leaps from an observation platform close to a deep wooded gorge.
LOCATION *Off the B864, 1 mile N of the junction of the A836 and A837 at Inveran.*

SILBURY HILL *Wiltshire*

What the great man-made mound of turf-covered chalk and rubble, 130 ft high, 200 yds in diameter and 100 ft across the top, is doing brooding above Marlborough Downs no one really knows, but it is possibly connected with nearby Avebury. No evidence of burials has ever been found, but Silbury Hill may have begun as a Neolithic round barrow and been added to during the Bronze Age. It is clearly seen from the Neolithic causewayed camp at

Windmill Hill and is situated just across the A4 from West Kennet, a Bronze Age chambered tomb. This is one of the most impressive of all English chambered tombs, being 8 ft high, 330 ft long and 20 ft wide. It is well lit so that its internal structure can be easily studied.
LOCATION *Off the A4, 1 mile W of West Kennet.*

SKARA BRAE *Orkney*

Almost 4,500 years ago a sandstorm engulfed the village of Skara Brae. The people fled in haste, leaving behind their belongings and treasures. When the village was dug out of the sand thousands of years later, excavators found the huts and their furnishings – all made of stone – intact.
LOCATION *On the B9056, 7 miles N of Stromness on the A967.*

SKIDDAW *Cumbria*

The top of Skiddaw (3,054 ft), Lakeland's third highest mountain, can easily be reached by a walker. The summit, called the High Man, was the site of a medieval lookout post and beacon. The view is one of the most stirring in Lakeland. Derwentwater, Helvellyn and Borrowdale are almost always seen, but on a good day the Cheviots, Ingleborough, the Isle of Man and even Ireland may be visible.
LOCATION *Off the A591, 4 miles N of Keswick.*

SKOMER *Pembroke*

South of St Bride's Bay is a group of islands of which Skomer, a nature reserve administered by the Nature Conservancy Council and the West Wales Naturalists' Trust, is the most prominent. It abounds with seabirds, has a wide variety of sweet-smelling flowers and offers shelter to breeding seals. The Skomer vole, a sub-species of field vole, is unique to the island. A flat plateau only 200 ft above the sea still affords excellent views, and the long island is divided into two by a narrow isthmus. As on many Welsh islands, there is evidence of extensive Iron Age settlements, but the wildlife has been alone for centuries.
LOCATION *On Broad Sound to the west of Wooltack Point on a minor road off the B4327 from Haverfordwest.*

SMOO CAVE *Highland*

The township of Durness gives its name to the local limestone from which sea and

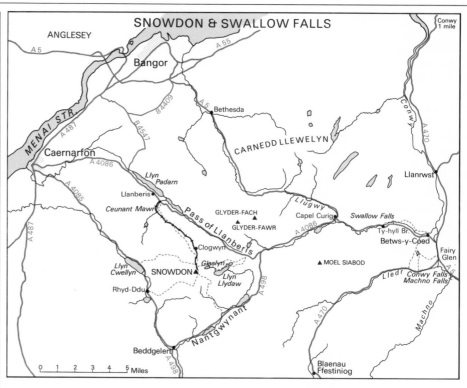

river have carved Smoo Cave. Smoo, derived from *Smuga*, the Old Norse for 'a cleft', has three chambers but only the outermost is accessible at low tide through a 33 ft high arch. Potholers can ford the Allt Smoo to the middle chamber where a river cascades down a 30 ft shaft. The innermost cave, a grotto of weird shapes of eroded limestone, is 120 ft long and 8 ft wide.
LOCATION *Off the A838, 1 mile E of Durness.*

SNOWDON *Gwynedd*

See page 64.

STAC POLLY *Highland*

See page 72.

STENNESS *Orkney*

On Mainland island close to Stenness and Harray, Orkney's two largest lochs, lies a mysterious complex of monuments very similar to the Wiltshire system at Stonehenge. The Orkney complex consists of one of the finest chambered tombs in Europe at Maes Howe, the Stones of Stenness which are connected by an avenue leading to the Ring of Brodgar.
LOCATION *Off the A965 from Kirkwall.*

STIPERSTONES *Shropshire*

Legend says that if England is ever

threatened, Wild Edric the Saxon earl will rise from Stiperstones to defend his country. The surface of the 1,762 ft hill, the second highest in Shropshire, is pockmarked by disused lead mines once worked for the Romans. There is a curious rock formation called the Devil's Chair where it is said Old Nick sits when cloud covers the summit. Stiperstones is owned by the Nature Conservancy Council, and looks west into Wales and south-east to The Long Mynd.
LOCATION *At Bridges on a minor road 5 miles N of Eaton on the A489.*

STONEHENGE *Wiltshire*

Outlined by the setting sun against the

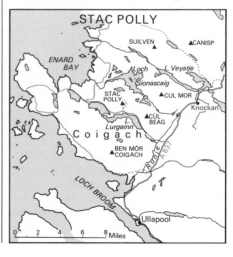

backdrop of Salisbury Plain, Stonehenge looks just what it is – an imposing Neolithic to Late Bronze Age monument. By day it buzzes with visitors who pass through a turnstile. The oldest section, dating back more than 4,500 years, is the outer ditch, inside which is a double circle of 80 blue stones brought by raft and sledge from the Prescelly Hills in Wales, a distance of more than 200 miles. About 1640 BC renovations took place and the blue stones were replaced by sarsen stones from Marlborough Downs. Sarsen derives from the word Saracen, meaning foreign. In the centre are the altar stone and the heelstone or sunstone. This is struck by the first ray of dawn's light on the longest day, June 21, and suggests that Stonehenge had an astronomical rather than a religious function. More than likely it had both, and judging by the number of barrows a large population relied upon it.
LOCATION *Off the A344 between the junctions of the A303 and A360.*

THE STORR *Highland*

Many who love mountains make the pilgrimage to Skye, look at the Cuillins and depart without realising that the north-east of the island has some of the most phenomenal rock scenery in Britain. The Storr at 2,358 ft is the highest point on the Trotternish peninsula, but its most spectacular sight can be reached long before the peak. The Old Man of Storr is a huge and solitary pillar of rock some 160 ft high.
LOCATION *Off the A855 about 2 miles N of Portree.*

STUDLAND HEATH *Dorset*

A short journey on a car ferry, then sand dunes and heathland, the buzz of bees and the soaring song of larks make the 1,570 acres of the Nature Conservancy Council's Studland Heath one of the finest nature reserves in Britain. The summer visitor can see all Britain's native species of reptile – three snakes and three lizards. In winter, a well-appointed hide overlooks a freshwater lake where goldeneyes and pochards dive for food, and shovelers shovel and filter food from the water through their huge spatulate bills.
LOCATION *About 4 miles N of Swanage on a minor road off the B3351.*

SUILVEN *Highland*

The two-peaked 'Matterhorn of the Highlands', Suilven, is not very high at 2,399 ft

but its shape ensures that it is one of the most impressive mountains in Scotland. In Gaelic it is called *Caisteal Liath* (the Grey Castle), and to the Vikings it was *Sul-fjall* (the Pillar Mountain). It is also known as The Sugar Loaf. Suilven, slowly eroding sandstone over the top of ancient rocks, can be reached by a strenuous walk from the village of Lochinver.
LOCATION *About 3 miles SE of Lochinver at the end of the A837.*

LOCH SUNART *Highland*

The 20 mile long gash of Loch Sunart cuts into the west coast of Scotland, separating the peninsulas of Morven and Ardnamurchan. A road runs along the often wooded north shore, with views across the loch to the hills of Movean. The road ends 2 miles short of the Point of Ardnamurchan, the most westerly place on the British mainland.
LOCATION *The A861 from Ardgour runs along the lochside to Salen. From here the B8007 continues westward along the shore.*

SWALEDALE *North Yorkshire*

There are delightful views of the river from Richmond where the impetuous Swale slows a little before reaching Grinton where it is joined by Arkle Beck cantering down from Arkengarthdale. Another spectacular sight is Ivelet Bridge, haunted, it is said, by a headless dog. At the northern end of the single-span bridge is a coffin stone, where the wicker coffins could be placed while those who had struggled down the dale carrying the weight could rest.
LOCATION *Ivelet Bridge is on the north side of the B6270 from Richmond to Kirkby Stephen.*

SWALLOW FALLS *Gwynedd*

See page 90. (Map, facing page.)

LOCH SWEEN *Strathclyde*

The ruin of Castle Sween, built in the 13th century, dominates one headland of Loch Sween and the restored chapel of St Maelrubha at Kilmory another. The chapel has some 'Celtic' slabs which actually date from the Middle Ages. Kilmory is noted for its lobsters which abound among the rocky weed-laden ledges of the loch.
LOCATION *East of the B8025 off the A816.*

SYMONDS YAT *Hereford and Worcester*

See page 94.

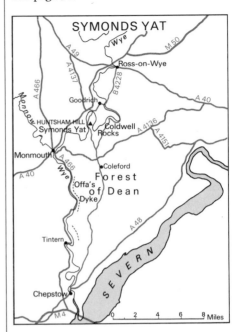

TAN HILL *North Yorkshire*

Tan Hill Inn, the highest pub in England, stands alone on the summit of its 1,732 ft hill, looking down on Stonesdale Moor. There is no village, but the moor was once the crossing point of several old drovers' roads, and the herdsmen could sit in the pub and see all the surrounding countryside. Tan Hill and its moor are still sheep country in the wild expanses of Swaledale.
LOCATION *4 miles N of Keld on a minor road off the B6270.*

TARR STEPS *Somerset*

The naturalist will find a walk from Tarr Steps along the wooded banks of the Barle always enjoyable and at times quite memorable, whatever the season. Kingfishers flash above the chuckling water, chaffinches sing from the trees and herons wait patiently by the deep swirling pools. Flowers grace the woods and red deer glide away through the trees. Man has known this spot for centuries, and has crossed the Barle by means of a clapper bridge called Tarr Steps. No one knows who built it, but it took some effort because the stones are not of local rock. Even the experts cannot agree. Some are sure that Tarr Steps is prehistoric; others are equally certain it is medieval.
LOCATION *By a minor road off the B3223, 1 mile SW of Liscombe.*

LOCH TAY *Tayside*

Loch Tay is 17 miles long with a scenic shoreline. The finest views are from the road along the southern shore looking across to Ben Lawers (3,984 ft). The peak and southern slopes are cared for by the National Trust for Scotland. Ben Lawers is known as 'The Echoing Mountain' and its views extend from the Atlantic to the North Sea. Kenmore is a fine resort at the eastern end of Loch Tay and the scene from its bridge so impressed Robert Burns that in 1787 he wrote a short poem about it which is displayed in the Kenmore Hotel. Nature trails lead through woodlands and along the loch banks.

LOCATION *The A827 runs along the north shore between Kenmore and Killin. A minor road on the south shore also links the two villages.*

TINTERN ABBEY *Gwent*

Whatever the weather, Tintern Abbey, set in a meadow below the wooded slopes of the Wye Valley, always looks majestic. It was founded by the Cistercians in 1131, substantially added to throughout the 13th and 14th centuries and dissolved in 1536. Much of the abbey remains intact and the Anchor Inn beside the bridge over the River Wye was almost certainly the abbey's watergate. Two nature trails lead through the woodlands which are rich in wildlife. A visit to the abbey inspired the poet William Wordsworth to write his famous *Lines composed a Few Miles above Tintern Abbey, on revisiting the Banks of the Wye during a Tour, July 13, 1798.*

LOCATION *On the A466 about 5 miles N of Chepstow.*

LOCH TORRIDON *Highland*

Wild mountains surrounding a tree-lined loch close to the old Caledonian Pine Forest ensure Loch Torridon's scenic reputation. The village of Torridon huddles beneath the big Beinns of Eighe (3,312 ft), Liathach (3,456 ft), Alligin (3,232 ft), and Dearg (2,995 ft). The rock is Torridonian sandstone which is laid down in horizontal strata, giving the slopes a banded appearance. There is a switchback road along the north shore of the loch from Torridon to Inver Alligan and a single track over Bealachna Gaoithe from where the Pass of the Wind goes on to Diabaig.

LOCATION *Off the A896 between Annat and Shieldaig.*

TREGARON BOG *Dyfed*

See page 122.

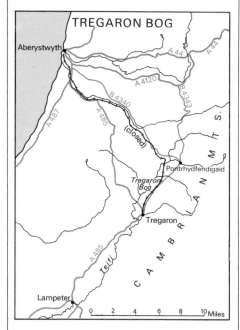

TRE'R CEIRI *Gwynedd*

Wind blasts across the hills, curlews cry and buzzards play in the gusts. Few people brave the 1,600 ft climb towards the three summits which dominate the Lleyn Peninsula. The Welsh call them *Yr Eifi* (the fork), while the English have named them The Rivals. No one lives up here and the walker is alone, but this has not always been so. An examination of the summit of the most easterly prong of the fork reveals a human presence of long ago, for here is Tre'r Ceiri, the Giants' Town. Huge stones have been skilfully slotted between natural formations to enclose an Iron Age settlement. This could well have been a stubborn Celtic outpost determined to resist the Roman forces. For the views alone – the Isle of Man and Ireland are visible on a clear day – a climb up to see The Rivals is worth it, but the eastern fork to Giants' Town is an exceptional bonus.

LOCATION *On the B4417, 1 mile W of Llanaelhaearn on the A499.*

TROUGH OF BOWLAND *Lancashire*

The best way to appreciate the wonderfully varied scenery of the Forest of Bowland is to follow the narrow winding road from Dunsop Bridge to Quernmore near Lancaster, through the Trough of Bowland, which climbs to more than 1,000 ft. On the Lancaster side of the summit the Wyre has its origins in two streams, the Marshaw and the Tarn brook. It flows through Abbeystead, Dolphinhome and Garstang and then to Fleetwood. On the Dunsop Bridge side are the infant feeder streams of the River Hodder, which chuckles its way over a stony bed to meet the Ribble, flowing through Whitewell, Dunsop Bridge and Bashall. The Wyre and the Hodder are good salmon streams flowing through areas rich in bird life, including goosanders, dippers and grey wagtails. The area also caters for walkers, and splendid views over to the Irish Sea in one direction and the Yorkshire Dales in the other make the effort of climbing to the 1,000 ft summit well worth while.

LOCATION *On a minor road off the A6 at Caton.*

ULLSWATER *Cumbria*

See page 97.

URRA MOOR *North Yorkshire*

See page 126. (Map, page 177.)

LAKE VYRNWY *Powys*

Lake Vyrnwy, a reservoir lying in a deep valley surrounded by spectacular mountain scenery, supplies water to Liverpool. A well-marked path leads through wooded valleys full of streams. One of the most attractive of the valleys is a horseshoe, ending with a steep descent to the headwater of the lake. A road across the 390 yard long summit of the retaining dam allows motorists to make a complete circuit of the lake.

LOCATION *On the B4393 from Llanwddyn.*

WAST WATER *Cumbria*

The bed of Wast Water, the deepest lake in England, is 8 ft below sea level. It is 3 miles long and flanked by huge scree slopes which occasionally avalanche into the water. Stacks of mountains, among them Yewbarrow (2,058 ft), Kirkfell (2,631 ft), Great Gable (2,949 ft) and Lingmell (2,649 ft), enclose the lake and on a cold winter's day are reflected in it. The southern end is much more gentle and the woodland alongside a National Trust nature trail screens a pump house which delivers 4 million gallons of Wast Water to the nuclear power station at Calder Hall.

LOCATION *A minor road from Gosforth on the A595 runs alongside the lake.*

WATERSMEET Devon

There are few more exciting sights than the mingling of two urgent streams. A magnificent example of this is where the combined Farley and Hoaroak waters crash into the East Lynn river and accompany it to the sea at Lynmouth. Steeped banks of spring flowers line the gorge and their heady perfume hangs in the air while the birds sing a tune for the dancing waters. Hillsford Bridge is a vantage point to view the union of Farley and Hoaroak. A path leads to Watersmeet.

LOCATION *On the A39, 1 mile SE of Lynmouth.*

WESTLETON HEATH Suffolk

In medieval times Suffolk was a sheep county and Westleton Heath close to Dunwich Forest is a remnant of those days. Heathlands are fast disappearing, but Westleton now has a nature reserve to ensure its survival. Huge clumps of gorse and broom flood the summer months with a blaze of yellow flowers and feed a host of insects. Thus Westleton has a huge population of breeding birds – colourful linnets, stonechats and red-backed shrikes.

LOCATION *On the B1125, 1 mile N of Middleton.*

WEST LOCH TARBERT Strathclyde

The coast of Strathclyde is slashed into islands, inlets, isthmuses, isolated rocks and indented peninsulas. Mountains tower over the sea lochs. Every sheltered spot seems to have spawned its own village, every viewpoint its castle and every loch its fish. Tarbert has its ruined 14th-century castle, once a stronghold of Robert Bruce. But its industrial life began as a herring fishing port ideally situated on an isthmus linking Knapdale and Kintyre. West Loch Tarbert, sheltered by a headland, is rich in wildlife and unsurpassed in its scenery.

LOCATION *On the west side of the A83, between West Tarbert and Clachan.*

WHINLATTER PASS Cumbria

Braithwaite village is Norse in origin and its name means a stream running through a clearing in a forest. From the village, the Whinlatter Pass climbs to a height of 1,043 ft and is flanked by Grisedale Pike and Lorton Fells. Views of the tranquil Bassenthwaite Lake contrast with the savage grandeur of the 3,054 ft Skiddaw.

LOCATION *On the B5292 from Cockermouth or Braithwaite.*

WHITE HORSE HILL Oxfordshire

See page 156.

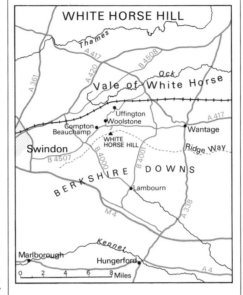

WINDERMERE Cumbria

Windermere, 10 miles long and 1 mile across, is not only the largest lake in England, but is also one of the most beautiful. Despite increasing numbers of visitors and the frequent steamer services between Lakeside and Ambleside it retains its majesty. There are views to the Langdale Pikes, woods sweep down to the shore and islands straddle the middle reaches. Fishermen trawl the depths for char, a trout-like fish found only in Windermere's deeps.

LOCATION *West of the A591 and A592 between Ambleside and Staveley.*

WIN GREEN HILL Wiltshire

Tree-fringed Win Green Hill, 910 ft, is the highest point of Cranborne Chase, a former hunting ground of King John where no village was permitted to be established. The forest laws were repealed in 1828, but the legacy remains. It is still difficult to penetrate the Chase, with its narrow roads and tiny hamlets hidden in folds of hills or behind shelter belts. This unusual pattern can be seen from the National Trust ground at Win Green summit. Even the Isle of Wight, 40 miles to the south-east, can be seen on a clear day.

LOCATION *On the B3081, 4 miles SE of Shaftesbury.*

WINNATS PASS Derbyshire

The wild, rugged nature of Derbyshire's countryside around Castleton can be appreciated in the staggering views from the summit of Winnats Pass. In the days of the stagecoach, highwaymen found the head of the pass ideal for ambushing the travellers struggling and pushing their tiring horses into the teeth of an apparently ever-present wind.

LOCATION *About 1 mile W of Castleton on the A625.*

WORBARROW Dorset

Worbarrow Bay is part of an army firing range but is seldom used as such at weekends or holiday periods. The views of the bay overlooked by the towering pyramid of Worbarrow Tout are magnificent. Worbarrow Bay, with Kimmeridge Bay, make up the Purbeck Marine Nature Reserve where the variety of underwater life is remarkable. Times of firing appear both in the local press and on specially erected army notice boards. Visitors are advised to keep to the paths because of unexploded shells.

LOCATION *On a minor road off the A351 from Wareham or Corfe Castle.*

WORMS HEAD West Glamorgan

Worms Head derives from the Old English for a dragon, an apt description since the area, once a coastal plateau of the Gower Peninsula, has been eroded by the sea and looks like a monster. The joints in the limestone have been widened by the sea. The head of the Worm is accessible for an hour or so at low tide. The humped body is formed by a limestone arch called Devil's Bridge. At the north face of the Worm is a blow hole which spouts spray at high water as formidably as any dragon of old.

LOCATION *On Rhossili Bay at the west end of the B4247.*

THE WREKIN Shropshire

The 1,334 ft Wrekin is formed from some of the earliest rocks in Britain, perhaps 900 million years old. Earthworks 2,000 years old cover 7 acres of the summit and it retains a feeling of mystery generated by great age, rich history and fascinating views.

LOCATION *On a minor road off the B4380 from Ironbridge to Wroxeter or on minor roads off the A5 W of Telford.*

INDEX

Main features are shown in CAPITAL letters and illustrations in *italic type*. All other places are shown in roman type.

ACKNOWLEDGMENTS

Front cover, Ogwen Falls, Snowdonia; page 3, Great Gable, Cumbria; pages 4/5 Cona Glen, Highland; pages 6/7 Rock strata at Friog Gwynedd.

Some of the illustrations in this book were previously used in the following books published by Drive Publications or Reader's Digest: *Book of the British Countryside, Discovering Britain, Illustrated Guide to Britain, The Last Two Million Years, Nature Lover's Library.*

The illustrations in this book were provided by the following artists, photographers and agencies. Work commissioned by Reader's Digest is shown in italics.

Except where otherwise stated, credits read from left to right down the page.

Front cover Andy Williams Photo Library. Back cover John Cleare/Mountain Camera. 3 John Cleare/Mountain Camera. 4–5 CLI/Keystone. 6–7, 8–9 Paul Wakefield. 10–11 *Michael Freeman.* 12 left, Scottish Tourist Board; right, Mansell Collection. 13 *Michael Freeman.* 15 Heather Angel/Biofotos. 16 right, Fotobank International Colour Library/A. W. Besley. 17 Richard Jemmett. 18–19 Ian Howes. 20 top, The British Library Board; bottom, Trinity College Dublin (The Green Studio, Dublin). 21 Michael Freeman. 22 K. M. Andrew. 22–23 Spectrum Colour Library. 24–25 John Watney Photo Library. 26 John Cleare/Mountain Camera. 27 Georg Gerster/John Hillelson Agency. 28 *Colin Molyneux.* 29 left, Colin Molyneux; right, artist *Trevor Boyer.* 30 top, John Cleare/Mountain Camera; bottom, artist *Bob Hook.* 31 *Paul Wakefield.* 32–33 Airviews Ltd. 34–35, 37 K. M. Andrew. 38–39 Peter Barker/Sefton Photo Library. 39 top right, artist Ray Burrows; bottom right, West Highland Museum, Fort William. 40–41 *Colin Molyneux.* 42–43 Patrick Thurston. 45 *Colin Molyneux.* 46–47 M. P. L. Fogden/Bruce Coleman Ltd. 48–49 John Cleare/Mountain Camera. 50 artist *David Baxter.* 50–51 Noel Habgood/Derek Widdicombe. 52–53, 54–55 *Jon Wyand.* 56–57, 58 John Cleare/Mountain Camera. 59 *Jon Wyand.* 60 artist *Ray Burrows.* 60–61 Michael St Maur Sheil. 62–63 K. M. Andrew. 63 right, artist Tim Hayward. 64–65 Philip H. Evans/ Bruce Coleman Ltd. 66 artist Victoria Goman. 66–67 Paul Wakefield/Bruce Coleman Ltd. 68 Stewart Galloway/Susan Griggs Agency. 69 David Williams/Sefton Photo Library. 70–71 Philip H. Evans/Bruce Coleman Ltd. 71 artist Ivan Lapper. 72–73 John Cleare/Mountain Camera. 74 Geoff Doré/Bruce Coleman Ltd. 75 artist *Graham Allen.* 76–77 CLI/Keystone. 78 artist *Jill Tomblin.* 79 left, *Paul Wakefield;* right, *Penny Tweedie.* 80–81 Robert Matassa/Fotobank. 82 top, *K. Wilson;* bottom, *P. O'Conner.* 83 Derek McDougall/Wade Cooper Associates. 84 top, Mansell Collection; middle and bottom, Mary Evans Picture Library; right, Bob and Sheila Thomlinson. 85 *Paul Wakefield.* 86, 87 *John Wyand.* 88–89 John Bethell. 89 artist *Ray Burrows.* 90–91 Andy Williams Photo Library. 92 artist *Ray Burrows.* 93, 94–95, 97 Andy Williams Photo Library. 98 artist *Robert Morton.* 99 Jorge Lewinski. 100–1 *Malcolm Aird.* 102–3 CLI/Keystone. 104 C. M. Dixon. 105 Adam Woolfitt/Susan Griggs Agency. 106, 107 Derek Widdicombe. 108 Spectrum Colour Library. 109 British Tourist Authority. 110–11, 112–13 Malcolm Aird. 114–15 Andy Williams Photo Library. 116 artist *Ray Burrows,* courtesy of Vindolanda Trust. 117 Janet and Colin Bord. 118–19 K. M. Andrew. 120 left, artist *Ray Burrows;* right, Adam Woolfitt/British Tourist Authority. 121 K. M. Andrew. 122–3 Paul Wakefield. 124 artist Ken Wood. 124–5 Colin Molyneux. 126–7, 128 *Jon Wyand.* 129 artist *Tim Hayward.* 130–1 *Trevor Wood.* 132 artist *Ray Burrows.* 133 CLI/Keystone. 134 British Tourist Authority. 135 Heather Angel/Biofotos. 136 artist Victoria Goman. 136–7 CLI/ Keystone. 138–9 John Woolverton. 140–1 Michael St Maur Sheil/ Susan Griggs Agency. 142 Scottish Tourist Board. 143 Michael St Maur Sheil/Susan Griggs Agency. 144–5 Aerofilms Ltd. 147 CLI/ Keystone. 148–9 Spectrum Colour Library. 150 Derek Widdicombe. 151 left, Heather Angel/Biofotos; right, artist *Colin Emberson.* 152 Derek Widdicombe. 153 Mike William/Sefton Photo Library. 154 Marcus Brown/Northern Picture Library. 155 Mike Williams/Sefton Photo Library. 156 Spectrum Colour Library. 157 CLI/Keystone. 158 Patrick Wise/Fotobank. 159 Janet and Colin Bord.

The publishers also acknowledge their indebtedness to the following publications which were consulted for reference:

Across Northern Hills, Geoffrey Berry, Westmorland Gazette; *The Adventures of Conan Doyle,* Charles Higham, Hamish Hamilton; *Along the Pennine Way,* J. H. B. Peel, David & Charles; *Along the South Down,* David Harrison, Cassell; *Ancient Mysteries,* Peter Haining, Sidgwick & Jackson; *The Archaeology of Southwest Britain,* Susan M. Pearce, Collins; *Argyll & Bute,* Nigel Tranter, Hodder & Stoughton; *Around Historic Somerset & Avon,* Colin Wintle, Midas Books; *Around the Lizard,* Tor Mark Press; *The Ascent of Snowdon,* E. G. Rowland, Cidron Press; *Axbridge Rural District Official Guide,* Home Publishing Co.; *Betws-y-Coed and the Conwy Valley,* I. W. Jones, John Jones; *Beyond the Great Glen,* James R. Nicholson, David & Charles; *AA Book of the British Countryside,* Drive Publications; *Brecon Beacons National Park,* ed Margaret Davies, HMSO; *Broadway Tower Country Park,* Michael Kirke, Beagle Education Services; *Canal,* Anthony Burton & Derek Pratt, David & Charles; *The Canals of the West Midlands,* Charles Hadfield, David & Charles; *The Cairngorms,* Desmond Nethersole Thompson, Adam Watson, Collins; *Cairngorms National Nature Reserve,* The Nature Conservancy, Amesbury Press; *The Central Highlands,* Ian Finlay, Batsford; *The Central Highlands,* Campbell R. Steven, Scottish Mountaineering Club Guide; *Cheddar Caves, Illustrated Official Guide,* Dr W. I. Stanton, Photo Precision Ltd; *The Cleveland Way,* Alan Falconer, HMSO; *The Coastline of Scotland,* J. A. Steers, Cambridge University Press; *A Coast to Coast Walk,* A. Wainwright, Westmorland Gazette; *Collected Poems,* T. S. Elliot, Faber; *Collected Shorter Poems of W. H. Auden,* Faber; *The Companion Guide to the Coast of North East England,* John Seymour, Collins; *The Companion Guide to the Coast of South East England,* John Seymour, Collins; *The Companion Guide to the Coast of South West England,* John Seymour, Collins; *The Companion Guide to Northumbria,* Edward Grierson, Collins; *The Companion Guide to North Wales,* Elizabeth Beazley & Peter Howell, Collins; *The Companion Guide to South Wales,* Peter Howell & Elizabeth Beazley, Collins; *The Companion Guide to the West Highlands of Scotland,* W. H. Murray, Collins; *Complete Cotswolds and Shakespeare Country,* Reginald J. W. Hammond, Ward Lock; *Complete Dorset and Wiltshire,* Reginald J. W. Hammond & Kenneth E. Lowther, Ward Lock; *Complete Yorkshire,* Reginald J. W. Hammond, Ward Lock; *Cornwall, A Shell Guide,* John Betjeman, Faber; *Cornwall Coast Path,* Edward C. Pyatt, HMSO; *Cornwall's Structure & Scenery,* R. M. Barton, Tor Mark Press; *Cors Caron,* Nature Conservancy Council; *Cors Caron National Nature Reserve – Old Railway Walk,* Nature Conservancy Council; *Cors Tregaron,* Nature Conservancy Council; *The Cotswolds,* J. Allan Cash, Spur; *The Cotswolds,* Brian Smith, Batsford; *Country Walks around Broadway,* The North Cotswolds Walkers' Group; *Dartmoor National Park,* Professor W. G. Hoskins, HMSO; *AA Discovering Britain,* Drive Publications; *Dorset – Thomas Hardy's Country,* Arthur Mee, Hodder & Stoughton; *The Drovers' Road of Wales,* Fay Godwin & Shirley Toulson, Wildwood House; *East Anglia,* Paul Fincham, Faber; *East Anglia,* Peter Stegall, Robert Hale; *Exploring Britain,* Garry Hogg, Shell/John Baker; *Exploring Wales,* William Condry, Faber; *The Face of North West Yorkshire,* Arthur Raistrick and John L. Illingworth, Dalesman Books; *The Face of Scotland,* I. G. McIntosh and C. B. Marshall, Pergamon; *Folklore, Myths and Legends of Britain,* Reader's Digest; *The Footpaths of Britain,* Michael Marriott, Queen Anne Press; *Freeman of the Fells,* A. H. Griffin, Robert Hale; *Geology and Scenery in England and Wales,* A. E. Truman, Penguin; *Geology and Scenery in Scotland,* J. B. Whitton, Pelican; *Geology of Symonds Yat and the Wye Gorge,* Forestry Commission, Chequer Press; *A Guide to Prehistoric and Roman Monuments in England and Wales,* Jacquetta Hawkes, Chatto & Windus; *Guide to Prehistoric England,* Nicholas Thomas, Batsford; *A Guide to the Cleveland Way,* Malcolm Boyes, Constable; *Guides to the View from the Summit of Snowdon,* Chris Jesty, Vector Promotions; *Guinness Book of Records;* *Hadrian's Wall,* A. R. Birley, HMSO; *Hadrian's Wall,* David J. Breeze and Brian Dobson, Pelican; *Hand-picked Tours in Britain,* Reader's Digest; *The Heritage of Yorkshire,* E. F. Lincoln, Oldbourne; *Highland Autumn,* W. R. Mitchell, Robert Hale; *Highland Landscape,* W. H. Murray, National Trust for Scotland; *The Highlands and Islands,* Francis Thompson, Robert Hale; *Highways and Byways in Dorset,* Sir Frederick Treves, Macmillan; *Highways and Byways in the West Highlands,* Seton Gordon, Macmillan; *Hill Walking in Snowdonia,* E. G. Rowland, Vector Promotions; *History, People and Places in Dorset,* Garry Hogg, Spur; *History, People and Places in East Sussex,* Iris Bryson-White, Spur; *The History of the Guydir Family,* Sir John Wynn, David & Charles; *The Holy Island of Lindisfarne and the Farne Islands,* R. A. and D. B. Cartwright, David & Charles; *Island Quest,* Prunella Stack, Collins; *The Islands of Western Scotland,* W. H. Murray, Eyre Methuen; *The Isle of Mull,* P. A. Macnab, David & Charles; *Kidnapped,* R. L. Stevenson; *Lake District,* Reginald J. W. Hammond, Ward Lock; *The Lake District,* James Buntin, Batsford; *The Lake District,* Sean Jennett, Darton, Longman & Todd; *The Lake District,* W. H. Pearsall and W. Pennington, Collins; *The Lake District, A Century of Conservation,* G. Berry and G. Beard, Bartholomew; *The Lake District National Park,* HMSO; *Lakeland Discovered,* Margaret Slack, Robert Hale; *A Lakeland Notebook,* A. H. Griffin, Robert Hale; *Land of Scott,* Scottish Tourist Board; *Landscapes of Britain,* Roy Millward and Adrian Robinson, David & Charles; *Long Distance Paths of England and Wales,* T. G. Millar, David & Charles; *Maiden Castle,* Sir Mortimer Wheeler, HMSO; *Malham,* Dalesman Books; *Mendelssohn, his life and times,* Mozelle Moshansky, Midas Books; *The Mendelssohns,* Herbert Kupferberg, W. H. Allen; *Mendip, A New Study,* Robin Atthill, David & Charles; *The Mendips,* A. W. Coysh, E. J. Mason and V. Waite, Robert Hale; *Mountaineering,* John Cleare, Blandford; *Mountains and Hills of Britain,* Michael Marriott, Willow Books, Collins; *Mountains and Moorlands,* W. H. Pearsall, Collins; *Mysterious Britain,* Janet and Colin Bord, Garnstone Press; *The National Trust Guide,* Robin Fedden and Rosemary Joekes, Cape; *The Natural Wonders of the British Isles,* Charles Walker, Orbis; *The New Shell Guide to England,* John Hadfield, Rainbird; *The New Shell Guide to Scotland,* Donald Lamond Macnie, Ebury Press; *Norfolk and the Broads,* Reginald J. W. Hammond, Ward Lock; *Northern Scotland,* Reginald J. W. Hammond, Ward Lock; *North York Moors National Park,* Arthur Raistrick, HMSO; *North Wales (Northern Section),* Reginald J. W. Hammond, Ward Lock; *The North Country,* G. Bernard Wood, Robert Hale; *The North York Moors,* NYM National Park; *No Through Road,* Reader's Digest; *Observer's Book of Butterflies,* W. J. Stokoe, Warne; *Observer's Book of Wild Flowers,* W. J. Stokoe, Warne; *On Wings of Song,* Wilfrid Blunt, Scribner's; *Orkney,* Ronald Miller, Batsford; *Orkney and Shetland,* Eric Linklater, Robert Hale; *The Other Orkney Book,* Gordon Thomson, Northabout; *The Peak District,* Roy Millward and Adrian Robinson, Eyre Methuen; *The Peak and the Pennines,* W. A. Poucher, Constable; *Pembrokeshire,* R. M. Lockley, Robert Hale; *Pembrokeshire,* Brian John, David & Charles; *Pembrokeshire Coast National Park,* Dillwyn Miles, HMSO; *The Pembrokeshire Coast Path,* John H. Barrett, HMSO; *The Pennine Way,* Tom Stephenson, HMSO; *The Pennine Way,* Christopher John Wright, Constable; *Portrait of the Border Country,* Nigel Tranter, Robert Hale; *Portrait of Broadland,* S. A. Manning, Robert Hale; *Portrait of the Brecon Beacons,* Edmund J. Mason, Robert Hale; *Portrait of Cornwall,* Claude Berry, Robert Hale; *Portrait of Cumbria,* J. D. Marshall, Robert Hale; *Portrait of the Dales,* Norman Duerden, Robert Hale; *Portrait of Dartmoor,* Vian Smith, Robert Hale; *Portrait of the Lakes,* Norman Nicholson, Robert Hale; *Portrait of North Wales,* Michael Senior, Robert Hale; *Portrait of South Wales,* Michael Senior, Robert Hale; *Portrait of Sussex,* Cecile Woodford, Robert Hale; *Portrait of Yorkshire,* Harry J. Scott, Robert Hale; *Portraits of Mountains,* Eileen Molony, Dobson; *Prehistoric Dartmoor,* Paul Petit, David & Charles; *A Prospect of Britain,* Andrew Young, Hutchinson; *Rievaulx Abbey,* Charles Peers, HMSO; *Ring of Bright Water,* Gavin Maxwell, Longmans; *Ryedale Country,* Ryedale Printing Works; *Scotland, the Blue Guides,* John Tomes, Ernest Benn; *Scotland: The Northern Highlands,* J. Phemister, HMSO; *The Scottish Border and Northumberland,* John Talbot White, Eyre Methuen; *Scottish Climbs,* Hamish MacInnes, Constable; *The Scottish Highlands,* John A. Lister, Bartholomew; *The Scottish Peaks,* W. A. Poucher, Constable; *The Scouring of the White Horse,* Thomas Hughes, Macmillan; *The Shell Book of Exploring Britain,* Garry Hogg, John Baker; *The Shell Book of the Islands of Britain,* David Booth and David Perrott, Guideway; *Snowdonia National Park,* G. Rhys Edwards, HMSO; *The Snowdon Log,* Connie Williams and Helen Light, Merseyside Youth Hostels; *Snowdon Paths,* Snowdonia National Park Publications; *Somerset and Avon,* Robert Dunning, Bartholomew; *South Downs Way,* Sean Jennett, HMSO; *South Wales,* Ruth Thomas, Bartholomew; *The South West Peninsula,* Roy Millward and Adrian Robinson, Macmillan; *The Story of Scotland's Hills,* Campbell Steven, Robert Hale; *Sunday Times Book of the Countryside,* Macdonald; *Sussex,* John Burke, Batsford; *Symonds Yat,* Wyedean Tourist Board; *Symonds Yat Tourist Trail,* Forestry Commission, Chequer Press; *Talking of Wales,* Trevor Fishlock, Cassell; *This Beautiful Britain,* Marshall Cavendish; *A Topographical Dictionary of Wales,* Samuel Lewis, S. Lewis & Co.; *Upland Britain,* Roy Millward and Adrian Robinson, David & Charles; *Viewpoints of England,* Garry Hogg, Shell Guides, Osprey; *A Visitor's Guide to the Lake District,* Brian Spencer, Moorland Publishing; *A Walk Along the Wall,* Hunter Davies, Weidenfeld; *Walks in the White Horse Country,* Nigel Hammond, Countryside Books; *Walking in the National Parks,* Alan Mattingly, David & Charles; *Walking on the North York Moors,* The Ramblers' Association, Dalesman Books; *Walking Through Northern England,* Charlie Emett and Mike Hutton, David & Charles; *Walks for Motorists – County Durham,* Keith Watson, Frederick Warne; *Walks for Motorists – Lothian and the South East Borders,* Raymond Lamont Brown, Warne; *Walks for Motorists in Snowdonia,* J. T. C. Knowles, Warne; *Walks in the Wye Valley and the Forest of Dean,* Roger Jones, Roger Jones Books; *Waymarked Paths – Highmeadow Woods,* The Ramblers' Association; *West Cornwall,* Reginald J. W. Hammond, Ward Lock; *The Western Isles of Scotland,* Arlene Sobel, New English Library; *Western Scotland,* Ward Lock Red Guide; *The White Horse and other Hill Figures,* Morris Marples, Alan Sutton; *Wild Flowers of the Wayside and Woodland,* T. H. Scott and W. J. Stokoe, Warne; *Wild Wales,* George Borrow, Collins; *Wonders of Britain,* Eric Newby and Diana Petry, Hodder & Stoughton; *Wordsworth – Poetical Works,* Thomas Hutchinson, OUP; *A Year in the Fells,* A. H. Griffin, Robert Hale; *Yorkshire,* Maurice Colbeck, Batsford; *Yorkshire Moorlands,* Maurice Colbeck, Batsford; *Yorkshire – North Riding,* Arthur Mee, Hodder & Stoughton; *Yorkshire – The West Riding,* David Pill, Batsford.